The

AUTOMOBILE

ADVANCE PRAISE FOR THE BOOK

'It is so good to see a book which covers all aspects of the automobile sector in India, and it does so with such splendour and flourish. My favourite part was the bit about the *bikerni*s!'

—Anil Dharker, writer, and founder of
the Mumbai International Literary Festival

'What a wonderful journey. Gautam has found a way to navigate through the history of the automobile in India in a way that is fun and exciting, without being intimidating.'

—B.V.R. Subbu, former president, Hyundai Motor India

'Few writers have been impassioned to trace the journey of the automobile through Indian life, history and culture. Gautam Sen stands tall.'

—Muzaffar Ali, film-maker, poet and painter

'Gautam's long-time love affair with cars and his deep knowledge of them, as well as their impact on Indian society, shine through this most readable and instructive book.'

—Rahul Singh, columnist, former editor of
Reader's Digest, Indian Express and others

'What I liked best about this book was the effortless anecdotal tone the author has taken when tracing the historical relevance of automobiles in India—whether it is the royal period of the maharajas or the glamourous Bollywood era.'

—Shobhaa Dé, columnist and author

'What fascinated me while reading the book is the influence cars have had on the evolution of our culture. *The Automobile* is the perfect guide to the history of the automobile and the role it has played in India's cultural and industrial growth. And in Gautam's voice, the story is as thrilling as it is knowledgeable!'

—Shriji Arvind Singh Mewar of Udaipur,
76th custodian of the House of Mewar

The
AUTOMOBILE
An Indian Love Affair

GAUTAM SEN

PENGUIN
VIKING
An imprint of Penguin Random House

PENGUIN BOOKS

USA | Canada | UK | Ireland | Australia
New Zealand | India | South Africa | China

Penguin Books is part of the Penguin Random House group of companies
whose addresses can be found at global.penguinrandomhouse.com

Published by Penguin Random House India Pvt. Ltd
7th Floor, Infinity Tower C, DLF Cyber City,
Gurgaon 122 002, Haryana, India

Penguin
Random House
India

First published in Penguin Books by Penguin Random House India 2021

ISBN 9780670092246

Typeset in Adobe Garamond Pro by Manipal Technologies Limited, Manipal
Printed at Thomson Press India Ltd, New Delhi

www.penguin.co.in

Contents

Preface

Art, from the Latin *ars*, *artis*, meaning 'skill, craft or technical knowledge', is a human activity, which by 'aggregating a set of elements', creates an object, that arouses reflection and emotion in a human being or group. The meaning, naturally, varies from one place to another, from one culture to another, and from one era to another. It is, therefore, impossible to agree on a universal definition, the very notions of beauty or aesthetics, which appeals equally to all. There is, however, a certain consensus around the 'fine arts' of painting, sculpture, music, dance, literature and poetry. Other areas, such as theatre, printmaking, photography, cinema, comics, and even cooking, are today accepted as art.

When, at one of the oldest and most respected museums in the world, an object comes up for display, it surely cements the opinion that that object could very well be close to art, and thus, an important part of culture. The Musée des Arts Décoratifs (MAD), in Paris, is not the Louvre, but it is a part of the entire complex, the gigantic building, which includes the Musée du Louvre. It is in an extension of the northern wing, of what was the main palace of the French kings from the late twelfth century to the late eighteenth century, after which it became a museum.

During the summer of 2011, over a four-month period (from 28 April to 28 August 2011), as many as seventeen automobiles were on display at MAD, at a special exhibition of the personal collection of American fashion designer Ralph Lauren, as exquisite examples of the art of art deco, from the earlier part of the twentieth century. The MAD was not the first art museum—outside of the automotive museums—to exhibit automobiles. A few of Ralph Lauren's cars were on exhibit in a museum in Boston, in 2005. The famous Museum of Modern Art (MoMA) in New York has long been home to a few cars in its permanent design collection: a 1946 Cisitalia 202 GT, which was a milestone design, from immediately after the War, and a sleek Jaguar E-Type, added in 1996. Since then, they have added several more cars to the display, including an early Porsche 911 and a '73 Citroën DS.

Though some objects are considered art, functional objects, such as furniture, household items, crockery, cutlery, come more into the realm of design. Engineering products from the twentieth century, such as refrigerators, cooking ovens, washing machines, and most white goods are, at best, conveniences.

The automobile, though, goes well beyond being just a convenience. It is true that for some it remains just a device to transport people from point A to point B. For thousands of others, it has been and it yet remains an object of pleasure, pride, status, sports, excitement, emotion and passion. Arguably, the automobile has been the most important invention of the twentieth century. Not only has the automobile given the hoi polloi freedom, mobility and liberty, it has changed our lifestyles, the way we live and interact, the way we work, the kind of jobs that we do, and has led to an evolution of our cultures. It has changed the cities, the countryside, the way they are conceived, designed and constructed, the way our houses and apartment blocks are configured, as well as the technology involved therein.

The changes wrought about by the automobile have been for the better, as well as for the worse. Congestion, pollution, the need to feed one's ego, to show off, are a few of many ills that the automobile has been blamed for, and rightly so. Yet, looked at objectively, the benefits of the automobile far outweigh the shortcomings and the problems.

With the thousands of visitors to the MAD going mad over Ralph Lauren's cars, followed by the hundreds who were as fascinated by a special exhibition of a selection of cars and motorcycles at UNESCO's world headquarters in Paris, in 2016, the automobile, as an intrinsic part of the history of mankind during the twentieth century, needs to be recognized.

For certain nations, though, the automobile has perhaps played a much greater role than for the others. For the United States, the automobile has as good as defined the nation and its people. Not only was it a symbol of independence and personal freedom, the automobile gave Americans unprecedented mobility, transformed their society and shaped their modern culture.

Jack Kerouac's 1957 novel *On the Road*[1] spoke for an entire generation of Americans. Other examples of influential/popular American road-trip literature include John Steinbeck's *Travels with Charley*[2] (1962), Tom Wolfe's *The Electric Kool-Aid Acid Test*[3] (1968) and Robert Pirsig's *Zen and the Art of Motorcycle Maintenance*[4] (1974). In many of America's best movies, the automobile has played an important role: Dennis Hopper's seminal *Easy Rider* (1969), the post-apocalyptic science fiction *Mad Max 2: The Road Warrior* (1981), as well as *Duel* (1971), the movie which launched the career of Steven Spielberg. Similarly, American popular music has provided innumerable paeans to the automobile, from Chuck Berry's 'Maybellene' (1955), to Janis Joplin's achingly desperate 'Oh Lord, Won't You Buy Me a Mercedes-Benz' (1970).

Similarly, the automobile has had a pronounced impact upon the cultures of the English, the French, the Germans and the Italians. Even countries which are not known to be significant automobile producers, such as Argentina, Austria, Belgium, Brazil, Canada, the Netherlands, Mexico, Poland, Switzerland, and many others, all acknowledge that the automobile has indeed transformed them, as people and as a culture.

The influence of the automobile on Asia has been relatively recent. It was only after the Second World War that Japan took to the automobile in a very big way, and by the end of the twentieth century, the automobile not only became the backbone of the country's recovery, but the symbol of its international influence. Along with that, the cultural impact of the automobile on the Japanese has been no less important.

The only other country in Asia which has felt a profound influence of the automobile is India. Initially, as a very significant market for some of the finest bespoke automobiles the world has ever known, and then later, in more recent times, as a producer, mass consumer and user. In the early part of the twentieth century, the rajas, maharajas, nawabs and the nizam acquired some of the most extraordinary automobiles the finest of carmakers ever constructed. Matching them were the highly educated lawyers, doctors, professionals and merchant classes from the cities of Calcutta (now Kolkata) and Bombay (now Mumbai), who ordered some of the most tasteful bolides, enjoying and appreciating the joys of motoring and motorsport.

Post-Independence, the automobile played a very important role in India's industrial growth, as well as a hero in many Bollywood movies. The automobile is yet transforming India, as it connects the remotest corners of our vast nation, providing mobility, freedom and jobs to millions. It has acted as an emancipator for women in many parts of the nation, allowing them to go to school and university, commute to work and to the marketplace.

Well into the twenty-first century, the automobile has provided India with an industry (one of very few which is a genuine case of 'make in India') which is one of its most important 'engines of growth'. Not only are we the world's biggest manufacturers of motorized two-wheelers, we are also one of the five biggest carmakers.

It is true that India, as a nation, is also one of the major polluters, and the automobile has been one of the bigger culprits. At the same time, the automobile has wrecked traffic in most Indian cities, and been the cause of over a lakh and a half deaths every year—yet another shameful world leadership.

We cannot, however, deny the fact that it has and will be changing India—hopefully—for the better. There is a tendency to condemn and blame the automobile for all our ills and problems, without understanding or appreciating the many benefits. Even if a few naysayers complain, the fact of the matter is that most Indians are yet, fascinated by the automobile. As the West has been falling out of love with the automobile, India has rediscovered its love for the automobile. This book is about that.

1

A Love Affair Begins

The very first Indian to drive his own automobile may well have been Kumar Shri Ranjitsinhji Vibhaji Jadeja, otherwise (and better) known as Ranji. Yes, the same Ranji of Ranji Trophy fame. Ranji became the Maharaja of Nawanagar, a minor princely state in Gujarat, in 1907, but before that, he was already famous as one of the world's finest cricketers.

In fact, even before that, when he was in the United Kingdom studying at Cambridge, between the years 1889 and 1893, he acquired a very early automobile, which was the cause of much excitement and consternation in that quaint university town.

The first vehicle (mind you, not a car) acquired by an Indian in India, however, may have been a steam-powered, two-cylinder three-wheeler, a French De Dion-Bouton, which Maharaja Rajinder Singh of Patiala purchased in the early 1890s. Around 1893, an Olds steam car, made by the pioneering American Ransom E. Olds, was shipped out to India for the Bombay office of Francis Times India, but the car never arrived as the ship it was on sank. This car is recorded[1] as the first ever export of a car from the USA. It was perhaps the first time an automobile sank as well . . .

It was also in 1897, when a Benz was imported by an Englishman in India, J.B. Foster, a senior executive at Greaves Cotton & Co. The car arrived in the city of Bombay (now Mumbai). It seems that the first car seen on the streets of Calcutta (now Kolkata), the capital of British India then, may have been from a year earlier, in 1896. What was the model of the car is not known. In 1898, a European firm imported three 'horseless carriages", which found their way to some petty royal states, and the Indian maharajas' love affair with the automobile began.

But that love affair was limited to mainly the maharajas, the wealthier English families residing in India and the merchant class from the cities of Calcutta, Bombay and Madras (now Chennai), as the motor car then was not only a very pricey piece of kit, but was also way beyond what most of India's 200 million poor could afford. With an average annual per capita income of less than Rs 200 and a car costing upward of Rs 5000 then (the equivalent of twenty-five years of salary!), for most of India's 238 million[2] people at the turn of the century, the automobile was nothing more than an object of reverential curiosity.

In the same year that the three horseless carriages found their way to some Indian potentate, 1898, a car was also imported into India by a certain H. Hewitt. Though the model is not known, it has been speculated that it may have been another Olds (the branding of Olds evolved into Oldsmobile post-1901). Around 1901 or so, three more Oldsmobiles were imported into Bombay: one was for the legendary industrialist Jamsetji Tata, the founder of the Tata Group of companies, the second was for an attorney, Rustom Cama, and the third was for the owner of Bombay Garage, Kavasji Wadia. Tata and his wife were also photographed driving another American car, a Rambler. This image is from a couple of years later.

At that point of time, the cars were mainly playthings, hardly a means of transport with which one commuted, or shopped. Yet, there was no stopping the handful of the rich and the famous of India from acquiring scores and scores of these 'toys'. So much so that the most prestigious carmakers of the world would proudly announce when a car was delivered to one of the many Indian princes, or, when one won a reliability trial with a maharaja connection. Advertisements like the one put out by Automobiles L Pierron in France,[3] which claimed that one of its cars had won the Concours de Bombay, and that the car had been awarded the Coupe de Maharaja, were not unusual, even if the real story was not quite that.

This advertisement was reinforced by a report in the same issue of the magazine *La Pratique Automobile*, which printed: 'The Maharajah of Cooch Behar won the Bombay Reliability Trials in a Mass powered by a 16/20hp Ballot after driving 500 miles non-stop.'[4] The report was about the 1908 edition of the Bombay to Kolhapur reliability trials, held on 2–5 February 1908. Though the information regarding the presence of a Ballot engine-powered car in India was not untrue, the details were not quite correct. A 15-horsepower (hp) Mass did win its class, which was the Class 3 (a category of vehicles with a selling price of less than Rs 7000, or £466), and the Mass was nothing else than a rebadged Pierron.

A bit of misreporting, given that mass communication had its limitations those days, was not all that unusual. The Mass, though, was not, in all likelihood, the only Ballot-powered car sold in India. French Motor Company in Calcutta was the importer and distributor of a whole host of French marques. Indeed, several other French cars took part in this same trial: Lacoste & Battmann, La Buire, Peugeot, Panhard et Levassor and Clément-Bayard.

At the turn of the century, France was the leading carmaker in the world, and even if India was not part of its empire, many of the early French brands made inroads into India, as the crown jewel of the British Empire had the reputation of having enough wealthy people who could afford these new playthings.

Thus, unsurprisingly, many of the fledgling makers of these playthings thronged to India, appointing dealerships in the port cities of Bombay, Calcutta and Madras. All kinds of cars were imported— electric, steam and petrol—as it still was not clear which was going to work the best. At the beginning, European manufacturers took the lead, specifically the French, with importers and dealers selling Chenard et Walcker, Clément-Bayard, Darracq, De Dion-Bouton, Delaunay-Belleville, Hotchkiss, Mors, Panhard et Levassor, Renault and Richard-Brasier.

Soon, the slower-starting British industry laid claim to the important market represented by the crown jewel of the empire, with

marques like Daimler (which were being constructed under licence
from Germany, in the United Kingdom), Humber, Lanchester,
Napier, Rolls-Royce, Standard, Star, Thornycroft, Vulcan, Wolseley
and Wolseley-Siddeley. American brands like Olds, Rambler, Cadillac
and Studebaker followed, as well as cars from Italy, such as the Fiat and
the Bianchi, as well as the Minerva from Belgium.

The beginning of the legends

Despite the importance that the carmakers gave to the Indian princes,
there seem to have been moments of embarrassment too. One story
that has become part of the folklore of India was about the maharaja
from eastern India who was visiting London sometime in the 1920s.
The man being a follower and admirer of Mahatma Gandhi believed
in dressing simply. Perhaps not as simply as the 'half-naked fakir', in
the words of Winston Churchill, but simple enough in a long white
kurta, and a plain white dhoti, in a length, which was 'decently' longer
than what the Mahatma preferred to be in. Though he was not one
bit ostentatious in his outward appearance, he still had the taste of his
forebears, a penchant for things expensive. So, like many of his kind, he
decided to pay a visit to one of the London showrooms of Rolls-Royce,
a marque whose cars he traditionally patronized.

Unfortunately, the elegantly attired salesperson at the showroom
did not take the Indian very seriously and decided to show him the door
instead. Furious at the insult, the maharaja sent his (presumably better-
dressed) minister to that same Rolls-Royce showroom to order three
cars, and arrange for them to be shipped to India, sans coachwork. On
their arrival at Calcutta, these three cars were converted into garbage
trucks and gifted to the Calcutta Corporation, the city's municipality.
Rolls-Royce had no option but to buy back these three vehicles, have
them re-bodied and then sold off (at a hefty discount, no doubt) to
other royalty in India. Of course, this maharaja never bought another
Rolls-Royce for the rest of his life . . .

This is how the legend goes. In all likelihood, it is just a legend,
not necessarily true, as no clinching evidence has ever been unearthed.

Yet myths, stories and legends abound about the maharajas and their passion for cars, some untrue, many fascinatingly real.

The introduction of the 'horseless carriage' changed completely the lifestyle of Indian royalty, and with it began an enthralling new passion that was to endure for many decades. The choicest of cars with the most unusual of coachworks made their way to India to satisfy the varied tastes and demands of the rajas and the maharajas. Some were ceremonial throne cars; several hunting cars with Stephen Grebel search lamps and gun racks were made. Then, there were cars for wedding and state processions, even special automobiles for the 'ladies of the house' to travel in secluded 'purdah'. Most importantly, each one of the princes had one objective: to outdo the other in terms of pomp, glamour and splendour.

Not all the cars specially constructed for the Indian princes and the wealthy merchant class were in agreeable tastes. For instance, a Ford Model A, which then was a relatively 'middle-class' car, was custom-made for a wealthy landowner in Gujarat, in overpowering silver repoussé decorative work and lace curtains. Then there was (it still survives) this rather flashy, gold-plated Daimler of Seth Hukumchand of Indore. The strangest of them all, though, was the famous Swan Car of Calcutta, a 1910 Brooke with the front of the car made to look like a swan that would hiss steam from the nostrils. Ironically enough, it was not the fancy of an Indian eccentric, but that of a wealthy British resident of Calcutta—perhaps the Indian sun had finally affected him!

Journalist Elizabeth Blackstock wrote in the popular web magazine Jalopnik, on 17 November 2018: 'There's plenty to criticize about the British rule in India, but I think I've found its most redeemable factor. I'd like to introduce you to the 1910 Brooke Swan Car, designed by a very wealthy engineer named Robert Nicholl "Scotty" Matthewson. It is absurd. It is hilarious. It is the only thing I ever want to drive for the rest of my life.'[5]

The reaction in the local media then was even more amusing: 'Women screamed. Carriages went careering off the road. Water buffalo, oxen, goats, donkeys, elephants, camels and natives, after one glance, took off at top speed in every direction,' ran a report[6] from

Calcutta, in April 1910, describing the effect the Swan Car had on the people of the city. It was a strange piece of rolling fantasy that had not just the hoi polloi, but also the rich, the aristocracy and the gentry of the city astounded. The people of Calcutta were used to the automobile, with the first car having arrived more than a decade earlier, the very first reliability trials having taken place in 1904, and the streets already clogged with tramcars, horse carriages and automobiles.

Yet that still did not prepare them for what may truly be the most extraordinary car ever to take to the road. The brainchild of a wealthy and eccentric resident of Calcutta, Robert Nicholl 'Scotty' Matthewson, the Swan Car was one crazy device. Calcutta's society had fallen in love with the automobile and some very fine cars were already to be seen on the streets of the city. Matthewson had a different idea of how to make an impression. Determined to eclipse the extravagant automobiles of the local moneyed set, Matthewson decided to get himself something different.

Travelling to England in 1909, Matthewson commissioned J.W. Brooke & Company of Lowestoft, Suffolk, to build him a car in the shape of a swan. Why a swan remains a mystery. Apparently, Matthewson had a thing or two about swans: he lived in Swan Park, in the chic district of Alipore, next to the Calcutta zoo (which has always had one of the biggest collections of birds, especially swans!)

Why Matthewson opted for Brooke is not clear either. Brooke was no Rolls-Royce or Daimler. It had a better reputation for marine engines and motor launches, a business that it had embarked upon in 1874. By 1900, it was making engines for cars too, and in 1902, it designed a triple-cylinder engine for powering cars. J.W. Brooke & Company was also one of the earliest to develop an inline six-cylinder engine, for powering motor launches. From 1906, Brooke decided to rationalize and made just the six-cylinder engine for both marine use and for its cars, in various sizes and power outputs. Matthewson opted for the less powerful version. (Incidentally, Brooke ceased making cars altogether by 1913.)

It is possible that Brooke was the only one who agreed to work on such a strange commission, one which called for considerable effort.

Made out of thick wood, the body was hand-carved and patched with plaster by master artisans to create the effect of feathers. The front—above and ahead of the engine and radiator—became the neck and head of the swan, and electric bulbs (one of the very early uses of electrics in a car!) made the swan's amber eyes glow eerily in the dark. The rear half of the car was decorated with a carved pattern of lotus plants and fishes picked out in gold and silver leaf. As the lotus was symbolically significant to the Hindu majority, it is quite possible that Matthewson deliberately chose to have them emblazoned on to the car.

The special features of the car did not end with that. Matthewson had a multi-note Gabriel Horn—a sort of pipe organ driven from the exhaust—that, with a keyboard in the rear of the car, allowed him to play chords and make bugle calls. And if that was not annoying enough, the swan's beak, on the press of a button, sprayed scalding water (fed by the pressurized engine cooling system) in a wide arc to clear the way. The idea was not just to frighten away the little people, but also to scandalize high society.

The powers that be in Calcutta were not amused. The authorities got in on the act, the police intervened, and the Swan Car was banned from the city's roads. Matthewson, who had spent the considerable sum of £10,000–15,000 (the cost of at least two new Rolls-Royce Silver Ghosts those days) decided to sell the Swan Car.

Not surprisingly, Matthewson's pride (and considerable joy, no doubt) was bought by Ripudaman Singh, the Maharaja of Nabha. In keeping with the saga, Ripudaman Singh decided to commission a companion for the Swan Car. A three-fifths scale version of the Swan Car was developed within the estate of the maharaja, in the 1920s. The body was hand-beaten from steel sheet and the vehicle was fitted with an electric motor. A single-seater, the 'Baby Swan' or the 'Cygnet', as it was referred to, was for the personal use of the maharaja, for tootling around in his estate.

Around the time when the Swan Car was terrorizing the genteel folks in the city of Calcutta, or a couple of years thereafter, by the start of the Great War, by now the ex-capital of British India had a vehicle parc of over 2000 automobiles, with as many as 3000 in the

Bengal Presidency. The Bombay Presidency had a similar count, too, though Bombay itself had about 1000 vehicles registered in the city. An article in the *American Commerce Reports* said: 'Motor cars are now extensively used throughout India. In Calcutta about 2000 motor cars are registered and in Bombay about 1000.'[7] Madras, by then, had less than a thousand, and Karachi and Lahore together had another thousand.

The early enthusiasts

With the shift of the capital of British India to Delhi, and the famous Coronation Durbar of December 1911, when King George V, and his consort, Queen Mary, were officially crowned the Emperor and Empress of India, the seven-times-seven city of the Sultanates and Mughals became an important 'destination' for brand new cars too.

Rolls-Royce put at the disposal of their Majesties as many as eight cars, all with identical landaulet-style bodies. Standard Motor Company supplied some seventy vehicles (sixty cars and ten trucks) for the Durbar, and Madras-based coachbuilders Simpsons, coach-built fifty landaulet and tourer bodies on Darracqs for the same event.[8] It was also an occasion for a motor show to be held in Delhi, where Daimler, Lanchester and several other carmakers had their models on display, mostly supplied through their distributors in India.

With almost all of the 560-odd princes of India in attendance at the Durbar, to pay obeisance to their English masters, the automobile became the perfect symbol for Imperial England, the ultimate expression of the technological superiority of the West, as well as an object of immense desire and prestige. Every prince worth his salt needed to have one. Yet there was one problem: many of the princely states in the remoter parts of the country hardly had any 'motorable' roads. To be able to use the cars, which these enthusiastic princes acquired, the first set of macadam roads were constructed in the interiors of the country. Yet many made do with the dirt tracks of ages bygone, from ancient times.

Amongst the many princes, several were motoring pioneers, with the most notable being Ranji, the Maharaja of Nawanagar. Long before cricket became the king of games in India, it was essentially a game for the kings, the rajas and the maharajas. Of them, the most famous, without any doubt, was Ranjitsinhji Vibhaji Jadeja. Born on 10 September 1872, Ranji became the Maharaja of Nawanagar, a thirteen-gun-salute state in Gujarat, in 1907. Before that, though, he was already famous as one of the world's best cricketers, if not the best.

After attending Trinity College, Cambridge, where he bought the first automobile as a plaything, he played for the cricket team of the county of Sussex in the United Kingdom and served as the team captain. In 1896, Ranji joined the English cricket team, becoming the first Indian to play top-level international cricket, and he went on to play for England until 1902. Widely regarded as one of the greatest players of all time, Ranji's playing was described by Sir John Frederick Neville Cardus, an English writer and critic, best known for his writing on music and cricket, as 'the Midsummer night's dream of cricket'.[9] Unorthodox in technique and with exceptionally fast reactions, he brought a new style to cricket and revolutionized the game. Always held in very high esteem, the most important first-class cricket tournament in India, the Ranji Trophy, was named in his honour.

Playing and staying in England at long stretches, Ranji befriended brothers Frederick, George and Frank Lanchester, who, in 1896, were the first to make an all-British car. Ranji bought his first Lanchester—a 12hp twin-cylinder motor car—in 1904, with which he competed in the Delhi-Bombay Reliability Trials in 1904. Since the first Lanchester 12hp, whenever a new model was introduced by the English carmaker, at least one was shipped to India to add to Ranji's Lanchester collection. It's not that the Maharaja of Nawanagar bought only Lanchesters—he had a fine collection of cars from other marques, too. Marques like Bentley, Bugatti, Chevrolet, Delahaye, Lagonda and Rolls-Royce. But his collection of Britain's oldest was the most extensive. As well as being a good friend of Frederick Lanchester, who spent many summers with Ranji in India, the maharaja may have also had some shares in the carmaker, explaining his desire to be a good client by example.

As the Maharaja Jam Sahib (a title specific to the state of Nawanagar), Ranji was a very progressive ruler and statesman. As well as modernizing the capital of Jamnagar, and developing the seaport of Nawanagar, he built roads, railways and irrigation facilities. During the First World War, he was a British army staff officer in France, attaining the rank of colonel. In 1920, he represented the Indian states at the League of Nations Assembly, Geneva, and in 1932, he became chancellor of the Indian Chamber of Princes.

Ranjitsinhji died in 1933, aged sixty. As he did not have any offspring, Ranji was succeeded by his nephew, the thirty-eight-year-old Digvijaysinhji Ranjitsinhji Jadeja, who remained the Maharaja Jam Sahib of Nawanagar until 1947, when Nawanagar was merged into the newly independent India. Continuing his uncle's policies of development and public service and upholding the cricketing tradition of his uncle (he served as President of the Board of Control for Cricket in India during 1937–38), Digvijaysinhji also served on the Imperial War Cabinet and the National Defence Council, as well as with the Pacific War Council during the Second World War. Most importantly for this book, he carried on with Ranji's penchant for Lanchesters: by 1940, at least forty-two Lanchesters had found their way to the Nawanagar stable of cars![10]

Not unlike Ranji, the Maharaja of Patiala, Rajinder Singh was another early enthusiast. As we know, the maharaja may have imported a steam-driven De Dion-Bouton as early as 1892, or around then. A petrol engine De Dion-Bouton may also have been imported around 1901. This, though, must have been by his son, the young Bhupinder Singh, who was crowned the maharaja when his father passed away in 1900. Two years later, another French car model, the single-cylinder Cottereau 7hp was imported. Featuring wooden wheels, the Cottereau looked a lot like the De Dion-Boutons from then.

'The Cottereau had two gear levers: one was for changing gears, the other for reverse,' explained English restorer Julia Williamson (who has restored this particular car, in recent times) to the author,[11] adding that the car also had pedals, 'the left foot for the clutch, which beyond a certain point also applies the transmission brake. The right foot pedal applies the rear brakes, which can also be applied with the hand brake lever. At the steering wheel, there are three levers: one for throttle, one for advance/retard and one for the valve lifters. A hand pump as well, to deliver the oil to the gearbox as well. That's six levers and a hand pump, all to be used correctly!'

The way Ranji had a passion for Lanchesters, Bhupinder Singh (who, incidentally, instituted the Ranji Trophy!), had an obsession with Rolls-Royces. As per André Blaize, the eminent Rolls-Royce archivist, Bhupinder Singh ordered—at the very least—twenty-five Silver Ghosts, four Phantoms, ten Twentys, one 20/25hp and two Phantom IIs. Eventually, the Patiala stables may have had more Rolls-Royces than the number of Lanchesters at Nawanagar, but then the Patiala stables were reputed to be 186 cars strong!

Competing with the Maharaja of Patiala was the man who, in all likelihood, may have been richer than he, the Nizam of Hyderabad, the Asaf Jah VI, Mir Mahboob Ali Khan Siddiqi Bayafandi. Fief over a land mass of 2,12,000 square kilometres, bigger than the size of England and Scotland together, the sixth nizam also took to the automobile in a big way, acquiring a French Richard-Brasier 16/24hp around 1906, followed by a set of six Napier cars in quick succession. Napiers then were the most luxurious English cars, and predated Rolls-Royce's rise to the top. Other cars followed—apparently, thirty cars were bought in a span of three years—before Mahboob Ali Khan passed away in 1911.

Mir Osman Ali Khan Siddiqi, Asaf Jah VII, the seventh nizam, had a different kind of passion for the automobile, preferring to acquire the most elaborate, and the most lavish. By the time the nizam was acknowledged as the wealthiest man in the world by *Time* magazine[12] (circa 1937), this was not just reflected in his famed mountain of pearl or the 162-carat Jacob diamond that he owned, but in the 200-odd cars that were part of the palace stables. The royal mews housed dozens of Bentleys, Buicks, Delahayes, Duesenbergs, Cadillacs, Humbers, Jaguars, Mercedes-Benzes, Napiers, Oldsmobiles, Packards and, of course, Rolls-Royces, including the famous 'throne car'.

Ordered by Osman Ali Khan soon after he had ascended the throne, this Rolls-Royce 40/50hp (better known as a Silver Ghost later on), from 1913, featured a rear section which was raised to take on a regal throne-like seat, the upholstery in brocade and gold. In the *American Commerce Reports*, the description of the car is: 'a car that was imported from England for the use of the ruler of the largest Native State in India is given: It has a 40 to 50 horsepower, six-cylinder chassis, detachable wheels, and groove tyres. The rear part of the body is raised, giving a higher seat for the nizam, and the back cushion is fitted with double folding arm rests, which when down afford an extremely comfortable armchair seat in the centre. There are also in the interior of the car four small collapsible seats for the officials of his highness. The "celestial" or domed roof is finished with silver beading and bordered with silver fender plating of fleur-de-lis pattern. The ornamentation on the top of the domed roof is a silver "cap of maintenance", an emblem of local significance, which adds to the dignity of the car's appearance.'[13]

'As related by Hyderabad automotive enthusiast and authority, Deepak Gir, to the author:[14] 'Legend has it that on the nizam's return once from a trip to Delhi, he was received at the Hyderabad station in the Rolls-Royce. The crowd was so large that it was impossible to drive, and the car ended up being pushed all the way to the palace.' Which may also explain why this highly purpose-built ceremonial car has less than 400 miles on the odometer, as of 2020!

Of much more modest means (and much better taste), yet another early adoptor of the automobile was the Maharana of Rajpipla, Chhatrasinhji. Competing in the same Bombay-Mahabaleshwar Trials of 1906 as had Ranji, Chhatrasinhji participated with a French Clément-Bayard 16hp. Unlike Ranji, Chhatrasinhji drove exceedingly well and so did not lose a single point, winning the class for cars costing between £253 and £450, and was one of only two in those trials who was not penalized. Three years earlier Chhatrasinhji had bought a Wolseley 6hp, which he drove around himself, dispensing with the need for a chauffeur.

One of the earliest Wolseley-Siddeleys imported into India, a 15hp landaulet from 1906 was also acquired by the maharana. With his fleet of cars expanding, the maharana hired K. Messia as a motor engineer and chauffeur to maintain them. Messia received a salary of Rs 300 per month (when the per capita was Rs 200 per head per year), as well as free board and lodging. He had five cars in his charge, and apparently, he 'overhauled and repaired a Clément-Bayard car in a satisfactory manner'.

The passion for fine cars carried on to the next generation, and the Rajpipla family owned several very fine cars, with Maharana Vijaysinhji owning twelve Rolls-Royce cars at various points of time, from a 1913 Silver Ghost to a 1937 Phantom III, as per the records of Rolls-Royce archivist André Blaize. He also acquired a Daimler, a Bentley and a Riley, amongst others.

The reliability trials from Delhi to Bombay at first, and then the later ones from Bombay to Mahabaleshwar and to Kolhapur, acted as incentives for some of the other no less enthusiastic princes to partake in the sport of the automobile. The Maharaja of Cooch Behar, Nripendra Narayan Bhup Bahadur, was one such early adept of the automobile. For the reliability trials of 2–5 February 1908, from Bombay to Kolhapur and then back via Mahabaleshwar, the trophy for the winner of Class 3 was given away by the Maharaja of Cooch Behar. Class 3 was a category of vehicles with a selling price of less than Rs 7000, or £466, and the trophy itself was valued at the equivalent of Rs 1000, which was a considerable sum of money then.

The legend of the Rolls-Royce

The overall winner of the same reliability trials was a Rolls-Royce 40/50hp Silver Ghost; in all likelihood, one of the very early Rolls-Royces imported into India. Brought in by a merchant trader Frank Norbury, and showcased at the Bombay motor show, where the car garnered a 'best of show', it was entered for the Bombay-Kolhapur Reliability Trials, which it won, for its completely trouble-free performance.

Very impressed, the Maharaja of Gwalior, Madhavrao Scindia, bought the car, and had it repainted from its original cream to a silver-white hue, which may have been powdered pearl mixed with pigment. The maharaja, Madhavrao Scindia, not surprisingly, had a passion for pearls. With its striking pearlescent livery, this 1908 40/50hp Rolls-Royce, the thirty-seventh car in the series, was soon rechristened the

'Pearl of the East', and was one of the first Rolls-Royces to be given a name, a rare tradition, which in time made certain Rolls-Royces legendary in the history of the automobile. It was also the car, which set off the craze for Rolls-Royces amongst Indian royalty.

Over the years, the wealthiest of the Indian princes competed with each other in the number of Rolls-Royces they acquired, so much so that India became one of that British prestige carmaker's most important markets. Yet, with some 900-odd finding their way to India before the start of the Second World War, the numbers were not all that significant, given that Rolls-Royce had produced more than 20,000 cars by then.

For that matter, Rolls-Royces were not the only great automobiles—there were so many during the pre-War era and, truth be told, just a handful of the Indian princes had the knowledge and the discerning taste to identify and acquire the most innovative or the finest.

One such early aficionado of thoroughbred automotive machinery was Maharaj Man Singhji Dowlat Singhji, the brother of the maharaja, His Highness Himat Singhji Dowlat Singhji of Idar, a fifteen-gun-salute state from Gujarat. The maharaj's son, Maharaj Umeg Singhji, explained to this author that his father was a true-blue enthusiast, who not only had a passion for exciting cars, but also had an abiding interest in aviation, as did his brother, the maharaja. The maharaja was a founder member of the Bombay Flying Club and his love of flying and speed must have reflected in their choice of cars. The Idar roll call of cars was not unusually long, but was most tasteful, and amongst the several fine ones that they acquired, there were American rarities in the form of an Auburn Speedster, as well as the most prestigious American, a Duesenberg, plus, several French beauties such as a Bugatti and a Delage. The rarest and the most extraordinary of their stable, though, was another French car, called Farman.

Brothers Henri and Maurice Farman initially sold and raced bicycles, then cars later. Soon, the brothers' interests turned to the latest mechanical adventure: aviation. On 13 January 1908, Henri won the Archdeacon Cup for successfully completing the first official flight of over a kilometre, in a southern suburb of Paris, flying a Voisin, with a

Gnome engine. The Wright brothers had flown farther, but not under official sanction. Subsequently, Henri was credited with coining the term 'aileron'—the small, hinged sections on the outboard portion of a wing that is used to control the direction of an aircraft. A few months later, on 30 October, Henri, in a Voisin again, made the first intercity flight ever: a 27-km run from Bouy to Reims, France. Soon after, the brothers decided to start making planes, and with the advent of the First World War, Farman became a significant aircraft maker, making 12,000 aircrafts by the end of war.

In 1919, the brothers turned once again to the world of automobiles. They wanted theirs to be the very best around, and given their aircraft-making background, materials, technology and aerodynamics from the more exacting world of aviation became the starting point of the cars that Farman made. The Farman A6, launched in 1921, was one of the most powerful and luxurious cars ever, and was befitting of their slogan, 'A car rolls, a Farman glides', which was a tongue-in-cheek reference to their main rival from across the channel. Selling from the brothers' palatial showroom at the Champs-Élysées, Farman became the car to have for those who knew their automobile, and soon the list of a very exclusive clientele included the likes of cinema's first woman star Pearl White, and royalty such as the Shah of Persia, Ahmad Shah Qajar, and the Sultan of Morocco, Youssef Ben Hassan.

As the Idar brothers were into aviation, they must have been well aware of Farman's technological capabilities, and were, in all likelihood, a fans of the marque. Their knowledge and enthusiasm is borne out by the fact that the maharaj (maharaja's brother) chose to have his Farman coach built in a most unconventional body style. Most of the Indian princes tended to have their cars in a tourer or a closed body saloon style—the Farman (an A6B, which was an evolution of the A6) features a most unusual four-door torpedo body style with a tapering boat-tail.

Well-known car designer and journalist Robert Cumberford, whilst speaking to the author, had this to say of the Idar Farman: 'The boat-tail shape is unusual on a car with four seats; usually boat-tail speedsters were two-seaters. The lines of this A6B are graceful and rather advanced.' Points out Cumberford: 'There is no hiding the fact that the car is tall and looks heavy, but the flowing lines of the wings and the straight waistline are to its advantage, giving it the appearance of a car made ten years later.'[15]

Barely 100-odd Farmans seem to have been manufactured between 1921 and 1932, when the carmaker ceased activities, and just a few are extant today. The Idar A6B, unquestionably the most attractive amongst all Farmans, survives to this day.

Similar impeccable taste—and not a reflection of numbers—is to be seen in the cars acquired by the Maharaja of Wankaner, Pratapsinh Jhala. The maharaja owned a series of exciting, lightweight sports cars including the French Amilcar CG6 (a sort of a 'poor man's' Bugatti), a very early Bentley 3-Litre, from 1924, as well as an astoundingly beautiful Castagna-bodied Lancia Astura super sports car, plus several delectable English sportsters: a Lea-Francis, an MG and a Riley Imp.

Of course, it would be unfair to suggest that numbers reflect poor taste, as many of the wealthier princes managed to have both numbers and excellent taste in automobiles. A good example of that would be the Darbhanga family, who were, technically, very large landowners, zamindars that is, since the time of Akbar.

Maharaja Kameshwar Singh Bahadur, who 'ruled' from 1929 until India's Independence in 1947, was an avowed car enthusiast. Over the years, he acquired scores of cars that eventually grew to a collection of some ninety-odd, of which more than thirty were Rolls-Royces alone. Though he had a penchant for the English, including Daimlers and Bentleys, Kameshwar Singh also bought Buicks, Cadillacs and Packards. Yet, these cars were hardly used—with just 16 miles of paved roads within the estate, most of the cars covered very little mileage ever!

Some 2400 km south of Darbhanga was the much richer princely state of Mysore. With his personal wealth estimated at $400 million then (and $7 billion in 2020 prices), the Maharaja of Mysore, Krishnaraja Wadiyar IV, was considered the second richest man in India, after the Nizam of Hyderabad. Yet his interest in automobiles was restricted to the usual fleet of Rolls-Royces and other 'standard-issue' luxury marques. It was his successor, his nephew, who would become a very fine connoisseur of the automobile.

Jayachamaraja Wodeyar Bahadur, the twenty-fifth and the last Maharaja of Mysore, was one of the most knowledgeable collectors of cars. He was also one of India's more illustrious princes, who was acknowledged as a philosopher, a musicologist, a political thinker, as well as a philanthropist. Graduating from the Maharajas College in Mysore in 1938, Jayachamaraja Wodeyar won five awards and gold medals for academic brilliance. That same year he was married off, and in 1939, he toured Europe, visiting many associations in London and becoming acquainted with many artists and scholars. He was just twenty-one years old when he ascended the throne on 8 September 1940 after the demise of his uncle Maharaja Krishnaraja Wodeyar.

A true-blue automotive aficionado, the Maharaja of Mysore bought some of the most interesting of cars in the immediate post-War period. The maharaja, when he had taken to a marque, believed in acquiring them in numbers: at the least, six Bentleys and around five Daimlers were acquired during the late 1940s, early 1950s.

In fact, two of the largest Daimlers ever, the DE36, were bought by default. These cars were prepared for the Australian tour of King George VI. The tour never went ahead though because of the king's illness. The Australian government had ordered six large DE36 Daimlers: three landaulet, two tourers and one limousine, with coachwork by Hooper for all of them. With the cancellation of the tour, there was no immediate need for the pricey Daimlers and the cars were disposed of. One of the tourers and one of the landaulets were sold, either through Hooper, or by the Australian government, to the Maharaja of Mysore.

A 2.8-tonne mammoth, one of these DE36s was used for many years by the maharaja for his annual Dussehra festival procession to the temple of the family's deity, Chamundeshwari. With the ceremonial elephants in tow, the car matching the elephants in size and presence, the procession always made for great photography.

In the post-War period, when car manufacturing resumed, the basic Bentley Mk VI 'Standard Steel saloon' came with factory-fitted bodywork, which was discrete, yet elegant. And in being more low profile and understated, the Bentley was the right car at the right time—post-War austerity was the mood of the moment, and the Rolls-Royce was seen as more ostentatious. In all likelihood, Maharaja Jayachamaraja Wodeyar, with his refined tastes and his regular exposure to Europe, preferred the discretion of the Bentleys over Rolls-Royces, which may explain why he went and acquired as many as six of them in a short span of time.

At the same time, the maharaja fell in love with the rather flamboyant Figoni et Falaschi-bodied Delahaye 175 from the 1949 Salon de Paris. One of the more famous French marques from the pre-War era, Delahaye launched the 175 in 1947, as a development of the pre-War 135 model. Featuring six-cylinder engines, mated to a pre-selector-type semi-automatic gearbox, the Delahaye 175 was a complicated (and finicky) piece of high technology. A shorter wheelbase version, the 175 S, was developed for competition and one such car was entered for the 1951 Monte Carlo Rally, where it finished first in the hands of drivers Jean Trevoux and Roger Crovetto.

When the 175 was launched in 1947, at the Salon de Paris, to showcase the all-new car, Delahaye commissioned France's most prominent coachbuilders, Figoni et Falaschi, to come up with one of their most flamboyant and inimitable designs. The show car took pride of place at the Delahaye stand, placed as it was on one of the very first rotating turntables at a motor show. The car featured a flowing coupé body style in which the front fender flowed down and merged into the rear wheel spats, the rear sloping down to a wedge. With a removable transparent Plexiglas top over the front half of the greenhouse, the car was easily one of the most distinctive at the show. The interior was done up in Hermes leather.

Two years later, for the 1949 edition of Salon de Paris, Figoni et Falaschi unveiled a very similar Delahaye 175 coupé. This one was almost identical to the '47 Salon car, but instead of the transparent Plexiglas, it was a regular hardtop coupé with a more practical removable sunroof. Painted a light metallic blue, which gave the effect of diamond powder lacquering, it was undoubtedly a very striking car, and the Maharaja of Mysore acquired the car right after the show.

The car was taken out of India in the 1970s, and was eventually owned by Elton John. Now it is one of the star cars at the famous Petersen Automotive Museum, in Los Angeles.

The other unusual car which the maharaja owned was an Invicta Black Prince, a car that the maharaja bought when he was planning a nice long holiday touring Europe, in 1948. For that drive around the Continent, he decided upon a car touted as the ultimate state-of-the-art automobile, in a United Kingdom fresh out of war, victorious and ready for the most modern in technology.

Though Invicta had closed shop in or about 1935, the brand was rejuvenated in 1946 when it was relaunched as the Invicta Car Development Company. The Black Prince (as the new model was named) featured a very modern engine from engine specialists Meadows, as well as several other advanced features, such as all-round independent suspension, built-in jacks and a battery charger, an electric immersion heater for oil and water, a Smiths heater and a radio.

The technological talking point of the new model, though, was the gearbox. A fully automatic transmission, the Brockhouse Hydro-Kinetic Turbo-Transmitter offered an infinite variety of ratios, controlled by a simple forward-and-reverse switch. The problem was that the gearbox had not undergone any protracted testing or development. So going forward was no problem, but the pawl catch that engaged reverse was notoriously liable to failure, which happened to most of the Black Princes soon after delivery.

The maharaja's Black Prince rolled out of the Invicta factory on 30 June 1948. First time out on the road, the maharaja found driving an automatic a dream, but the car just would not reverse. There was no way that the maharaja could take the car for his tour of Europe—instead he had it shipped out to India, to Bangalore, leaving him with no choice but to buy another car, a Bentley once again, for his European holiday. Barely sixteen to eighteen Black Princes were ever manufactured, before word got around and potential buyers disappeared. By 1950, Invicta was bankrupt once again.

Of the sixteen-odd cars, thirteen are extant as of 2019, of which a bare half a dozen are convertibles, one of them being the car that the

Maharaja of Mysore had bought. The car survives, in Mumbai, with a Parsee family, which has owned it since 1961. It is one of the few which still run—this almost one-of-a-kind Black Prince is taken out on occasional weekends for a salubrious drive on Worli SeaFace, or on Marine Drive.

The decade or two before the Maharaja of Mysore was impressing all with his automotive taste and flamboyance, the two scions of the Nizam of Hyderabad, Azam Jah, Damat Walashan Sahebzada Nawab Sir Mir Himayat Ali Khan Bahadur Bey Effendi and Moazzam Jah, Walasham Shahzada Nawab Mir Sir Shuja'at Ali Khan Siddiqui Bahadur, went on a splurge. Respectively the elder and the younger sons of the Nizam of Hyderabad, Mir Osman Ali Khan, Azam Jah and Moazzam Jah acquired some of the most expensive and rare automobiles ever to grace the roads of India.

The Ottoman factor

Though India did not have much to do with the Ottoman Empire, a spectacular double marriage hit the headlines in early 1931. On 21 February 1931, Princess Hadice Hayriye Ayshe Durruhsehvar and Princess Niloufer Khanum Sultana were married to Azam Jah and Moazzam Jah, respectively. The sublimely beautiful Princess (or Sultana) Durruhsehvar was one of the daughters of Abdul Mejid II, the last Ottoman Caliph and cousin and heir of the last sultan of the Ottoman Empire, Sultan Abdul Aziz. Though the princess was born in Turkey in 1916, when the Ottoman Empire was passing through its last phase, her family eventually went into exile in Nice after the abolition of the Caliphate by Mustafa Kemal in 1924. Sought by the Shah of Persia and King Faud of Egypt as a bride for their respective heirs, Mohammed Reza Pahlavi and Farouk, it was the Nizam of Hyderabad who 'won' Durruhsehvar over for his elder son, hoping that the family would eventually 'inherit' the Caliphate.

To make things doubly sure, the nizam got his second son Moazzam Jah to wed Durruhsehvar's cousin Princess Niloufer, the great-granddaughter of Sultan Murad V, the Ottoman Emperor for a brief period in 1876, and the (deposed) brother of Sultan Abdul Aziz. Moazzam Jah and his brother Azam Jah, unlike their father, who was known to be very tight-fisted, enjoyed the good life, spending lavishly, holidaying in Europe with their beautiful wives, and buying many fancy bolides. Amongst the cars that the two brothers bought was a pair of Duesenbergs, a Mercedes-Benz SS, an Auburn V12, Cadillacs, Bentleys, Packards, Jaguars and sure enough, several Rolls-Royces.

The most spectacular of Azam Jah's many Rolls-Royces was a Phantom III. With a Windovers cabriolet body, the car was finished in mustard yellow, with the rear wings, dual spare wheel covers, full rear spats and a broad side swage line in maroon. The hood was in a dark-red material, stored in a dark red mohair envelope at the rear of the car. Crests and monograms in gold were painted on the front doors. A Lalique glass mascot could be illuminated either red or blue. The interior was fitted in gold-coloured leather, piped in dark red. There was red leather flooring to the front compartment and red carpet to the rear. The steering wheel rim was in ivory. All the side windows of the car were of red-tinted Triplex glass. Inside, there was a cocktail cabinet with a soda bottle and three large cut-glass tumblers. There were Thermos flasks to each elbow of the rear seat, and to the offside, there was a detachable spittoon made to look like a speaking tube. Noteworthy were the revolver holsters fitted to each side of the dash!

Moazzam Jah's Rolls-Royce Silver Wraith was relatively mundane, one of the twenty-five Park Ward saloon coachworks built to design number thirteen. More interestingly, Moazzam Jah ordered a pair of identical cars, with the other one for his wife Niloufer, but there is some doubt whether he took delivery of the car (instead, it may have been picked up by the Bhavnagar royal family.) With the upheavals of history and the vicissitudes of time, Moazzam and Niloufer went their separate ways eventually (with Moazzam marrying twice again). The former passed away in 1987 in Hyderabad, the latter dying in Paris two years later. Azam Jah and Durruhsehvar also parted ways.

During those same years, the story of love and the automobile, some 1500 km north-west of Hyderabad, in Jaipur, was taking on a different hue. After being adopted to become the Maharaja of Jaipur,

Madho Singh II had numerous (no less than sixty-five) children by various concubines, but the highly superstitious maharaja was warned by a sage against having legitimate heirs and thus took great care not to impregnate his five wives! Thus, on 24 March 1921, Madho Singh II adopted his kinsman, the ten-year-old Mor Mukut to be his son and heir. The boy was renamed Man Singh upon his adoption. Madho Singh II died a little over a year later, and in 1922, was succeeded by Man Singh as the Maharaja of Jaipur. The new maharaja was just eleven years young.

Upon his ascension, Sawai Man Singh embarked on a programme of modernization, setting up infrastructure and founding numerous public institutions, which would later result in Jaipur's selection as the capital of Rajasthan. Recognized as one of India's best polo players, Sawai Man Singh also won, among other trophies, the World Cup in 1933. Incidentally, in 1970, Man Singh had a fall while playing polo in England and he died later the same day. He was survived by his third wife Gayatri Devi and four sons.

Though he was married twice to 'suitable' brides, his most famous relationship was his courtship and subsequent espousal of the legendary beauty, Gayatri Devi of Cooch Behar, daughter of Maharaja Jitendra and Indira Raje. Much younger than Sawai Man Singh, Gayatri Devi, who was once described as one of the most beautiful women in the world, survived the maharaja by several decades, and passed away on 29 July 2009, aged ninety. Very elegant, she retained a few of the beautiful cars which Sawai Man Singh had acquired over the years. One was a Bentley 4½ Litre MX Series from 1937 (which was bought two years before she got married to the maharaja), the other being a Jaguar XK120 from 1950.

There is a legend around this. When Gayatri Devi and Sawai Man Singh were holidaying in Europe, once on an outing, a sports car flashed past to which the maharani exclaimed: 'What was that!' The next morning the doorbell rang, and the maharani opened the door to be greeted by Jaguar officials who were there to deliver a stunning, brand new XK120 to the young lady. It was a gift from her doting husband. Gayatri Devi retained the car until her death.

Just 160 km north-east of Jaipur, in the state of Alwar, the maharaja's taste in automobiles was rather special. The only son of the previous ruler, Sir Mangal Singh Prabhakar Bahadur, Colonel His Highness Raj Rishi Shri Sawai Maharaja Sir Jai Singh Veerendra Shiromani Dev Bharat Prabhakar Bahadur (to spell out his full name!) was made the Maharaja of Alwar when he was only ten-years-old, in 1892. Initially noted as brilliant, erudite and charming, Maharaja Jai Singh, however, was also known to be cruel and profligate, deifying himself and using the wealth of the state for his own needs. Whenever British inspectors arrived, he turned his charm on them to show that conditions in Alwar were quite good, despite whatever stories there may have been told to the contrary.

Yet an incident on 7–8 January 1933, when more than thirty people were killed, forced the British authorities to convene a board of inquiry against the maharaja, where he was found guilty of mishandling the situation. Instead of prosecuting him, the English deposed him, and then exiled him from India altogether, to the city of his choice, Paris.

Despite his eccentricities—and there were legions, as legends go— the maharaja was quite a big spender as far as cars were concerned, and over the years, before he was banished, he had acquired quite an interesting collection of cars. Some have mentioned that he did not care all that much for Rolls-Royces, yet Maharaja Jai Singh did buy, at the least, nine new Rolls-Royces (six Silver Ghosts, two Twentys and at least one New Phantom). His real passion, though, was for Hispano-Suizas, the French-made rival to the Rolls-Royce, and considered by many to be significantly more sophisticated. By the time he went into exile, he had at least fifteen of them, making him one of the biggest collectors of Hispano-Suizas ever.

Most of his Hispanos were huge, stately affairs, though he did order them in various wheelbases and body styles, his favourite being the H6Bs. As per legend, he bought his cars in threes, used them for three years and then had them buried. So, digging around Alwar you may not strike gold, but perhaps rusted metal. In all likelihood, another unsubstantiated legend, perhaps not true at all.

One of the more spectacular Hispano-Suizas in the Jai Singh stable was an H6C, from 1927, with the registration plate reading

Alwar 3—thus it must have been an important car in the scheme of things during Maharaja Jai Singh's time, believes marque historian and expert Hans Veenenbos.

Alwar 3 may have been used for hunting, too, going by the gun cases mounted on the running boards and the powerful Stephen Grebel spot lamps. Riding on a specially stretched wheelbase chassis of 3.37 metres long, this Hispano featured an H.J. Mulliner Salamanca limousine coachwork, which was flexible enough to convert the car into a 'throne' car, too (which again seems to be a questionable use, as the maharaja had a very elaborate Lanchester throne car specially made as a throne car). It is also possible that the car was used as a 'zenana' car, a car for the women to travel in 'purdah' privacy.

Incidentally, the maharaja was a strict vegetarian (despite which he seemed to love hunting or were the guns there just for effect!), and so all his cars featured fabric wherever leather needed to be used. For instance, the leather inserts between the leaf springs were replaced by poor-surviving fabric, which needed replacement regularly, and the interiors of his cars were always done up in silk and brocade, never leather.

A little over 100 km to the east of Alwar is Bharatpur. For reasons similar to that of Jai Singh's, the Maharaja of Bharatpur, Sir Kishen Singh, was also exiled in 1924, five years before he passed away. Maharaja Brijindar Sawai Ram Singh Bahadur Jang, the father of Kishen Singh, had developed the famous wetland, the Bharatpur Bird Sanctuary, for the private entertainment of his family and friends. In 1921, one of the most famous hunts of all took place when the Prince of Wales (who later became—for a rather short period—King Edward VIII) visited Bharatpur as part of a royal tour of India. On the morning that the Prince of Wales visited Bharatpur, 1721 birds were shot, of which sixty-four were shot by the prince, and seventy-three by the maharaja. (It is difficult to imagine it today, but during his Indian tour, Prince Edward shot thirty tigers, six leopards, three bears and ten rhinoceroses as part of his total kill of ninety-five game animals!)

Important enough amongst the many princely states of India, the royal family of Bharatpur, accorded a nineteen-gun salute by the viceroy, trace their ancestry to the eleventh-century Sinsiwa Jat clan, a fierce, warlike people from the dusty plains of northern India. They achieved prominence in the late seventeenth century under a Jat freebooter who harassed the armies of Aurangzeb, and carved out a swathe of territory for his clan between Delhi and Agra.

The communitarian Kishen Singh, seventeenth in the line of rulers, was reputed to have kept as many as two dozen Rolls-Royces in his royal mews, including five of the smaller model, the Twenty, some of which were there to be part of the fleet of luxury cars to transfer his guests from the palace to the wetlands. One of the Rolls-Royce Twentys was specially equipped for tiger shooting.

Kishen Singh's specially bodied Rolls-Royce Twenty was one of the few genuine hunting cars, with the body by George Wilder of Kew Gardens, in Surrey, United Kingdom. A very unusual body style, termed a 'howdah' (a seat for elephants usually!), the four-door car has a folding dicky seat at the rear, that when opened out, faces backwards so that guarding against a tiger attacking from the rear becomes easier . . . The car also has a sunroof that opens out for the maharaja to be able to take pot shots at tigers and other animals, standing up within the car, the roof acting as a turret from where to swivel around and shoot all and sundry.

Described as eccentric and extravagant, the maharaja bought game animals at inflated prices and let them loose in his game park for his shikar trips. A spendthrift, Kishen Singh beggared Bharatpur by spending Rs 7.8 million, more than twice its revenue, in 1924. Ultimately, he was deposed by the British colonial authorities—he died four years later in 'exile', in Agra, just 62 km from Bharatpur (!) in 1929. Of course, all this did not stop him from sending his son, the young prince Vrijendra Singh, to gain an English education. Starting off at the exclusive Bryanston School in England, Vrijendra Singh completed his education at the other end of the world, at Wellington, in New Zealand. Although he was clearly being groomed for the position of maharaja, the youth had to wait until 1939, when he turned twenty-one, before the British administration would allow him to assume the full responsibilities of the position.

In the meantime, the maharajkumar, Vrijendra Singh, led a good life, organizing shoots at his sanctuary, as well as buying the automobiles he fancied. One of them was a Horch 480, a rare and expensive German supercar from the period, a true rival to the fastest cars produced by Mercedes-Benz and Bugatti then. The maharajkumar's Horch was the twenty-fifth car built out of a total production run of only a few more than fifty, in this model's two-year production life (1931–32), so even in the 1930s these were rare cars indeed. For that matter, cars from the Auto Union group, to which Horch belonged (the others were Audi, DKW and Wanderer) were very rare in the subcontinent.

Around 1933 or 1934, the 1931 Horch was given away to Robert Gove, an Australian who dealt in horses, and was a good friend of the Bharatpur family. The details are sketchy today but the seventeen-year-old maharajkumar and the veteran horseman agreed to an arrangement, which saw Robert Gove take possession of the 1931 Horch 480 from the maharajkumar's garage as a gift or in part payment for a prize horse. The Horch left India for Australia around then.

In all likelihood, the young maharajkumar would have barely missed the car in the enormous garage, given that Vrijendra Singh, years later, in lieu of payment for a stay at New Delhi's luxury hotel Claridge's, had left behind one of his Rolls-Royces to adjust against his bill, a Horch for a horse (or horses) does not sound at all improbable.

The true connoisseurs

In contrast, the maharajas of Indore and Kapurthala were true automotive connoisseurs, real enthusiasts, who were very particular about the automobiles they owned and used. Kapurthala, formerly a thirteen-gun-salute princely state, is one of the smallest districts of Punjab. Originally founded by Nawab Kapoor Singh, it was made the capital of a new state founded by S. Fateh Singh Ahluwalia in 1772. Situated at a distance of 19 km south-west of the city of Jalandhar, Kapurthala was already famous for its architectural monuments and beautiful gardens. Once called the Paris of Punjab, it was not unusual

for the heir apparent of Kapurthala—the Tika Raja, as he was titled—
to be in Paris, the city, which was a favourite of the family.

Jagatjit Singh, the Maharaja of Kapurthala from 1877 to 1949,
was an unabashed Francophile, and a regular in Paris. Unlike so
many Indian princes, Maharaja Jagatjit Singh was a globetrotter and
was out of the country for at least six months in a year, the summer
invariably being spent in Europe, specifically Paris and Nice and on
the Cote d'Azur. Fluent in French (he wrote his personal diary in that
language), the country left an indelible impression on the tastes and
predilections of the maharaja in as much as that the palace, which
he constructed for himself (and designed by the French architect
Alexandre Marcel), was largely influenced by the architectural features
of the palaces of Fontainebleau and Versailles. An honorary colonel in
the Indian Army, the maharaja was also awarded a Legion d'Honneur
by the French in 1924.

Contrary to popular legend, Maharaja Jagatjit Singh did not have
several hundred women at his beck and call—he had six wives over
the years. Of these, the last two were European: a very young Spanish
beauty called Anita Delgado, whom he married on 28 January 1908,
and who was the subject of a book (*La Pasión India*)[16] by Spanish writer
Javier Moro, and Evgenia Grosupova, the daughter of a Czech count
and Nina Grosupova, an actress.

Jagatjit Singh's son, the Tika Raja (which was equivalent to the
maharajkumar title) Paramjit Singh, was also a regular in Europe,
specifically Paris, and who appreciated the good life, beautiful women
and gorgeous cars. Even though Paramjit Singh was already married
to Brinda Devi, a princess from the royal family of Jubbal who 'with
her princely husband destined to be maharaja, was the toast of Paris,
the 'jewels in the crown' of French society, mingling with deposed
European crowned heads, including King Alphonso of Spain and
Queen Marie of Romania'.[17]

Yet the Tika Raja could not resist the charm of Astella Alice
Mudge, an Englishwoman, who eked out a living dancing in Paris'
famous Folies Bergère. Thus began an intense relationship that lasted
some fifteen years before the Tika Raja decided to marry Stella (as Astella

preferred being called) in 1937, making her his third wife, and renaming her Tika Rani (eventually becoming the maharani when her husband became the maharaja in 1949) Narinder Kaur.

As a wedding gift, Narinder Kaur née Stella Mudge, received a car from the smitten Tika Raja. Not just any old car, but arguably the most beautiful car which was on sale anywhere in the world in 1937: a Talbot-Lago T150-C-SS sports coupé. Whose choice was the Talbot-Lago is not known, but the Kapurthala family was known for their classy taste, which differentiated them from many of the other princely families of India. Maharaja Jagatjit Singh did not care for Rolls-Royces, the staple transport for most of the Indian maharajas, and instead preferred French and European marques such as Hispano-Suiza, Peugeot, Minerva and Lancia. The Tika Raja had already been a client of coachbuilder Joseph Figoni, having purchased a Delage *conduite intérieure* in May 1932, as pointed out by Figoni's son, Claude Figoni to this author. Thus, it is quite possible that the Tika Raja, given his eclectic taste, as a gift for his favourite wife, chose the swankiest car on the planet.

The Talbot-Lago was an absolute stunner. With a 'goutte d'eau' (teardrops in French) body style, just fourteen of these spectacular cars were ever made. Stella's gift, chassis number 90107, is considered to be the most unique of the series: the only one with fully skirted front and rear aluminium fenders, all aluminium body, a sunroof, painted wheels and a cloisonné hood ornament in the shape of a royal crown, testifying to the car's royal Indian connection.

Stella (who was known in Paris as the 'Rose of India') kept the car for at least two years, often competing at concours d'elegance events in France, reputedly changing the colour and upholstery to match her gowns (though this does not seem to be true), and winning several 'best of show' prizes. Sometime in 1939, Stella de Kapurthala (as she was often called) decided to unload her wedding gift, and Luigi Chinetti, the famous Italian-American racer and importer of exotic cars, arranged to have the Talbot-Lago sold to a wealthy Southern Californian playboy called Tommy Lee.

The Maharaja of Kapurthala Jagatjit Singh died on 19 June 1949. His son, Paramjit Singh became the maharaja (in name only, as

Kapurthala had merged into independent India) in 1949, but lived for another six years only. His long-suffering first wife, Maharani Brinda Devi, died in 1962.

Stella, though, outlived them all. Accumulative and self-centred, Stella stayed on in India, living at first in Delhi, and then moving to the hill station of Shimla. It was in Shimla that in January 1984, she 'fell in her flat in a drunken stupor and lay unconscious for several days', according to the fascinating story recounted in the pages of Coralie Younger's book, *Wicked Women of the Raj*. The police found her, took her to the Shimla Sanitarium, from where she was transferred to St Stephen's Hospital in Delhi. Stella never recovered, and passed away on 23 February 1984, in Delhi, where she is buried.

The story of the Yashwantrao Holkar II, the Maharaja of Indore, is less dramatic. Yet his choice of wheels and his involvement in their design and coachbuilding makes him the finest automotive aesthete India has ever had. Named after his most famous ancestor—the legendary sixth ruler of Indore Yashwantrao Holkar, who ruled from 1798 to 1811 and was considered by many as the Napoleon of India for his exploits at successfully winning a series of wars against his neighbouring states with the objective of building up an empire—Yashwantrao Holkar II found himself on the throne in 1926 at the tender age of eighteen due to some infamous indiscretions of his father, Tukajirao Holkar III. The accession ceremony took place on 11 March 1926 at the Juna Rajbada (the Old Palace), and on 22 May 1926, Yashwantrao returned to England, where he had done his schooling at the posh public school of Charterhouse, to complete his university graduation at Christ Church college, Oxford.

During his stay in England and his travels in Europe, Yashwantrao Holkar was influenced considerably by the Art Deco movement. At the same time, he also gained considerable knowledge and a fine taste in the newly blossoming art of automotive design. One of the very first cars that he purchased was a Delage D8 with exquisite Figoni coachwork. The car was on display at the stand of the French coachbuilder Figoni, at the 1931 edition of London's motor show, at Olympia. Partial to beautiful French cars, the maharaja also had a Bugatti, a Delahaye and a Hispano-Suiza J12, as well as a very handsome, bespoke Mercedes-Benz 540K and an astoundingly beautiful Alfa Romeo 8C2900B Spider with Carrozzeria Touring coachwork, a car, which had the reputation of being the fastest production car in the world in the 1930s.

A true aficionado, what really made Yashwantrao Holkar a talking point amongst car enthusiasts was his patronizing of the English coachbuilding firm of J. Gurney Nutting, and specifically the kind of connection he had with both of Gurney Nutting's renowned stylists A.E. 'Mac' MacNeil and John Blatchley. The latter took over as Gurney Nutting's chief designer, when MacNeil left for rival coachbuilder James Young in 1936.

MacNeil and Blatchley could be considered two of the best pre-War English stylists, and both apparently worked to Yashwantrao Holkar's very succinct briefs. The result was a series of superb-looking cars that rolled out of J. Gurney Nutting's coachbuilding facilities: amongst them a beautifully proportioned 4 ½ Litre Lagonda, a stunning Duesenberg on a SJ chassis and a 4 ¼ Litre Bentley Aerofoil coupé.

In fact, it was Bentleys which the young maharaja was a great fan of—he acquired as many as seven of them over the years. The first was a supercharged Le Mans type 4 ¼ Litre from 1930 (which caught fire; the engine then was put into a speedboat, which ended up at the bottom of Mumbai harbour!), and the last one was a Bentley R Type Continental bought in 1954. The R Type Continental was an H.J. Mulliner-bodied car, but most of the others sported J. Gurney Nutting coachworks. Of them, one of the most notable was a 3 ½ Litre Bentley from 1935, which embodies the perfect leitmotif of the Holkar-MacNeil style: with superb two-toning amplifying the flowing lines of this (originally) cream-coloured (now green) coupé.

Given the distinctive designs and the sheer aesthetic perfection of most of the Holkar cars, several of them have found their way abroad, with most placed in famous international collections. Quite a few of the most remarkable cars which came into India—a few of the Duesenbergs, the Idar Farman, an amazing Cadillac V16 with body by Farina in Italy, innumerable Rolls-Royces and Bentleys, several of Alwar's Hispano-Suizas, Nawanagar's Lanchesters, as well as many others were exported out, or smuggled out, of India, reaching Europe, the United States and elsewhere. At the same time, a few of the families of the princely kind have managed to retain some of their family 'autolooms', the most noteworthy being those of Gondal, Udaipur and Jodhpur.

Those who never let go

Located on the caravan route to Delhi, Central Asia and China, Jodhpur, a city perched on the edge of the Thar Desert, grew in wealth and power. Since 1459, when Rao Jodha, the local Rajput chieftain, shifted the capital from Mandore to Jodhpur, giving the place its name, and constructing the Mehrangarh Fort, the city grew over the years to become Rajasthan's second most important city after Jaipur.

Major H.H. Raj Rajeshwar Saramad Raj-hai Hindustan Maharaja Dhiraj Maharaja Sri Sir Umaid Singh Bahadur, the twenty-second in line after Rao Jodha, became the maharaja in 1918. One of the more enlightened amongst all the Indian princes, Maharaja Umaid Singh (to use the more convenient short form), as well as being the president of the British Royal Institute of Architects, was also a real 'car guy'. With its beautiful balconies, charming courtyards, green gardens and stately rooms, the Umaid Bhavan Palace sure made a fine example of Indo-Saracenic architecture, but Umaid Singh's car collection was no less eclectically tasteful.

In the years during which he was the maharaja—1918–47— Umaid Singh acquired a very wide collection of cars ranging from mundane Morrises to a fleet of very special Rolls-Royces. In his rather diverse bunch consisting of cars like Rovers, Chevrolets, Cadillacs and even a Talbot, Umaid Singh also had a Bugatti, as well as several Bentleys, including an exquisite 3 ½ litre Aerofil coupé with J. Gurney Nutting coachwork. Another delectable piece of machinery was a very stylish Vauxhall boat-tail speedster, a 13/98 from 1925. Yet it was his penchant for Rolls-Royces, with very tasteful coachworks, which really stands out.

One of the very first Rolls-Royces that Umaid Singh acquired was a Silver Ghost, a Barker-bodied car in polished aluminium, in 1920. He went on to own two more Silver Ghosts, three Rolls-Royce Twentys, as well as two Phantoms. A '27 Windovers limousine-bodied Phantom, with a very nicely proportioned design, in polished aluminium coachwork remains with the family.

With the launch of the Phantom II, Maharaja Umaid Singh bought a very stylish drophead coupé with French Binder coachwork in 1934. This car was taken out of India decades back, and in the early 1980s figured in the American TV serial *Bring 'Em Back Alive* as the car from the royal family of 'Bundi', an imaginary princely state from somewhere in the Far East. In the following year, the maharaja ordered another exquisite car, a J. Gurney Nutting Streamline Coupé—which is with a collector, Amir Ali Jetha, in Mumbai, at the time of writing, in 2020—as well as a Windovers drophead coupé, based on a Continental chassis, just like the Streamline Coupé.

This beautiful blue-coloured Windovers drophead coupé is still very much in the Umaid Bhavan Palace garage. A distinctive design, this Rolls-Royce exemplifies the best of 1930s car design, with a most unusual running-board step, which pops out as the door is opened: most convenient and mechanically a simple, but brilliant piece of engineering. Still 'residing' within the garages of Umaid Bhavan Palace, this one-owner car is a remarkable example of automotive history.

Maharaja Umaid Singh died on 9 June 1947, a couple of months before India became independent, and his eldest son, Hanwant Singh became the maharaja soon after. An automotive enthusiast too, his main passion though was polo, a sport which he was a champion at, the other interest being magic!

Hanwant Singh, in his short reign as maharaja (he died in a plane crash in 1952), acquired several cars from the General Motors' family, most specifically a beautiful two-tone Buick Roadmaster convertible, a couple of '47 Cadillacs, both Series 62s, as well as a 1948 Packard. All these cars remain at Umaid Bhavan. The most astounding automobile which he bought, though, was a Delahaye 135 MS, bodied by Figoni et Falaschi, which he acquired from

Bombay-based dealer Bachhoo Motors. This car remains in Jodhpur, but with Hanwant Singh's youngest brother Maharaj Dalip Singh. Arguably, this Delahaye is one of the most beautiful and valuable pre-War cars in India today.

A similar respect for history and the importance of family heirlooms—as well as 'autolooms'—can be seen with the princely family of Udaipur. Arvind Singh Mewar, popularly known as Shriji, is another aficionado, having opened one of India's first historic vehicle museums, in February 2000. With twenty-three-odd vehicles (twenty-one cars, one truck and one bus) in the museum, most are very special, in the sense that almost all are cars which have never changed hands, belonging to the family of the Maharana of Udaipur, cars which were acquired by Shriji's ancestors, the preceding maharanas, and then retained by the family over decades. Many more than the twenty-three on display were purchased by the maharanas since the earlier part of the twentieth century, but some were scrapped, some were disposed of and many were given away, to temples, staff, friends and family.

A feeling for history and a cognizance that automobiles have played a significant role in the history of princely India in the last one century have motivated Arvind Singh Mewar to preserve and restore the cars which remained in the ownership of the family. The cars range from mundane Morrises to regal Rolls-Royces.

Reflecting the simplicity of the maharanas, specifically that of Bhagwat Singh, who was the titular maharana from 1955 till his death in 1984, the collection includes two Morrises, one a 1950 Morris Tiger, the other a 1000 Traveller from 1959, though a Mercedes-Benz 180 D was the everyday-use car for the maharana. A Mercedes-Benz 190 Db and a 200 were also used by the maharana and his family. All three Mercedes-Benzes are in perfectly original state and are maintained as runners, with not very much mileage on them—the 180 D, for instance, has just a little over 36,000 km on the odometer. Similarly, a 1961 Austin Cambridge and a 1965 Rambler Classic also were runabouts for the family. There are even a Chevrolet truck and a bus (respectively from 1946 and 1947), which were used when the royal family went camping, the truck carrying the camping gear, the bus the retinue.

When the British authorities curbed Maharana Fateh Singh's powers in 1921, he remained the head of the state of Mewar, though in name only, until his death in 1930. Fateh Singh may have bought a Rolls-Royce 40/50hp Silver Ghost, in 1914 (the Udaipur Palace Motor Garage, though does not have any record of this car). It was his son Maharajkumar Bhupal Singh, who in 1921 was requested by the British to take over as the 'ruler' of Udaipur, who ordered at least three Rolls-Royce Twentys soon after he came to power.

The first of these was a Barker-bodied barrel-sided tourer that he acquired in 1922. The second, in 1923, was a most unusual one— another Barker-bodied tourer, but with a special hand control system for use by a differently abled person, the car was ordered so that the maharajkumar could use it. Paralysed from the waist down from the early age of sixteen, Bhupal Singh was nevertheless an expert hunter, going out on hunts strapped on to his horse. Even though most of the time he was chauffeured around, Bhupal Singh also wanted to be able to drive at least one of his Rolls-Royces, so this one came specially equipped for use by the prince himself.

In that same year, the Maharaja of Bharatpur, Sawai Kishen Singh, gifted Maharana Fateh Singh a brand new Rolls-Royce Twenty, again another Barker-bodied tourer. In 1927, the maharajkumar ordered a new Phantom with very elegant Hooper tourer coachwork, which was registered as Udaipur 3.

On the death of Maharana Fateh Singh in 1930, Bhupal Singh became the maharana officially and remained the 'ruler' of Udaipur until the state merged with India upon the country's Independence, making him the last 'official' Maharana of Udaipur.

After he officially became the maharana, Bhupal Singh bought at least three more Rolls-Royces. The first was a 20/25hp tourer with a Hooper body, ordered in 1930. The car arrived in 1931 and it received the registration plate of Udaipur 4. Three years later, the maharana ordered another Rolls-Royce 20/25. This time he got coachbuilders Thrupp & Maberly to make the limousine body. This car arrived in 1934, and received the registration number Udaipur 5.

In July 1936, the Udaipur stables acquired a 1924 Rolls-Royce Twenty, which used to belong to the Jodhpur princely family. This car received the registration plate of Udaipur 2. Restored during the beginning of the twenty-first century, Udaipur 2 has travelled everywhere, including Pebble Beach, where it won a special trophy, the Lucius Beebe Trophy.

Udaipur 4 and Udaipur 5 had different destinies. During the late 1960s, the then Maharana Bhagwat Singh decided to put the chassis of Udaipur 4 to a different use. The body was removed, and the garage at the palace converted the Rolls-Royce into a light truck-type design with two additional rows of bench seats aft of the driver-passenger cabin. Made into a 'safari' vehicle with a removable canvas top, the Rolls-Royce was used to ferry important guests to the forests and reserve parks near Udaipur. Though it has been called a 'shooting brake', the design is more pick-up than shooting brake (the car was used for the hunting of small game at most).

Udaipur 5 also had the mechanics at the palace garage giving it an interesting makeover—converting it into a Jeep-style design to carry the Mewar cricket team! From an original seven-seater limousine with elegant Thrupp & Maberly coachwork, this Rolls-Royce Twenty has become a (rather tight) eleven-seater Jeepney. Maharana Bhagwat Singh, a great cricket enthusiast, believed that his cricket team deserved, at the least, a Rolls-Royce to get them to the cricket grounds! The result is one of the most unusual body styles ever on a Rolls-Royce. Sure, the conversion may have most purists frowning, but the shape is distinctive, to say the least.

The fourth Rolls-Royce in the Udaipur palace museum is a 1934 Phantom II, which used to belong to Lieutenant Colonel Sir Vijaysinhji Chhatrasinhji Sahib, the Maharaja of Rajpipla. In the early 1960s, the car, in all probability, was gifted to the Rajmata (Queen Mother) of the princely state of Kolhapur, Raj Dadi Saheba Indumati Devi, and Arvind Singh Mewar bought it from her in 1973. With very elegant sedanca de ville coachwork by Windovers, this car is a famous one, having starred in the 1983 James Bond movie *Octopussy*, where the car and Udaipur (specifically the fascinating Lake Palace) figure prominently. The car again starred in the ITV television serial The Jewel in the Crown.

Sadly, at least five of the Udaipur Rolls-Royces are no longer with the family, having been disposed of or given away many years ago. The 1914 Silver Ghost was taken out of India around 1969 and the car is now in the United Kingdom. The 1922 Rolls-Royce Twenty was picked up by Rolls-Royce authority John Fasal in 1967 and that too is in the UK. The 1923 hand control car was gifted to the maharaj shree (the head priest) of Kankroli Temple. At some point the temple sold the car, and the car was for several years a part of the Shashi Kanoria collection in Kolkata. As of 2019, the car is with Bhubaneswar-based collector Dharmaditya Patnaik, who bought the car from Kanoria. The 1923 Twenty with Barker tourer body is with Delhi-based collector Sudhir Choudrie (when sold in September 1931, the asking price was Rs 5950!).

The two Cadillacs in the museum are of special significance too. On 29 February 1940, the daughter of the Maharajkumar of Bikaner, Sir Sadul Singh Bahadur, Bhanwar Baisaheb Sushila Kumariji was married to the Maharajkumar Bhagwat Singh Bahadur of Udaipur. Typical of elaborate Hindu weddings, the bride arrived laden with gifts for the groom's family, and amongst them were a closed palanquin, a closed carriage, an open carriage, a Rolls-Royce Twenty and an elephant. Plus two more cars: two Cadillacs, one a Series 61 four-door convertible sedan, and the other a Series 75 seven-seater formal sedan.

These Cadillac V8s, both from 1939, are handsome cars on long, yet not unwieldy wheelbases, and offered a broad selection of body styles, including semi-custom types by Fisher and Fleetwood, both of which were in-house coachbuilders. The top-of-the-line Series 75 was offered with a plethora of Fleetwood custom bodies on a long 3.58-metre wheelbase. About nine different body styles were available, with a multiplicity of possibilities in terms of seats and limousine divisions that gave the buyer a choice of at least fifteen models. One of two Cadillacs gifted was for the use of the future maharani. For the young bride, the Bikaner family chose a seven-seater formal sedan version with Fleetwood customizing the car with deep tinted windows that ensured 'purdah' privacy. Additionally, curtains too were fitted.

Powered by the more powerful 140bhp version of the engine, this car has been used occasionally, essentially to ferry special guests, including the likes of Jackie Kennedy. With just 26,293 miles (47,142 km) this Cadillac is special, all the more so given that only forty-four seven-seater formal sedans were produced (amongst a grand total of ninety-seven formal sedans including the five-seater version) made in 1939.

The other Cadillac, a Series 61, was available in four body styles of sedan, coupé, convertible sedan and convertible coupé. Very successful, as many as 5974 of the Series 61 were produced in 1939. Of these, just 140 were the four-door convertible sedans, though, and very few survive today. Used very occasionally as a ceremonial car by Shriji, this Cadillac comes out when there are special state visits and when dignitaries need to be ferried around in public. With just 20,186 miles (32,485 km) on the odometer, this car has starred as a ceremonial car with visitors such as Queen Elizabeth, when she was a guest of the maharana in Udaipur.

Amongst all the princely families, the one which has managed to retain the most of its automotive jewels, is the one from Gondal, an eleven-gun-salute princely state from Gujarat. The family are a part of the Jadeja clan, which is the name of a major clan of Chandravanshi Rajputs who claim descent from Chandra—the clan, by the fifteenth century, were ruling over a large tract of land, which included a large part of the Kathiawar peninsula and the region of Kutch, which is today in the state of Gujarat. The princely states of Kutch and Nawanagar were the most prominent of them all, and around the beginning of the seventeenth century, a branch of the Nawanagar family left to form the princely state of Rajkot, another to create the 2562-square-kilometre principality of Gondal.

At the advent of the automobile era, the Maharaja of Gondal was Bhagvatsingh Jadeja. Though he had a deep interest in medicine and was most concerned about alleviating disease and suffering of his subjects, the maharaja reluctantly took to the new-fangled toy of the rich, though he still preferred horse-drawn carriages. Over the years, he acquired a Minerva, a Humber, a Clément-Bayard, a De Dion-Bouton, a Renault, a Wolseley and a Lanchester. One of the earliest cars acquired, though, was a strange beast called the New Engine, from 1907. Rated as a 40hp model, the New Engine was fairly advanced for its time and had a better suspension system than a Rolls-Royce, but like many other early starters, this English carmaker—the New Engine Company (NEC)—disappeared soon thereafter, though the car that the maharaja bought is still very much there in the Gondal palace garages.

In 1930, one of the maharaja's sons, Maharajkumar Bhupatsingh, when returning from England after his studies, acquired a beautiful Delage D8S from Delage's London dealers George Newman and Company. This stylish sports coupé is another car which is still with the family. In 1938, a Packard One Twenty convertible coupé with rumble seat joined the other cars in the Gondal palace garages as the car arrived as a wedding gift from the Maharaja of Bhavnagar.

When Maharaja Bhagvatsingh died in 1944, his eldest son, the sixty-one-year-old Bhojrajsingh became the maharaja. As an engineer, Maharaja Bhojrajsingh was very fascinated by the automobile, more specifically American cars. A year after his reign began, with the War ending, Maharaja Bhojrajsingh decided it was time to augment his palace garages. Thus, fifteen cars were acquired from the Maharaja of Bhavnagar, and amongst them was a Mercedes-Benz 290 Nürburg seven-seater limousine.

Of the remaining fourteen, the most special was a Bentley 4 ½ Litre from 1929, a four-seater with Vanden Plas body, which the maharaja gave to his son Shivrajsinhji, who then sold it to the thakursaheb of the neighbouring princely state of Wadhwan. The thakur saheb sold the car too and it went out of India in 1970. The other very rare car acquired at that time was a 1930 Daimler Double Six. In a production run that lasted from 1926 to 1935, at the most just seventy-five of these V12-engined Daimlers were manufactured. Very rare and bespoke, the Daimler Double Six was originally ordered by the Maharaja of Bhavnagar, from whom it was acquired by the Gondal family in 1945. The car remains with the family.

In that same year, 1945, Maharajkumar Shivrajsinhji received from his sister a wedding gift: a fabulous 1935 Mercedes-Benz 500K, the fastest car in the world then! This car is one of two 500K extant in India.

Maharaja Bhojrajsingh also acquired several new cars, including a Buick Series 50 Super convertible and a Studebaker Commander Regal Deluxe convertible coupé, both bought in 1947. A Cadillac Series 62 convertible coupé and a rare Frazer Manhattan sedan, both from 1947, were acquired later. In May 1952, the maharaja bought an Invicta Black Prince—the ill-fated car which had been acquired by the Maharaja of Mysore in 1948—for Maharajkumar Shivrajsinhji.

Maharaja Bhojrajsingh died in 1952, when he was just sixty-nine years old. His eldest son, the thirty-seven-year-old Vikramsinhji Bhojrajjisinhji succeeded him as the titular 'maharaja'. Maharaja Vikramsingh had two sons (as well as two daughters), and both the sons were diehard car enthusiasts. In 1958, his eldest son, Jyotendrasinhji Vikramsinhji, bought himself a Mercedes-Benz 300 SL Roadster, which he raced very successfully for a few years, and of which he remains a proud owner.

His younger son, 'Maharaj' Ghanadityasinhji Vikramsinhji, popularly known as Ghanu, also raced very successfully for several years, most notably campaigning a home-grown single-seater with a Jaguar engine, named Godfather. Later, Ghanu set the tracks afire with a Formula 5000 Surtees, a TS11, in races across India during the 1970s and early 1980s. This car, too, remains with the family.

In fact, the car bug has also caught the son of Jyotendrasingh, Himanshusinh Jadeja, and the tradition of acquiring fine cars and keeping them in the family remains to this day. In the garages of the palace of the Gondal family, one will come across one of the largest collections of single-owner historic vehicles anywhere. A few of the cars may have been acquired pre-owned, and a few of the less interesting cars may have been disposed of, over time, but most of the fifty-odd cars housed in the garages of the palace are pristine single-owner automobiles with fascinating one-family histories.

Marques and models such as Buicks, Chevrolet Camaros, Corvettes, Cadillacs, Jaguars and Mercedes-Benzes are well represented in the Gondal mews. As well as a '47 Buick Super convertible, there is also a rare '34 convertible sedan and an Electra 225 from 1960. Camaros include a good-looking '69 and a handsome '71, as well as a more recent '96. Corvettes are a '79 L82 and a '92 ZR-1. Other than the '47 Cadillac, there is a '41 sedan and a 1955 Cadillac Series 75 eight-passenger limousine too.

Of the three Jaguars, the oldest is a 1946 3.5 Litre saloon, the other two are XK150s from 1958 and 1960. The 1960 XK150 is an S version—a 252bhp derivative of the standard XK150—and just nineteen of these were ever made in right-hand-drive drophead form. How the car was acquired is a story in itself. The deal was made to buy the Jaguar XK 150S from the Maharaja of Dharampur and the car was to be delivered by the morning of the practice session, a week before the race day, as it happened to be the eighteenth birthday of Maharajkumar Ghanadityasinhji. The car was given as a birthday gift to him from his father, Maharaja Vikramsingh. Ghanu did go on to win a race in the Jaguar, and his brother, the Yuvaraj Jyotindrasingh, went on to win the other race in his Mercedes 300 SL Roadster.

Of the several Mercedes-Benzes, one has a very colourful history: a 1979 280 S, which used to belong to former Bollywood star Zeenat Aman. In recent times, Himanshusinh has added a '97 Buick Riviera, which many believe is a 'future classic', and a Dodge Viper to the collection. A derestricted version of the CLS 63, the very hot AMG version of the Mercedes-Benz CLS, undoubtedly one of the fastest four-door cars in India today, joined the garage a few years ago. Plus, a Mercedes-Benz SLS, to carry on the tradition of buying exceptional cars, ones which will surely be future classics.

Retaining these historic vehicles and preserving the automotive history of princely India is one of the many ways that India's social-industrial history of the early part of the twentieth century needs to be recognized, so that future generations will have the opportunity to understand and appreciate the role the automobile played in defining India's social fabric.

2

The Love Affair Continues

It would be unfair to deduce that the rajas and the maharajas, the Indian princes, had a monopoly in acquiring the finest of automobiles. Some of the most tasteful of bolides were also purchased by the merchant classes, the lawyers, doctors and the newly successful professionals, in the cities of Calcutta and Bombay. In fact, the Parsees of Bombay were (and remain to this day) some of the most enthusiastic of automotive aficionados, acquiring and maintaining the finest of vehicles, both cars and motorcycles.

One of the most exceptional cars in Bombay was a Mercedes-Benz SSK, owned by Manek Petit. It is a convertible, from either the late 1920s or early 1930s, which he bought from Daimler-Benz distributor, Dadajee Dhackjee. The fastest car in the world at that point of time, just a handful of them found their way to India.

No less extraordinary was the distinctive Bugatti Type 46, with what seems like a unique Bombay-built body style, concocted between the owner of the car, Adi Bhiwandiwala, and D.R.D. Wadia of Auto Cars, Queen's Road, Mumbai, who had imported the car on Bhiwandiwala's behalf.

In an article on the cars of the Parsees,[1] Ali Rajabally described the Bhiwandiwala Bugatti: 'This epitome of expensive motoring was a three-tone sports job. A pearl white aluminium body, over-painted across the bonnet and part of the front doors in electric blue, a silver streak of lightning, separating the two colours. Four doors with a tiny footstep under each door, two spare wheels on the sloping back, bulbous wings over big wired-wheels. And inside, steering-wheel and gear-lever knob made of ivory, dashboard inlaid with mother-of-pearl, upholstery from pig-skin, soft as a baby's bottom.'

Of a more sporting nature were the other two Bugattis of Bombay, a Type 35A, owned by the young industrialist Jehangir Ratanji Dadabhoy Tata (better known as J.R.D. later), as well as the Type 39A owned by Homi Batlivala. J.R.D. even raced his car regularly. Acquired when he was just twenty-one years old, J.R.D. Tata's Bugatti Type 35A was procured—much against the wishes of his father—when he was still studying in France, in the year 1926. Though J.R.D. was best known for his abiding interest in aviation, his real passion was for quick and dynamically delightful automobiles, as he enjoyed the act of driving and racing, as much as flying a plane.

The brothers D.R.D. and A.R.D. Wadia, who owned the aforementioned Auto Cars dealerships, were also into racing, competing in a sleek all-enclosed Austin Seven. As well as being agents for Austin, they were also importers for Cord, and thanks to them, several of the legendary coffin-nosed Cord 810s made it to India. D.R.D., or Dady Wadia, as he was referred to, owned a shiny black Cord, and as a sales gimmick, told everyone that only distilled water was to be used for the radiator.

The above-mentioned German, French and American cars should not detract from the fondness the Parsees had for all things English. Two remarkable Vauxhalls, both redoubtable 30/98 sports cars, were brought in by Parsees. At first, it was Faly Petit who brought back one from Blighty, and at that point of time it was perhaps the only one of its kind in the country. The baronet Petit, though, had to come to terms with Manek Powvala, who stole his thunder, when he returned from Cambridge with another Vauxhall 30/98.

Rajabally's description of the Vauxhall was striking: 'Picture a slim low-sided, elegant sports job with a bonnet-strap, handsome flared wings and rakish lines. A fast touring car but a car less for the track and more for the road. To my mind, the kind of a car that went with suede shoes, cavalry-twill trousers, split-back jacket, silk handkerchief popping out of the breast pocket. A four-seater with three doors, the space for the driver's door being taken up by a long hand brake bristling like a sabre. There was no howl, no shriek, no wail, just power with decorum. A tranquillizing rumble of the exhaust and this marvellous little car was off. It had come to India with a heady reputation. In a trial run, it had lapped Brooklands at 107 miles an hour, the first British stock job to do so, a feat that had made the Bentley owners sit up and take note.'[2]

Could that be the reason why one of the most extraordinary Bentleys to come into India was brought in by another Parsee? In 1938, J.S. Vatcha bought a Bentley 8 Litre from Jack Barclay, in London. Probably mortified when his prized possession, a 4 ½ Litre Blower Bentley, caught fire and burnt down beyond repair, Vatcha decided that the only thing that could replace his Blower Bentley had to be the most powerful Bentley ever made, an 8 Litre. Curiously, the engine from the Blower was retrieved and fitted into a boat, which went down in the famous Bombay Dock explosion, in the early 1940s. An ill-fated car indeed!

Vatcha wanted something even more special than a 'normal' 8 Litre (if there was ever anything like that), so he went all the way. Before Vatcha had the car shipped off to India, he instructed L.C. McKenzie to work on the engine. A renowned tuner specializing in the preparation of Bentleys, Lewis Charles 'Mac' McKenzie was a prominent figure in Bentley circles during the 1930s. Best known for preparing the cars owned by 'gentleman racer' Forrest Lycett, 'Mac' had also built Lycett's famous racing 8 Litre, 'YX 5121', by shortening the chassis and tuning the engine to produce well in excess of 300bhp. The result was one of the fastest road cars of its day, which Lycett used to set class records at venues such as Brooklands, Lewes and Shelsley Walsh, amongst others.

Under McKenzie's care, Vatcha's Bentley received a new body, a two-door four-seater tourer style, as well as a new engine. The engine was a McKenzie masterpiece. Using three carburettors, this modified engine was noticeably more powerful than the standard 8 Litre's 180bhp, making these McKenzie-modified 8 Litres some of the fastest cars on the planet then. Thus, when this Bentley 8 Litre landed in Bombay, it must have created quite a buzz on its arrival. A late 1930s equivalent of a tuned Bugatti Veyron today, Vatcha must have enjoyed this supercar to the max before selling it off to another Parsee aficionado, P.D. Adenwalla in 1951.

Oh Calcutta!

The Parsee infection seems to have been carried across to Calcutta, too. Daddy Mazda, the Calcutta playboy, was another adventurous young man with a taste for the good, and the fast things of life, with the wherewithal to indulge in them. Though automaker Mazda was already producing three-wheelers in Japan, Calcutta's Mazda instead opted for a low chassis, long-nosed, eight-cylinder pre-War Jensen roadster, an S-Type, which was imported into Calcutta after the cessation of hostilities in 1945.

As Rajabally remembered, for his *Parsiana* article, 'The Jensen had a three-toned Stentor horn, huge Marchal lights with amber lenses and a cut-out loud enough to awaken the dead (this includes the Calcutta policeman on point duty). A car with a fast pick-up, touching 70 on the short Red Road or 10 miles more on the long stretch of the Strand, was easy. But when you were in the bucket-seat next to him, you rode in silence for it's difficult to talk, and harder to hear, when you've got the wind rushing past you, the bellow of two, three-inch exhausts only a foot or two away from your ears and 125 angry horses fighting mad to go places.'

Calcutta, though, had its own counterpart to the Parsee of Bombay, the Bengali brown sahibs (British-oriented Bengali gentlemen), with the appropriate English education at Harrow and Eton, followed by Oxford or Cambridge, a set of wealthy folks with Epicurean tastes and the aesthetic sensibilities of Europeans, with similar enthusiasm for the automotive wonders of the West. One such family was the Mitter family of Calcutta.

Right Honourable Sir Benode Chandra Mitter was one of Calcutta's most prominent lawyers. The son of Sir Romesh Chunder Mitter, a judge of the Calcutta High Court, who was for some time the first officiating Indian Chief Justice, Benode Chandra was born in Calcutta in 1870. By 1918, when Benode Chandra Mitter was knighted, he had served as a member of the Council of Governor of Bengal (1910–17), as well as serving as a standing counsel to the government of India (1910–16), and was then appointed the advocate general to the government of Bengal in 1917.

Later on, Sir Benode Chandra Mitter went on to become the law member of the Viceroy's Council of British India. No less prominent was his younger brother Sir Provash Chandra Mitter, who was a minister for local self-government and was a prominent leader of the Liberal Group in Bengal and president of the Indian Association and the National Liberal League, vice president and honorary secretary of the British Indian Association and president and patron of the Backward Classes Society of Bengal. Being a prominent member of Calcutta's high society during the inter-War years must have had its advantages—when Sir Benode Chandra Mitter passed away in 1930, he left behind substantial wealth in terms of properties and monies, which allowed the sons to indulge in some expensive toys.

The Mitter family's fascination for sophisticated cars began with a Duesenberg Model J, which the second-oldest amongst the five Mitter brothers (out of the ten children of Sir Benode Chandra Mitter), Satish Chunder Mitter, ordered in 1929. The beautifully finished Weymann-bodied Duesenberg sedan—then America's finest automobile by far—had been specially equipped with a variety of appointments (including 'airbags' in the seats!) to make travelling in India that much more comfortable. It was a big four-door sedan, which was not only luxurious and superbly well-finished, but was also powered by a most advanced in-line eight-cylinder engine. This engine was very developed (for its time), a mighty 265bhp, making these cars some of the fastest behemoths of the era.

The elegant and fleet-footed Duesenberg had all the younger brothers of Satish Mitter most impressed by its refinement and performance, triggering a buying spree of some of the finest automobiles in the world then. Brothers number three and four—Subodh and Sailen Kumar Mitter—opted for something from the old Continent, two cars from Germany's best, a pair of Mercedes-Benz SS 38/250s. So what if the elder brother had one of the most powerful cars in the world at that point of time, Subodh and Sailen decided to get themselves the fastest street legal cars in the world then: the Mercedes SS cars were capable of a top speed of 166 km per hour (kmph).

The youngest brother did not wish to get into a horsepower or max speed race. Instead, Provat Kumar Mitter decided to focus on cars with both grace and pace. The first car that he acquired was Italy's finest, an Isotta Fraschini Tipo 8A. Not quite as powerful as a Duesenberg, Isotta Fraschinis were beautifully constructed automobiles, which, at over $20,000 then, were pricier than a Model J Duesenberg in the USA.

'It was in the year 1931, when my father was just twenty-one years old,' recounted Provat Kumar's son Jayanta Mitter to this author in October 2018, 'that he came across this magnificent Isotta Fraschini parked in front of the luxury Delhi hotel, Maidens. Speaking to the chauffeur standing by, he was told that the car was for sale, as the car just wouldn't get into reverse!' That did not deter the young enthusiast, and Provat Kumar Mitter became the second owner of a relatively new Tipo 8A Isotta Fraschini 'for a song', as Jayanta Mitter relates. With the reverse gear problem addressed by one of Calcutta's many expert mechanics, the Isotta Fraschini regaled the cognoscenti of the city, and when it was time for Provat Kumar to get married in 1933, the Isotta served as the bridegroom's 'vahan' when getting to the wedding shamiana.

In the meantime, Provat Kumar Mitter heard that another Duesenberg, a Model J at that, was up for sale at a relatively reasonable 'pre-owned' price. An opportunity like that could not be missed, so Provat Kumar Mitter promptly picked up the Duesenberg of Hyderabad's Azam Jah. Chassis number 2222, with engine number J202, was the ninety-ninth Model J built—exactly six cars down the 'production line' from Provat Kumar Mitter's elder brother's Duesy! Azam Jah, better known as the Prince of Berar, had acquired what was Duesenberg's display car for their stand at the 1929 edition of the London Show, at Olympia. A right-hand-drive version with Murphy convertible sedan bodywork, this Duesenberg Model J featured the extra-long 3.9-metre wheelbase. Even if the car was exceptionally well equipped, the Murphy-bodied convertible was not as comfortable as the Weymann-bodied sedan, remembers Jayanta Mitter.

To Provat Kumar Mitter, though, being a true enthusiast, comfort was not very high in his list of priorities, as was made obvious when he decided to replace his big and elegant Isotta Fraschini with a very flamboyant convertible sportster, a Rolls-Royce Phantom I, but a very special one-off one, the legendary 17EX.

The genesis of the 17EX was all because of Bentley. With Bentley winning at the now-famous French race the 24 Hours of Le Mans, and stealing all the thunder, Sir Henry Royce decided that Rolls-Royce also needed to look at acquiring a slightly sporting image, and to that extent, the task was outlined to develop a series of cars, which would explore sporting possibilities. Rolls-Royce commissioned three experimental cars, and the 17EX was the last and most definitive version of the 'sports Phantoms' developed between 1926 and 1928. After extensive testing and development, the car was sold to the Maharaja of Kashmir, Hari Singh, in 1929, who had the Rolls-Royce brought across to Kashmir, in India.

A few years later, the car was acquired by Provat Kumar Mitter, and with the 17EX replacing the Isotta Fraschini, the Mitter brothers owned some of the most remarkable cars ever seen in India, as the one-off experimental Rolls-Royce shared garage space with two supercharged Duesenbergs and two Mercedes SS cars. As the 17EX took its vaunted place alongside the pride of Germany and the might of the United States, this veritable dragonfly of a Flying Lady became the cynosure of all eyes in the city of Calcutta. Even if the second city of the British Empire had enough wealth still to boast of some of the finest of automobiles in the Indian subcontinent, the one car that really stood out amidst them was Rolls-Royce's experimental special. More so when compared to the relatively staid and rather upright limousines and landaulets that most of the Rolls-Royce, Daimler, Cadillac and other luxury car owners seem to prefer.

The Mitter joint family—consisting of the five brothers, their spouses and their children, plus the retinue of domestics and chauffeurs—lived in a large villa with several outhouses in Loudon Street, a chic and very central locality of Calcutta. Though they had a few other 'ordinary' runabouts, the pride of place in the garages were allotted to the five cars, and even if the two pairs of Mercedes-Benzes and Duesenbergs made the Mitter garage a place worth a visit, the star of the garage was without doubt the 17EX.

The patriarch of the family, Sir Benode Chandra Mitter, had in his time acquired several properties, including three in the hill station of Darjeeling and one magnificent villa, Charu Villa, in the resort town of Hazaribagh, which he named after his wife Charushilla. Perched on the 600-metre-high Chhotanagpur Plateau some 400 km north-west of Calcutta, Hazaribagh (literally the City of Thousand Gardens), with its salubrious climate amidst lush verdant flora, forests, lakes and fauna was a peaceful haven away from the bustle and din of Calcutta, a delightful getaway for the family at least three times every year, during the cooler months.

'The first trip was typically after the festival of Durga Puja in October, the second in early December before Hazaribagh really became very cold and the third in February, before the drive became too hot,' recounted Jayanta Mitter to the author. For most of those getaways, these five cars would be the preferred drive. 'Most of the women preferred travelling in my uncle's Weymann-bodied Duesenberg,' explained Jayanta Mitter, 'as it was the most comfortable. The cooks and the helps were packed off in the two Mercedes-Benzes as no one wanted to go in them, as they had the hardest ride.'

Apparently, between Provat Kumar's Duesenberg and the Rolls-Royce, the younger members of the family clamoured for the privilege of travelling in the 17EX, even if it was not the most comfortable of the lot.

Leaving Calcutta, some 25 km down the Grand Trunk (GT) Road, the first town the entourage would encounter would be Serampore, a colony of Denmark from 1756 to 1845. The next town, 11 km farther down the GT Road from Serampore, would be Chinsurah. The most distinctive of these colonial towns would be the next one, though. Chandannagar—established as a French colony in 1673, when they obtained the permission from Ibrahim Khan, the Nawab of Bengal, to put up a trading post—became a permanent French settlement in 1688.

Leaving Chandannagar, a few kilometres up the GT Road (and 43 km from Calcutta), the convoy would pass through Bandel, a Portuguese colony founded in 1660. Once Bandel was crossed, the congestion would ease, and 'the next 70 kilometres or so of the GT Road, until the town of Burdwan [Bardhaman today], would consist of delightfully banked roads that would meander through the lush green Bengal countryside', remembered Jayanta Mitter, as he recounted the adventures to the author.

For the first time, the drivers of the five cars would get free rein. Provat Kumar Mitter would take both of his cars, the Duesenberg convertible sedan and the 17EX, with him driving one, a chauffeur doing duty on the other. From the ancient city of Bardhaman to the industrial town of Asansol would be an arrow-straight stretch where the cars would cruise at very high speeds, though 'one had to keep a sharp lookout for stray cattle and occasional people', recounted Jayanta Mitter to the author. 'The Calcutta to Hazaribagh drive was most enjoyable for an enthusiast, even in the industrial 1960s, due to its light traffic. But my father told me that what I enjoyed blasting down in the 1960s was nothing compared to the motorist's paradise it used to be in the 1930s when traffic was minimal,' said Jayanta Mitter.

Asansol, some 220 km from Calcutta, would be the regrouping point, which would be at the petrol pump owned by the Atwal Brothers, where the five cars would need to be tanked up, gobbling up gallons upon gallons of petrol. The pump needed to be warned in advance to stock up!

For the next 30 km,, the convoy would trundle through a rather congested urban sprawl up to Dishegarh. From Dishegarh the road started to get better and then from Gobindopur to Bagoder, which went not too far from the country house of the famous Calcutta doctor Sir Nil Ratan Sircar. The road for the next 50 km would be another fabulous drive, the stretches consisting of undulating straights up hill, down dale. The cherry on the driving cake, though, would be the last

50-km stretch to Hazaribagh, once the convoy would have turned left off the GT Road at Bagoder. 'A delightful combination of switchbacks and sharp turns that would bring out the best of the five cars, testing their speed, their acceleration, their braking, their roadholding and cornering abilities,' reminisced Jayanta Mitter.

Four of the five brothers and one of the expert chauffeurs would invariably race the last leg, with the Duesenbergs blasting away on the straighter stretches, the Mercedes-Benzes accelerating past with their supercharger howling away, the 17EX gracefully tucking and nipping within them. Forewarned, the denizens of Hazaribagh would line up by the road waiting for that magnificent convoy to come thundering by, flashing past in a blur of sound, fury, exhaust fumes and colour.

The run to Hazaribagh was not the only bit of touring that the Mitter family, the 17EX and the other four cars did. Three epic trips were made in the years 1934 to 1936. One was to the spectacular Kullu Valley, in what is today the state of Himachal Pradesh, at the foothills of the Himalayas and near the hill resort of Manali, some 1500 km away from Calcutta. Another was to Kashmir, some 2300 km away. The third was to the Khyber Pass, which is the motorable gap in the Spin Ghar range of mountains that marks the border between Afghanistan and Pakistan, and then through the Bolan Pass to Quetta, which is now in Western Pakistan, but this last epic journey started in Delhi, with the cars arriving by train from Calcutta.

It was on this last tour that the cars averaged well over 100 km/h during the Delhi to Ambala run of a little over 200 km, with Provat Kumar Mitter maintaining a steady 130 on his Duesenberg. The 17EX was very quick, without doubt, but not as quick as the Duesenberg, with Jayanta Mitter recounting to the author: 'My father saw several times 110mph (176 km/h) on the speedo, but the speedo error must have been considerable, as looking at milestones, my father felt that the speed was actually less than 100mph.'

By 1944, the 17EX was already sixteen years old and getting a little long in the tooth, so it was time for a new toy. Provat Kumar Mitter decided to acquire a Packard, which 'promised 100mph' performance, and the 17EX, sadly, had to go to finance the purchase. After spending almost a dozen joyful years in the City of Joy, the 17EX's new custodian was in the city of Allahabad, in India's northern state of Uttar Pradesh. Over the next two decades the Rolls-Royce Phantom I 17EX, changed hands several times, all the while moving around in Uttar Pradesh.

It would be a little more than ten years before the 17EX would be back in Calcutta for another prolonged stint. The credit for bringing the 17EX back to the great city would lie with another scion of a prominent Calcutta family, Protap Roy, who may have heard, as a young boy, about this amazing Rolls-Royce and how it had enthralled the aficionados of the city of automotive joy.

'It all began with my ambition to win the Best-in-Show award for my Doberman pinscher at Calcutta's championship dog show,' recounted Suchandra Roy, the wife of Protap Roy, to the author. 'In 1967, the Doberman was still a fairly new breed in India and my Simba was magnificent by any standard. Little did I know that Protap had ambitions of his own! Protap, as you know, tracked rare vintage and classic cars like a bloodhound.'

Born on 13 February 1930, Protap Roy was the eldest grandson of Maharaja Hon'ble Sir Manmathanath Roy Choudhary of Santosh, a princely state, which was in former East Bengal (Bangladesh today). His father was Maharajkumar Rabindranath Roy Choudhary, better known as Maharajkumar Robin Roy, a reputed sculptor and artist of the then burgeoning Bengal School of Art. Protap's grandfather became the first Indian president of pre-Partition 'undivided' Bengal's Legislative Council and as per his standing, drove to the Legislative Council in his Rolls-Royce Phantom I, despite owning several other cars.

The Phantom I wasn't his first Rolls-Royce; the Maharaja of Santosh had already owned two Silver Ghosts—a very early 1912 40/50hp (chassis number 2221), which was first ordered by a British resident of Calcutta, W.A. Duncan, from whom the maharaja had acquired this Barker-bodied tourer in 1920. This was followed by a brand new Silver Ghost (chassis number 47AG), in 1921. Ordered by Rolls-Royce's Calcutta agent, G. Mein Austin, 47AG received aluminium coachwork by Calcutta-based coachbuilders Steuarts & Co. It was in this kind of a background that Protap Roy was born. He collected paintings and was a very fine artist himself. He collected antiques, guns, dogs, but above all, classic and vintage cars—and these were the truest loves of his life.

That came later, though. With India's Independence, came the Partition of the country, and India was divided into India and Pakistan. Overnight, Protap Roy's home and the family's estate of Santosh was now a part of a 'foreign' country. With the death of Protap Roy's grandfather, the maharaja, financial implications were substantial. Roy had to start thinking of a professional career. Rather unexpectedly, he was pushed into advertising, landing a job with the advertising firm of J. Walter Thompson (JWT).

Later Protap went on to work for companies such as Nestlé, thanks to whom he was the first Indian to complete the higher management course at IMEDE (International Institute for Management Development), in Lausanne, Switzerland. Eventually, he joined Godrej Soaps, in a very senior capacity. He had finally reached the stage of his life and career when he could indulge in a serious interest in classic and vintage cars. This was also the time when his twenty-four-year-old fiancée discovered Protap Roy's other passion!

As Suchandra Roy related to this author, 'It was surreal, a mysterious bulky shape dangling from the hook of a massive crane silhouetted against a hot Delhi sky. A few days earlier, Protap had disappeared into the depths of Assam supposedly on work. He returned to announce that he had discovered a 500K!'

The Mercedes-Benz 500K, which Protap Roy had just acquired in 1965 (and which survives with a collector in Mumbai today), was to become the start of a small but select stable of very fine cars which would go on to include a Hispano-Suiza and a Rolls-Royce. The Hispano-Suiza was indeed very special—it was a short chassis Boulogne, one of just twenty-four ever made. Originally acquired by Francophile and Hispano fan, the Maharaja of Alwar, Jai Singh, Roy's Hispano was one of the most distinctive of the fifteen Hispanos that the maharaja had owned. This short wheelbase Kellner-bodied Hispano-Suiza features a bigger engine, and is, in all likelihood, the only survivor amongst all the short chassis Boulognes (and is in the famous Arturo Keller collection in California).

Roy's greatest love affair, though, was with the other car, the Rolls-Royce, a 1928 Phantom I Torpedo Tourer with bodywork by coachbuilder Hooper. Originally purchased by a certain H.R.P. Poddar, the car had been in the Santosh family for three generations and had been sitting in a garage in Calcutta after some cars were exchanged, and which Roy 'rescued' and brought to Delhi in 1966. The car sprang to life at the very first attempt and very little restoration work was required. It was painted a very dark purple to suit its sophisticated air; the colour matched one of Suchandra Roy's saris, incidentally!

The Hispano, the Mercedes and the purple Phantom were not just trophy cars. Indeed, none of Roy's cars were: Protap Roy preferred to drive his classics and vintages, not only because of their masterly craftsmanship but because they had been made to be used. The *Statesman* newspaper's annual classic and vintage car rally in Delhi became the event to debut the cars that Protap Roy would restore. The Mercedes-Benz 500K, painted a dark maroon with black mudguards, was taken to participate in the 1967 edition of The Statesman Vintage Car Rally in Delhi. 'The Mercedes cruised easily along through the rally until at the last stretch, from Faridabad to Delhi, Protap decided to turn on the supercharger,' recalled Suchandra Roy to the author. 'The car growled and began to devour the miles like a hungry cheetah!'

In 1968, it was the turn of the purple sari-inspired Rolls-Royce Phantom I to participate in The Statesman Vintage Car Rally, where it went on to win the concours d'elegance trophy. Over the years, Protap Roy also acquired some usable sportsters such as a 1934 Riley Imp and a 1947 MG TC. The former, acquired in 1969 from Delhi, participated in vintage and classic car events in Bombay. The Riley was also used for evening outings by the Roy couple, as was the MG.

More than acquiring, though, Protap Roy's true passion was tracing and locating rarities. His work took him around India and he made it a point to travel to the remotest of places, where he found cars, photographed them, and occasionally managed to ferret them out to enthusiasts who could buy, restore and use once again these beautiful machines. From an early Porsche 356A, through a Fiat 2300 S Ghia to Alfa Romeos, Bentleys, Cords, Duesenbergs, Hispano-Suizas, Isotta Fraschinis, Lagondas and scores of Rolls-Royces, Roy 'rediscovered' many of India's classic car wonders. The list of cars discovered and restored, acquired and lost is long.

The one that remains the most memorable for Protap Roy's wife Suchandra, though, is the Rolls-Royce Phantom I 17EX.

'Around that time, this was in 1967, amongst the many cars that Protap was tracking down was a Rolls-Royce Phantom I special, the car known as the 17EX,' remembers Suchandra. 'We already had a 1928 Hooper-bodied Rolls-Royce Phantom I and a super-charged Mercedes at home, and now he had heard of a Rolls with the 17EX nomenclature in the remote princely state of Bhadri.'

One of several princely states in north India, Bhadri was relatively small, located within the Pratapgarh district of Uttar Pradesh. Born about 1905, Raja Bajrang Bahadur Singh, the rajasaheb of Bhadri was a much-respected personality who, as well as founding Pant Nagar University, of which he was the vice chancellor, was also the governor of the state of Himachal Pradesh from 1955 to 1963.

The rajasaheb of Bhadri was also known to be a dog lover and was to judge the annual dog show held every year by the Kennel Club of India in Calcutta. 'This was Protap's opportunity!' explained Suchandra Roy to the author, adding, 'In the past he had made efforts to pin the Raja down and had even thought of travelling to Bhadri, but without success. So plans and railway bookings were made. We travelled the thousand miles from Delhi to Calcutta in our coupé, with Simba looking fit to ride a Rolls-Royce of his own.'

Suchandra Roy's dog Simba walked away with the Best-in-Show. 'And sure enough Protap began negotiations with the rajasaheb of Bhadri,' smiled Suchandra. 'He did part with the 17EX, but in addition to the agreed price, he wanted Protap to try and get hold of a pair of corgis!'

So how did that work out?

The 17EX arrived in Calcutta, but it was not in very good shape after years of being locked up in a dark garage. Yet Suchandra enthused:

'With her pointy back, high flared mudguards and the fairy on the tip of the hood leaning forward as if leading the way, the car looked like some extra-terrestrial dragon-fly!'

'Protap's mechanic—who didn't look as if he could put a bicycle together, leave alone an experimental Rolls—was actually an expert at restoring old cars,' explained Suchandra to the author. The mechanic and Protap Roy made a long list of what was required to get the 17EX moving. This was forwarded to the Rolls-Royce Enthusiasts Club (RREC) in England, together with a request for names and addresses of suppliers. Suchandra added: 'Protap also asked for advice on how to get hold of a pair of corgis.'

Within weeks, Protap Roy received a reply from the RREC congratulating him for finding such a rare car, remembers Suchandra Roy. All the names and addresses he needed were supplied, and so was advice for obtaining the rajasaheb's dearest wish: 'As for the corgis,' wrote the club, 'our advice is, try Buckingham Palace!'

Of sleuths and treasure hunters

One of India's first famous historic vehicle sleuths, Protap Roy went around the country locating and saving historic vehicles from being rejected and destroyed. Into the 1950s and 1960s, with India's Independence and a desire to etch out our own industrial future, automobiles from the pre-War era were seen as troublesome and expensive vehicles to maintain and use. In a desire to embrace modernity and convenience, many of the rich began to discard the troublesome automobiles of the past, favouring newer economical models.

Also, with a move to democracy and a more egalitarian society, the princes of yesteryears—the rajas, maharajas, maharanas and nawabs—began to lose their traditional sources of income and later, their privy purses, leading to a situation where they began selling off or even scrapping the older vehicles. Only a handful of the Indian princes were able to retain their wealth and lifestyles, as after India's Independence their royal privileges and titles disappeared over time, and so did their money and properties. Some, like the maharajas of Jodhpur and

Udaipur, have been able to capitalize on the newer industry of tourism, converting their sumptuous palaces into luxury hotels.

Others have seen their money draining away, their properties sold off and their cars disposed of. Some of the more exceptional cars found their way to collectors in the West, but with the ban on exports of classic cars since 1972, a few opportunistic collectors in India have managed to build up collections of some very fine cars.

Helping them in locating the cars were the sleuths like Protap Roy and Roni Khan, from Mumbai. Born in the year when India got its Independence, Roni Khurshedcher Khan (1947–2002) was one of the great stalwarts of this country's historic vehicle movement. Ahead of his time, Roni Khan almost single-handedly raised awareness about the importance and relevance of historic vehicles. At a time when people were looking to shed themselves of these wonderful cars due to maintenance costs, Roni rescued many. He would start by identifying their owners. He would then try to enthuse them into maintaining the vehicle. If that failed, he would then try to persuade another enthusiast to take the car into his or her permanent care.

In 1963, when just sixteen years old, Roni Khan founded the Vintage Car Club of Bombay (VCCB). An early pioneer of promoting the historic vehicle movement, VCCB was initially run from the Khan residence atop Malabar Hill, in Mumbai. Owning a dozen-odd historic vehicles, Roni, with his father Khurshedcher Khan's assistance, organized a number of historic vehicle-related activities, including a monthly newsletter, concours d'elegance and rallies.

It was also the VCCB which was responsible for convincing the Indian government of the importance of preserving India's historic vehicle heritage by ensuring that historic motor cars remain in the country, and numerous meetings with government officials were held at the Khan residence to urge them to consider taking steps to preserve the country's motoring heritage. Thus, the ban on the export of cars made before 1960 followed in 1972.

Guided by Roni, as well as Protap Roy, a number of collectors grew their collections, the most famous of them being Pranlal Bogilal (who acquired Khan's Invicta S Type, an AC and a Morris Bullnose

Cowley). Arguably the most important person in India's history with historic vehicles, Pranlal Bhogilal (1937–2011) was barely in his teens when he began acquiring arts and artefacts, jewellery and cars from the princely families, as their wealth diminished considerably in post-feudal Independent India.

Realizing the importance and the value of most of these historic vehicles, years before other collectors in India even thought of getting into the act, Bhogilal capitalized on the low prices for old items, which had no demand any more, building up, in the process, one of the biggest collections of historic vehicles in India. Bhogilal was loath to talk about numbers, but the grapevine mentions that he had collected more than 200 automobiles. For sure, Bhogilal never sold a single car—a few may have been gifted to friends, family, lawyers and doctors. The other way around, as his collection became famous, many people gifted him their cars for sentimental reasons and with the belief that their cars would receive the best of care, and that they were going to a good 'family'. 'Unless my car is between Rolls-Royces on a marble floor, my soul will not rest in peace, is what one elderly lady said to me,' Bhogilal explained to this author a couple of years before he passed away, 'insisting that I take her car. With such an explanation, it is difficult to say no!'

Having created the Vintage and Classic Car Club of India (VCCCI), as a follow-up of Roni Khan's VCCB, Bhogilal had been at the vanguard of the historic vehicle movement in India. He was personally responsible for 'convincing Prime Minister Indira Gandhi in the early 1970s to bring about the ban on export of cars from before 1960 as a part of Indian heritage', as Bhogilal claimed, when interviewed by the author.

His long-time dream was to create a museum. The Auto World Vintage Car Museum was opened in 2009, in Kathwada, on the outskirts of Ahmedabad. Placed within a beautiful 2200-acre estate, the partially open-air museum is a wondrous assembly of superb automobiles, and is set amidst manicured lawns dotted with fountains and sculptures, evergreen foliage and bright flowers, with peacocks and deer for company. The setting itself, called Dastan, is as overwhelming as the mind-boggling cars on display. The museum hosts the lion's share of Bhogilal's collection, a little over a hundred cars, a few motorcycles, several horse-drawn carriages and two traditional bullock carts. Though the condition of many of the cars is not the best, the museum is a 'must visit' for all fans of historic vehicles.

Another pioneer collector was Delhi-based Ramchander Nath (1928–2002). Born to Sham Nath and Pisto Devi, Ramchander Nath came from an old Delhi family, which had for centuries dealt with jewellery and ivory, at Delhi's Ivory Palace, a family business, which Ramchander Nath joined at the age of eighteen. Little did Ramchander Nath know that this early exposure and interest in automobiles would become a lifelong passion for him.

It was sometime in 1963 or 1964 that Ramchander Nath bought his first historic vehicle, a 1932 Mercedes-Benz. Over the years, more cars were added to the garage, and by the mid-1970s, Ramchander Nath had a sizeable collection of historic vehicles, most of which were very significant automobiles. Though he kept acquiring cars until about 1996, the cream of the collection is from the early years.

Amongst the fifty-odd cars in the Ramchander Nath collection, the most astoundingly beautiful is a French Delage D8 S, with exquisite Figoni coachwork. A very rare car, one which the world at large had believed had disappeared forever, this Delage is one of the most remarkable cars surviving in India today. No less important are a rare and elegant Auburn 850Y from 1934, a very impressive Maybach SW 38, and a flamboyant '55 Imperial, a rare American prestige car from the early 1950s.

The other pioneers

In the realms of the Indian historic vehicle movement, the name of Howrah-based Harish Chandra Agarwal should also be up there with stalwarts like Protap Roy, Roni Khan, Ramchander Nath and Pranlal Bhogilal, with the last named especially owing a lot to the former as many of Bhogilal's extraordinary cars came from Agarwal. From the early 1950s, Harish Chandra Agarwal located, sourced and traded in hundreds—if not thousands—of historic vehicles long before the rest of India woke up to the world of classics and vintages, long before the present-day punters realized the value of old precious metal.

Thus, when Shashi Kanoria, a twenty-two-year-old car enthusiast, became Harish Chandra Agarwal's son-in-law in 1969, he found in him a kindred soul, whose passion for modern rallying machinery was soon converted to that for historic matters. The first car that Shashi Kanoria restored was a 1926 Ford Model T. Through the years, as Kanoria added to his collection, identifying and picking up cars through his father-in-law, as well as doing his own bit of scouting and sourcing, the aspect of restoring the cars was what he found most fascinating, instead of just talking numbers. Yet, by the mid-1980s, Shashi Kanoria had a most impressive collection of some thirty-five-odd cars, ranging from a 1905 Darracq to a 1936 SS1, both of which have since moved to other collections.

Shashi Kanoria suddenly passed away on 25 March 2010. Fortunately for the historic vehicle movement, his son Shrivardhan Kanoria has taken on the baton and is full-time into restoring and refurbishing his and his uncle, Naresh Chandra Agrawalla's cars, as well as cars from other collectors. Shrivardhan, who learnt to drive a 1959 Ford Fairlane Galaxy when he was just eight years old, started restoring cars under his father's guidance and assistance in 2000, with more than forty-five cars restored until 2019.

The most famous of the Kanoria cars is a beautifully working Renault AX, from 1908 (or later), as well as a very rare Moon (from 1921–22). Other cars include a Chevrolet Six, a '48 Buick Eight, a '59 VW Beetle, a '61 Rover 3 Litre, an MG MGA, and a couple of Rolls-Royces, amongst several others.

Shrivardhan's father Shashi Kanoria provided the basis for another important Kolkata collection, the one of Pramod Mittal's (the brother of steel baron Lakshmi Mittal). With a score of cars acquired from the Kanorias, Mittal's collection includes a very rare SS1, a Crossley, a Nash, an early Standard and several other cars.

The other father-son team, which has been restoring and providing cars for other collectors, from Kolkata, are the Ghoshs, Sanjoy and his son Rajiv. For Sanjoy Ghosh, it was his grandfather, Justice J.P. Mitter, who gave him the collecting bug. It was after returning from Oxford in 1932, following the completion of his legal studies, that Justice Mitter decided to purchase a car, a Ford V8, a Deluxe Phaeton. As it had a V8, the car's lazy long-legged performance was most appropriate for comfortable long-distance drives around India, an activity which Justice Mitter adored. The Ford was used extensively until the Second World War.

With car production resuming after the War and sales of cars restarting, the trend was for the newer closed-body American saloons then flooding the Indian marketplace. The soft-top tourer Ford was by then rather passé, and as Justice Mitter by then had become a Calcutta High Court Judge, a closed-body (or a turret type, as General Motors called it) 'sedan' was what was deemed more in line with a High Court judge's standing. So a Chevrolet Fleetmaster was acquired, and the Ford was, sort of, abandoned.

Until 1972, that is, when Justice Mitter's grandson, twenty-year-old Sanjoy Ghosh, decided to get the Ford going, after receiving his first salary from his new job at Sinclairs. It was another ten years though and several false starts before the Ford received its first proper restoration in 1982. Since then, Sanjoy's Ford has won over sixty-five trophies in Kolkata's The Statesman Vintage Car Rally. The Fleetmaster, in the meantime, remained a favourite of Justice Mitter until he passed away in 1985. For the next seven-odd years Sanjoy used the car occasionally, and when in 1993, the *Statesman* decided to open the rally to post-War cars too, the Fleetmaster was readied and corrected, as it had the wrong colour, wrong seats, Ambassador tail lamps and Jeep carburettors. Since then, the Fleetmaster, too, has been dominating the classic section of the Statesman rally, and the same seems to augur for the two new cars in Sanjoy (and his son, Rajiv) Ghosh's stable, the 1949 Buick Eight and the 1949 Cadillac Series 62 sedans, both milestone cars, with both restored comprehensively.

With his reputation for resurrecting old cars spreading near and far, Sanjoy Ghosh quit his job with Sinclairs in 1977, to turn his passion into a profession as he opened a restoration workshop in Kolkata, at his residence. Since then cars from all corners of India have been restored at his facilities, including a striking Lancia Dilambda, one of Kolkata's most remarkable cars, an early Farina-bodied rarity, which survives in India.

The other Kolkata family with a passion for historic vehicles is that of the Boses. A keen rallyist himself when he was alive, the late patriarch Partha Sadhan Bose was a regular at the Indian national rally scene until the 1980s. Having competed in the Himalayan Rally, as well as the Eastern Safari Rally, the All India Safari Rally, The Karnataka 1000 and several others, Partha Sadhan Bose's trophy room reflects the success of his rallying career. In time, the passion moved from speed to elegant old ladies, triggered off when he first took the flag at The Statesman Vintage Car Rally way back in 1983 in a 1934 Daimler. That Daimler belonged to one of Bose's friends who had no idea of the treasure he owned. It was in 1984 that Bose finally acquired his first historic vehicle, a 1917 Canadian Ford Model T. Since then, his (and the family's) collection has grown to almost a dozen vehicles, consisting of the Model T, a Fiat 509A, a Buick 8, an SS1, an SS 1 ½ Litre, an MG TC Midget, a '53 Pontiac Chieftain, as well as a rare and pretty 1930 Auburn 6-85 and a Rolls-Royce 20/25 from 1931.

Mention also must be made of Pallab Roy, from the Cossimbazar zamindari family, who has retained and restored a historical car, a 1928 Studebaker President. As Roy explained to this author, 'The Studebaker was sent to India by Studebaker Corporation to demonstrate the advanced level of American engineering compared to contemporary cars made by other countries. The car had gone around the different cities before it came to Calcutta. As India was ruled by the British then, it was fashionable for most of the gentry to buy English cars. My grandfather, Raja Kamalaranjan Roy, was so fascinated by this car that he persuaded the dealer to get special permission from Studebaker to sell it to him!'

'The car was treasured by him and passed down, in the family,' related Roy to the author, 'and only with the Internet did I discover that this was indeed an extremely rare model and probably the only one that survives in the world now. In an effort to do justice to the restoration, I started searching for pictures of this model but none could be located.

The only original reference that I managed to retrieve were an owner's manual and the original coloured sales brochure from 1928, in which there is shown an illustration of this model, as well as others.' A very finely detailed restoration later, the Studebaker is a wonderful example of how automotive history needs to be conserved.

Similarly, some very fine cars have been saved and restored by the likes of Subrata Sen, Prithvi Nath Tagore, Souvik Ghose Chaudhuri, Rahul Sircar, Rishi Kumar, Sutanu Patra, Gadai Chand Dey, Golam Mommen, S.K. Karnani, Raja Mookerjee (and his family Rolls-Royce Phantom III), as well as Saikat Dutta and Sarojesh Mukherjee.

Calcutta also has been the source of several significant collections in India, such as the ones of Dr Ravi Prakash in Bangalore (now Bengaluru), or that of Dharmaditya Patnaik, from Bhubaneswar. Patnaik's collection has everything from that very rare hand-control Rolls-Royce Twenty, which used to belong to the Maharana of Udaipur, to an early-1990s Alfa Romeo Spider. As well as a Lancia Lambda, from 1926 (a seventh series car), an extraordinary 630K Mercedes-Benz, a Bentley 3 ½ Litre, from 1934, with exquisite Mann Egerton coachwork, a 1947 Cadillac Series 62 convertible, a delightful '56 BMW Isetta bubble car, a stylish Series 1 Jaguar E-Type from 1962, a '63 Triumph TR4, as well as a '65 Ford Mustang.

As mentioned, Dr Ravi Prakash from Bangalore sourced a significant number of vehicles from Kolkata. Now typically, collectors have been industrialists and business entrepreneurs, rarely professionals. Yet one of India's largest private collections of cars is that of a doctor, Dr Ravi Prakash, who owns well over 200 historic vehicles (as well as scores of motorcycles), which ranks him among the biggest collectors in India. As of 2019, most of his cars were housed in five garages in his farmhouse (on the outskirts of Bangalore), but the plan is to put them all in a purpose-built museum.

A 1937 Sunbeam Talbot willed by his mentor General Mahadevan, in 1979, jump-started Prakash to a new obsession. Over the years, Prakash has built up an impressive—and somewhat eclectic—collection, the range spanning several decades of the automobile. From a 1906 British Sentinel steam-powered truck to a 1982 Mercedes-Benz

500SEL, Dr Prakash has a whole host of interesting machinery, some very representative, such as a true veteran in the 1909 Wolseley, a 1915 Ford Model T, a path-breaking 1930 Lancia Dilambda, several Jaguars, as well as a very rare 1928 Lanchester Straight 8. A remarkable Delage D8, from 1930 (with Figoni coachwork), a Graham Blue Streak and a Lincoln-Zephyr V12 are the jewels in the crown. What began as a hobby in 1979 has grown into an engrossing pursuit, with the ambitious plans to build a museum, a project which is being pursued with the full cooperation of the family, as wife Sabena and daughters Rupali and Shefali are fully committed to it too.

The Bombay biggies

Once upon a time, Bombay led the numbers game, with Bhogilal's collection recognized as the biggest in the country. Though most of Bhogilal's cars have been moved to the museum at Ahmedabad, Bombay's collectors still have some of the bigger collections. Even after Vijay Mallya's amazing cars were auctioned, and have dispersed into other collections, some of the most significant cars in India remain in Bombay/Mumbai.

One of the most important collections in Bombay/Mumbai is that of Viveck Goenka, better known as the owner and publisher of India's most 'independent' newspaper, the *Indian Express*. His highly varied interests and passions go way beyond the business-entrepreneurial to subjects that range from wildlife photography to exploring inaccessible countryside with 4x4 off-roaders, to a fascination for historic vehicles. He spends many happy hours locating them, restoring them and enjoying them. In the process, Goenka has built up an amazing collection of 4x4s that range from a tiny Steyr-Puch Haflinger to a giant of a Unimog, the ultimate go-anywhere 4x4 of all time.

Goenka's collection of historic vehicles, in several ways, is very systematic. For instance, he has at least one representative model of every S-Class Mercedes-Benz manufactured since 1954! Goenka also has many models of the relatively modest automobiles made in India by the likes of Hindustan Motors and Premier Automobiles. Thus, the collection has each and every Fiat and Premier model made in India, plus the entire gamut from Hindustan Motors.

The other thematic 'plebs' in his collection include a very cute range of tiny Fiats, the 500s and the 600, several VW Microbuses, and a few Beetles too. The range also spans rare exotics, such as a sublimely beautiful '29 Mercedes-Benz Nürburg, a '33 Studebaker V8 convertible sedan, as well as a purpose-built Packard, a very attractive Pontiac Firebird convertible, a magnificent Imperial and two rare Nissan Presidents.

Undoubtedly one of the most diverse in India, Viveck Goenka's collection is arguably one of the most interesting too. In his obsession for perfection, Goenka has developed excellent facilities to restore his many cars, and in the process, has acquired enough knowledge of the engineering aspects of historic vehicles to undertake the restoration projects himself. Being extremely passionate in 'purist' restoration processes, he supervises the work on his vehicles personally.

Matching Goenka for range and eclecticism is the little-known collection of Harit Trivedi. When just six years old, in 1965, Harit's fascination for cars was triggered by a vision of a startlingly beautiful Ford Mustang, which he saw in the street in Zug, a town in Switzerland where Trivedi was living with his family. By the age of nine, Harit was cutting out pictures of historic vehicles from newspapers and magazines. 'I have no idea where this passion comes from,' explained Harit to this author, adding; 'it must have been from a previous life as no one in the family was really so passionate about historic vehicles!'

After the family returned from Switzerland and settled in India, in Bombay/Mumbai (Harit was nine then), the young boy made it a point to look for and spot historic vehicles on a regular basis. He also started attending every historic vehicle rally in Bombay/Mumbai as a spectator. It was while Harit was still in college that he acquired his first historic vehicle, a 1926 Fiat Tipo 509. After that, there was no looking back, as Harit has collected quite a significant number of vehicles. Several of Harit's cars include some very iconic American muscle cars from the 1960s, plus many cars that are rare in the Indian context. Amongst them is a stunning Lancia Astura-based racer, which has raced extensively in Kolkata, as well as a very rare Humber Snipe 80 Pullman landaulet, plus a sweeping Dodge Custom Royal coupé. Unfortunately, many of the other rarities with Harit are yet to be restored.

At some point, motorcycles also came into the picture and there are several two-wheeled rarities in Harit's collection too. Then a chance event of a distant cousin digitalizing his family photographs led to the start of a collection of old photographs. This cousin had photographed Queen Elizabeth being driven around in an early 1950s convertible Buick when she was visiting India in 1961. Gifted to Harit by the cousin, these photographs started off another collection: that of old photos of historic vehicles in India. Harit today has an amazing collection of archival material of automobiles in India, from the distant past. From photographs, it has expanded to historical literature, brochures, manuals, newspapers, magazines, anything remotely related to automobiles in India. This is one collection which keeps growing.

Rivalling Harit for old photos, catalogues, leaflets and historic documentation is the collection of Karl Bhote, who lives between Pune and Mumbai. Karl's car collection is specifically India-centric. He, however, credits his father for it: 'The seeds were sown by my dad himself being very fond of classics, and my parents encouraged me from a very young age. What was the definitive triggering point, I can't say, I was too young. The fondness specifically for Fiats was because of my grandfather's 1973 Premier President, which he bequeathed to me,' explained Karl to this author.

Prof. T.R. Sarkari, who taught automobile engineering at the Indian Institute of Technology, in Powai, Mumbai, was the one who had bought the Premier President in 1974 and had it with him for several decades, before gifting it to his car-crazy grandson Karl. That Premier marks the start of a passion for Premiers and Fiats, with Karl's collection sporting numerous Fiats/Premiers of all kinds, from a 1954 Fiat Millecento (the first of the series) to a 1996 Premier Padmini S1, the last of the line. Karl's paternal grandfather Russi Bhote bought one of the first Standard Heralds in Madras (now Chennai) in 1962, and Karl's father Bomi Bhote bought his first car, also a Herald, in the 1980s.

Bhote is one of several Parsees who keep contributing to India's automotive culture, with Behram Ardeshir (an Alfa Romeo specialist), brothers Kooverji and Faridoon Gamadia who own the regular-use evergreen Invicta Black Prince, Dinyar Jamshedjee and his rare Rolls-Royce Wraith, as well as Cyrus Dhabar, brothers Kaizad and Nekzad Engineer and Xerxes Master. One of the most enthusiastic of the Mumbai collectors, the late Fali Dhondy, and his tasteful collection of characterful cars—Alfa Romeo Spiders, Austin-Healeys, a Rolls-Royce Twenty, a Ferrari 308 GTS, a Volkswagen Karmann Ghia, and a Fiat 124 Spider with a personalized signature by the car's designer, Tom Tjaarda—must be mentioned too. Fortunately, his daughter Rashna has been taking care of them. It would also not be amiss to mention that one of India's finest, quality collections of historic vehicles (not by numbers) as of 2019, is owned by a Parsee in Mumbai who prefers to remain undisclosed.

Of course, Mumbai also has several small collections with many exceptional automobiles: Amir Ali Jetha and his exceptional Rolls-Royce Phantom II Continental, Sameer Kadam and his delightful Adler Trumpf Junior Sports, Harshit Merchant and his Saab 96, Jagdish Thackersey and his Bentley, Amit Sapre and his astounding 'resurrected from rust and dust' Bristol, and many others. The collection that one needs to look out for in the near future, is the one which is in the process of being put together by business tycoon Gautam Singhania.

Delhi, the new epicentre

In recent times, though, the epicentre of India's historic vehicle movement has shifted to Delhi, with some of India's most important collectors located in India's capital. The most prominent of them is star lawyer Diljeet Titus. 'As a kid I grew up with Ambassadors, Fiats and Standard Heralds around at home,' recounted Diljeet Titus to the author. 'My grandparents owned Chevrolets and Austins, classic cars as they are known now. We used to visit them during our vacations, which meant trips to Shimla, Manali and Mussoorie. For me classic cars came to symbolize freedom!'

Titus began driving his grandfather's car inside their compound when he was just eleven years old. Since he was not allowed to drive on the roads, he spent the next seven years cleaning the cars at home and standing around workshops whenever the family's cars were being sent for servicing or repairs. 'My mother Veena Titus remembers that as a boy of five, I used to plant little toy cars in our garden, in the hope that they would yield trees full of cars. Probably that dream never left me. I started collecting cars in 1999,' remembers Titus.

Though Titus had worked in a law firm from 1989 to 1997, he started his own law firm in 1997. In 2003, Diljeet set up The Titus & Co. Museum for Vintage & Classic Cars. Over the years, Titus built up a hundred at one point of time. 'During my initial years of collecting I bought almost every car that came my way. I have been much more focused over the past few years, buying only rare, custom-built, or low mileage cars, or ones with proper documentation and provenance,' explained Titus to the author.

Diljeet has now rationalized his collection to essentially the most important and interesting cars: Rolls-Royces, Packards, a Pierce-Arrow, an Auburn, Chevrolets, Dodges, Mercedes-Benzes, Buicks and Cadillacs, as well as a Stutz and a very rare and magnificent Minerva. The collection also extends to historic motorcycles, horse carriages, automobilia, books, manuals, posters, et al.

Outstripping Titus in sheer size is the collection of recent collector Madan Mohan, who reputedly has more than 350 vehicles in his collection as of 2020. He has also been acquiring vehicles internationally, and many have been imported into India. Most of the vehicles are undergoing restoration, so the world at large has yet to see them.

Delhi is also host to several important collectors and their collections, including the likes of Amitabh Adhar, Rajiv Kehr, K.C. Anand, Kishore Gidwaney, the Jaiswal family, Sandeep Katari, S.B. Jatti, Deepak Gupta, Ankur Bhatia, Sudhir Choudhrie and several others.

One of the most important collections in Delhi is housed in a building, which is not in Delhi, but some 50-odd km south of the capital of India. The Heritage Transport Museum, located at the village of Taoru, in Haryana, just a two-hour drive away, is a wonderful monument to India's automotive history. Founded by inveterate collector Tarun Thakral, the museum has been conceived to document, exhibit, educate and disseminate information about transportation and its history in India and elsewhere. The museum uses its open-plan space as a didactic and pedagogic experience showcasing the evolution of transportation in India.

The museum has on display several Indian vehicles: a Hindustan 14 from 1949, an Indian-assembled 1949 Studebaker Champion, Willys CJ 3-A Jeep from 1951, a '54 Hindustan Landmaster, a Fiat 1100, a Hindustan Ambassador Mark 2 from 1970, a Premier President and a very rare Badal three-wheeler from 1980. The international line-up consists of a 1946 Nash 600 sedan, a '48 Hudson Commodore, a '54 DeSoto Diplomat Convertible, a '57 Land Rover Series I, a '61 Renault 4, a '63 Volkswagen Beetle, a '64 Peugeot 404 and a Volkswagen Kombi Van T2 from 1968, amongst many others, including a very rare '57 Ford Fairlane 500 Starliner. Several cars that are on display at Thakral's museum are owned by other collectors, a concept that allows collectors to 'share' their cars, with the hoi polloi enjoying the museum that much more.

The other very impressive museum is the one in Coimbatore, the Gedee Car Museum. Founded in memory of Gopalswamy Doraiswamy Naidu (known to all as G.D. Naidu), who was a famous scientist, inventor, educationalist and philanthropist, one who had been called the 'Edison of India'. When G.D. Naidu set about collecting cars, it was with a clearly thematic and technical bent of mind. Given that Naidu played a very important role in the development of Tamil Nadu's second largest city, Coimbatore, by installing several industries and infrastructure, it is not surprising that his descendants chose to set up an automotive museum in this city, as a tribute to the inventor legend.

Set up by G.D. Gopal, the son of G.D. Naidu, the Gedee Car Museum features a rather modest collection of some seventy-odd cars, most of which belong to the GD Charitable Trust, as well as some cars donated by other enthusiasts. All are carefully labelled, with technical details and highlights, with the accompanying text narrating their historical significance. Unlike many other collections in India, most of the cars do not bear fancy badges, and in that sense, the Gedee Car Museum is unique in tracing the history of the people's car through time. Cars like the Ford Model T, an Austin Seven, a Citroën 2CV, a VW Beetle and the Mini have taken centre stage, instead of highfalutin luxury automobiles.

At the same time, it must be pointed out that there are two Rolls-Royces (a Twenty from 1925 and a more recent Silver Shadow), two recent Cadillacs (a 1990s Seville and a humongous stretch limousine), as well as the crown jewel of the collection, a magnificent ex-Maharaja of Mysore Hispano-Suiza H6B. The other star of the Gedee collection is a recent replica of the 1886 Benz Patent-Motorwagen, the three-wheeler that ushered in the era of the petrol-engine automobile, powered by an internal combustion engine. More fascinating are some of the unusual runabouts in the museum, such as the BMW Isetta, a Goggomobil 250, a Lloyd 250, a DKW F7, a Hanomag 1.3 and a Hansa 1100, as well as a very rare Indian-made Scootacar. With this brilliantly pedagogic approach to understanding the automobile and its technological history, G.D. Gopal has created a veritable learning experience that manages to be both educative and entertaining.

The movement continues

Chennai, too, has several important collections: those of M.S. Guhan, Shankar Sundaram, Rajiv Rai, eminent restorer C.S. Ananth, and Ranjit Pratap. Rajesh Malhotra and Anil Punjabi, between them, have a handful of some of the most significant cars in India, including a very rare Alfa Romeo Giulietta SVZ with racing history, a Bugatti and a Mercedes-Benz 600 Pullman, the latter belonging to the Shah of Iran's extraordinary fleet. Mention must also be made of Sumanth Chaganthi, who has a most impressive collection of motorcycles.

It's also heartening to note that the bigger cities do not have a monopoly on India's historic car movement. Harshvardhan Singh, from the town of Dungarpur, in Rajasthan, has converted his family palace's mews into a 'museum' for historic vehicles, as well as a 'car bar'. Located 120 km south of Udaipur, Dungarpur is a picturesque little town, the crown jewel of which is a beautiful palace, the Udai Bilas Palace, set next to the still waters of the Gaibsagar Lake. Renovated and refurbished into a hotel by Harshvardhan and his family, the mid-nineteenth-century palace mew boasts a collection of some forty-odd historic vehicles housed in a heritage building, which used to be the stable for the horses and the carriages of the Dungarpur princely family.

The collection includes a '47 Packard Clipper Deluxe, a '39 Fiat seven-seater saloon, a '42 Willys MB Jeep and a '52 Willys CJ2A, plus a 1950 Cadillac Series 62 convertible, a very original Standard Vanguard, a '49 Standard Flying 14, a '66 Volkswagen Beetle and a '75 Land Rover. The most special car in the collection is the beautifully preserved Steyr 220 cabriolet from 1937, a car which has been in the family since 1939.

Another delightful collection of historic vehicles is on display at Fateh Garh, a haveli perched on the top of a small abutment above Udaipur. Fateh Garh looks like it is centuries old—which it is, and which it is not . . . There are stones and pillars, and bits and pieces that date back to 1882, and then there are a whole lot of the masonry and material, statues and cornices, which are modern. An old haveli in Dharia Kalan, a village near Neemuch, was dismantled, stone by stone, and then rebuilt 150 km away in its current location.

Leading the project was Jitendra Rathore, who had supervised the 'rebuilding' of another interesting retro hotel, Fateh Bagh, in the nearby town of Ranakpur, the first of several such 'heritage renaissance' buildings across Rajasthan. Next, Rathore decided to create his own hotels, the first of which was Ram Pratap Palace, a beautiful old haveli converted into a tasteful boutique hotel, within the city of Udaipur. Then Fateh Garh followed, which has not only become a landmark for heritage tours, but is also an abode for an interesting line-up of historic vehicles. The cars on display include a 1929 Ford Model A, a rare MG PA from 1935, a Dodge, a couple of Chevrolets, as well as a 1938 Daimler DB 18 and a Jaguar Mk VII from 1951.

A similar passion for historic vehicles still runs deep amongst the descendants of the Idar family, with the son of Maharaj Umeg Singhji, Maharaj Narendra Singhji believing in retaining cars such as a '53 Buick Special, a '47 Buick Super, a '54 DeSoto Diplomat Deluxe, a '57 Dodge Kingsway and a '47 Pontiac Silver Streak. The palace garage also houses a '41 Cadillac Fleetwood, a '43 Ford Jeep, a '59 Morris Minor as well as a Mercedes 280S, from 1975.

Jaipur, too, has several significant collections—those of Vikram Singh, Sudhir Kasliwal and Avijit Singh Badnore. Ahmedabad boasts of Subodh Nath, and Nagpur has very keen collectors in Arun Upadhaya and Dr Anjan Chatterjee. Hyderabad has Pestonjee Bhujwalla, Deepak Gir and Zain Bilgrami. Chandigarh has Reeth Sarkaria and Karandip Singh. Pune, too, has several collections, with the most noteworthy being that of Zaheer Vakil's. Bengaluru has an impressively long list in Suleiman Jamal, Lokesh Laxmipathy, Pankaj Motreja, Naveen K., Srinand Piedpet, Vinod Hayagriv, T.R. Raghunandan, Christopher Rodricks, K.P. Subaiah, Suresh P.A., Tom and Tilak Thomas, Balachandra Yadalam, and several others, as the club in the city, Karnataka Vintage & Classic Car Club (KVCCC), is very active. One of India's biggest collections, reputed to be over 200 vehicles, is the Khoday collection in Bengaluru.

The Bollywood bandwagon

Then there are 'larger-than-life' collectors such as Bollywood star Jackie Shroff. A true-blue 'car guy', Shroff has owned some of the most important historic vehicles in India, including a Lotus Esprit, a Pontiac Firebird, a Citroën DS and one of the two extant Mercedes-Benz 540Ks in India, as well as the highly historic SS100 Jaguar, which had raced in Calcutta during the 1950s.

Bollywood actor, singer and director Mehmood Ali, better known as just Mehmood, personally raced a Jaguar, a XK120, at Pune's Lohegaon track in 1960s. As well as the Jaguar, the famous actor also owned a Chevrolet Corvette Sting Ray, the only one ever in India. In fact, the car was reputed to have been the actor's personal favourite, but it may have been, for tax reasons, registered in his second wife, Nancy Mehmood's name. A 1965 model year convertible, the car met with an accident (a family member was rumoured to have driven the car into a wall to prove the strength of the car's fibreglass body!), it remained unrepaired for some years until the owner of Mumbai's Mid-Town Motors, Abbas Jasdanwalla, came across the Corvette.

Jasdanwalla acquired the car in 1986, and, as Mid-Town Motors did not have much experience in repairing fibreglass, they fabricated the left fender of the car in steel (using the right fender as a reference), and had it bonded seamlessly to the fibreglass shell. Thereby, making this Sting Ray perhaps the only one in the world which does not have its entire body made out of that composite material!

Several other Bollywood stars had very interesting cars: Hamid Ali Khan, better known as the villain Ajit, also had a Jaguar XK120, Ashok Kumar owned a Rolls-Royce and a Bentley, Shashi Kapoor a Mercedes-Benz 190SL, Mohammed Rafi a Chevrolet Impala, and Nimmi a 1947 Cadillac. Bengali superstar Suchitra Sen had a very flamboyant Cadillac. Most of them, though, may have acquired these cars more as a reflection of status and wealth than as a passion for exciting automobiles. Prem Nath, though, must have been a serious enthusiast, as his collection included a rare Holden Monaro Coupé, a Lincoln Continental and a Ford Model T. Feroz Khan (1939–2009), who used cars and motor racing in his film (which we write about in the last chapter), owned a Mercedes-Benz 230SL.

The bedrock of the historic vehicle movement, though, has been the innumerable unnamed collectors with the most ordinary of vehicles. The ones who have collected, restored or preserved carefully the most mundane of automobiles, the ones who have done so for the sheer love and affection they have felt for their horseless carriages, the ones who refer to them as 'she', almost a person, alive, with moods, eccentricities and foibles of a human nature.

Yet, the Indian government and certain regularity bodies have been working towards destroying India's automotive heritage, by encouraging the concept of crushing vehicles which are more than a certain age. The intention is to keep older, more polluting vehicles off the road, so as to mitigate the pollution issues facing most Indian cities. These moves have been encouraged by the automobile industry, in the belief that it would contribute to improving sales of newer cars, two-wheelers and commercial vehicles.

A nation's wealth

It may be worth noting that several prominent economists have argued that it is economically inefficient to destroy cars and vehicles in an attempt to stimulate the economy, likening it to the 'broken window fallacy': the illusion that destruction and money spent in recovery from destruction, is a net benefit to society. A broader application of this fallacy is the general tendency to overlook opportunity costs or that which is unseen, either in a financial sense or otherwise.

This is obvious when one considers that in the United Kingdom alone, 'there are more than 1.5 million historic vehicles, or classic cars, in a total vehicle parc of 43 million cars', explains David Whale, the President of the Federation of British Historic Vehicle Clubs (FBVHC), estimating the 'worth of these vehicles at around £25 billion (Rs 2,40,000 crores)!'[3]

FBVHC is a member of the Fédération Internationale de Véhicules Anciens (FIVA, the international federation for historic vehicles), which defines all classics, vintages, veterans, old-timers, et al., as 'historic vehicles', and stresses the fact that these vehicles are part of our technical and cultural heritage. In 2016, FIVA became a non-governmental partner of UNESCO, with the latter, too, acknowledging that the automobile has for more than a hundred years now, had a hugely liberating effect on humanity. It recognizes that the owners of historic vehicles preserve motoring heritage and provide the public with a free museum (and sometimes, a free journey) of our motoring history and culture by using and showing their vehicles on public roads and at special events.

Malcolm Welford, FIVA's 'ambassador' for North America, estimates that the 25 million-odd historic vehicles in the United States are worth $100 billion. Similarly, the millions of old cars and motorcycles in France, Germany, Italy and other European countries, as well as the countries of Latin America, all add up to considerable value, as much as allowing us to glimpse an important slice of mankind's recent industrial past.

Moreover, the numbers and the values of these historic vehicles, what we call vintage or classic cars, motorcycles and other vehicles, which are more than thirty years of age, are growing every year, so much so that the governments of most European countries recognize these vehicles as national heritage, or treasures. India, too, has a significant number of 'historic vehicles'. It has been estimated that over 9 million vehicles in India are over the age of fifteen years. It would be safe to guess that at least 10 per cent of them—almost a million—are over thirty years of age, thus 'historic' as per the definition of FIVA, and so could be gaining in value. Thus destroying them would be a long-term loss to the nation. Restricting their use and, in the worst case, exporting them may be much better alternatives to destroying them.

All the older automobiles, whether cars, motorcycles, scooters, trucks and buses, all encapsulate the very essence of the history of the automobile in this country and its impact on contemporary culture and civilization. We believe that it is important to preserve not just the historic vehicles, but also related artefacts and records by researching and cataloguing the most authentic examples of our automotive past, so that they are available for future generations.

Despite the fact that a significant number of India's most important and historic vehicles have made their way abroad, some truly remarkable and rare automobiles remain in India, as do several milestone automobiles. No less deserving and important is the action of recording their histories, as well as encouraging the preservation of the ones which can be preserved. The story of the automobile, as well as of the associated people, is, in many ways, the story of twentieth-century India. This includes the fascinating personalities and the interesting anecdotes that go with these cars.

Following the definition of every vehicle which is more than thirty years old being a historic vehicle, automobiles such as Hindustan

Contessas, Premier 118NEs, Standard 2000s, even early Maruti 800s are all historic. Thus, the choice of historic vehicles in India today runs to tens of thousands of automobiles of all shapes, sizes and colours. Yet there exists a 'caste system', which discriminates against the commoner Indian-made automobiles. This attitude needs to change— the automobiles made in India are more important historically than the imported ones, as they are the true reflection of India's industrial history.

There is also a need for changes in other attitudes and obsessions; for instance, the need to establish the importance of preservation and patina over restoration. In India, there is an obsession with restoring cars to 'Pebble Beach standards', following the unhappy practice of over-restoring, which the Americans like doing. Most concours d'elegance events in Europe give much greater credence to preservation and the condition of a car in regular use than a freshly restored vehicle reduced to the role of a trailer queen, which is taken from one show to another on a trailer, instead of being driven. A good restoration is one that retains as much of the original vehicle as possible. Yet there is a tendency in India to 'recreate' vehicles, to make them look better than when they were new. By recreating—the skin and bones of an automobile—the history of a vehicle is partially and irretrievably lost.

At the Chantilly Arts & Elegance concours, held every alternate year at Chantilly, near Paris, the concours d'elegance competition is for brand new concept cars from the preceding year, following the tradition from the pre-War concours d'elegance competition for designs showcased by coachbuilders and carmakers from the immediate past. The main competition at Chantilly is about the condition of the historic vehicles on display, which is why the organizers call it a concours d'etat, a competition about the condition of a vehicle. Thus, the increasing importance of preservation and conservation over restoration and recreation.

A surprisingly significant number of historic vehicles in India have remained in the same family since new, and the documentation available for most of them is very impressive. Some of the collectors who have acquired their vehicles more recently have made considerable efforts at retracing the histories of their respective cars, and that is commendable indeed. Sadly, many have not. Then there are those collectors who have a tendency to 'invent' or 'rewrite' their vehicles' histories. Many ascribe the wrong age and/or date of manufacture, in an attempt to make their cars seem older or more important than they actually are. Either, they lack the knowledge and do not wish to make the effort to get the right information, or are just disrespectful in imagining that they will not be 'caught out'. Some even deliberately falsify. All of which is most shameful. Correct and appropriate documentation is essential for uncovering and/or rediscovering the true histories of the vehicles, as well as authenticating dates. All automobiles have a story to tell, and these stories must be told.

To that end, it is important for all concerned—the collectors, the owners and the enthusiasts—to unite and collaborate, at both the national as well as the international level. It is imperative to effectively address increasing legislation designed to keep historic vehicles off the roads of the cities of tomorrow, by spreading awareness and educating the 'non-believers' that historic vehicles are as much an intrinsic part of India's and humanity's cultural history, as are the seven arts.

3

Make in India

Englishman Samuel John Green, soon after arriving in India and joining the company Simpson & Co., in Madras, as a director in 1902, attempted to make a car with an engine, pump, boiler and gears. Constructed in-house at Simpson's facilities, this steam-powered car may have been the very first effort at making an automobile in India. The Green-Simpson steam car, in all likelihood, remained a one-off, and no further attempts seem to have been made for the next decade or so.

The next known attempt at making a car in India may have been around the years 1912–14, when a car badged the Morvi was constructed by another Englishman, Ralph Ricardo, who had arrived in India in 1911. This story seems very plausible when we learn that Ralph Ricardo was the cousin of Sir Harry Ralph Ricardo, who was the Ricardo in the famous automotive engine specialist Ricardo PLC, a company that still exists, making and consulting on internal combustion engines. Sir Harry Ralph had developed a 3.3-litre two-stroke engine for his cousin Ralph Ricardo's fledgling car-making venture Two Stroke Engine Company, in 1909. Though the cars were well made, the company went bust, as costs were higher than the prices the car could fetch. Thus, when in 1911, the Two Stroke Engine Company collapsed, Ralph Ricardo decided to leave for India, and try his hand at making his fortune in that British colony

5000 miles away, a part of the world which then was the jewel in the English crown.

Given his automotive background, Ralph Ricardo was, perhaps, better placed at realizing the dream of making a car in India than many others. A car with the registration number BOM 6666 was registered in the name of Ralph Ricardo, and the address on record was that of 'The Automobile Co. Ltd, Bombay'. The car, which Ricardo made was badged Morvi, and it is possible that the name came from the town of Morvi, in Gujarat, which at that point of time was a princely state, ruled by Maharaja Thakore Sahib Sir Waghji II Rawaji.

The fifty-three-year-old thakursaheb had the reputation of being very progressive, commissioning a horse-drawn tramway system in his state as early as the late nineteenth century. He was also reputed to be an early patron of the horseless carriage. It is highly possible that the thakursaheb commissioned Ralph Ricardo to develop the Morvi. Whether just one was made, or several, from the Morvi Motor Works (as the company may have been called), is not known. No doubt, the Morvi was indeed a very early attempt at making a car in India.

A couple of similar attempts were made in Calcutta, too, when a few years later, a cyclecar called the Russa was sold and registered for use in the city. Russa Engineering Works was a well-reputed dealership for several car marques, including Ford. In all likelihood, they had a coachbuilding facility in-house too, and not unlike several of the other dealers and distributors, offered the services of making the bodies. It is possible that the chassis and power train from a lesser-known cyclecar manufacturer in Europe was imported, and Russa fabricated the bodies on them and sold these lightweight cyclecars with its own badging. This was a rather common practice elsewhere in the world then.

In fact, the earliest form of 'car making' in India was mostly the coachbuilding activities. In most cases, complete (fully assembled and ready for the road) cars were imported and sold. Several of the carmakers also shipped out their cars in chassis-mechanical form, to be 'bodied' in India. Coachbuilding of bodies thus was perhaps the earliest automotive 'manufacturing' activity in India.

With a tradition for skilled woodwork, the art of coachbuilding had an early history in the subcontinent. The oldest known was that of Steuart & Co., from Calcutta. Established in 1775, over the years, Steuart & Co. built up a very fine reputation for its ornate and elaborate state coaches, howdahs for elephants and a variety of horse carriages, many sumptuously decorated with gold, silver and ivory. On special appointment to the Prince of Wales and the Viceroy of India, the list of Steuart & Co's clientele also included the who's who of princely India. With the coming of the horseless carriage, Steuart & Co. too realized that it had no choice but to embrace the new-fangled device, moving into the world of coachbuilding of automobiles, a service that it started offering with the advent of the motoring era in India. It also saw an opportunity in distributing cars and took up the distribution of several European brands including the British Thornycroft.

Established in 1862 by John I. Thornycroft, with plans to make steam-driven coaches, Thornycroft made its first steam car in 1895. By 1902, the company had moved to internal combustion power, launching its first car in 1903. Starting with a small 10hp two-cylinder car, Thornycroft moved to making bigger cars, which were a more than worthy rival to the Rolls-Royce Silver Ghost.

Thornycroft was one of the early carmakers to offer complete cars with standard bodies already installed. Naturally, complete cars cost more than the bare chassis, and the price of a complete car depended on the bodywork specified, of which there were several options (Victoria, landaulet, limousine, Roi-des-Belges, and so on). Thornycroft also sold bare chassis to those who wanted them, and so Steuart & Co., as well as selling complete Thornycrofts, imported significant numbers in chassis-mechanical form, building, at its facilities in Calcutta, the car bodies, as per the customer's requirements, or following the styles established by the carmaker.

As the popularity of the motor car increased, Steuart & Co. soon had competition. Not very far from its facilities, on Calcutta's chic Bentinck Street, French Motor Car Company Limited established a showroom, followed by a coachbuilding facility a few kilometres away. Starting with French car brands such as Panhard et Levassor, Mors and Berliet, French Motor soon added other European and American brands, including Armstrong-Siddeley, Bean, Bianchi, Minerva, Cadillac and Studebaker. As well as selling complete cars, French Motor also began bodying chassis-mechanicals shipped out by many of the carmakers. Business was so good that French Motor opened an important branch in Bombay soon thereafter. The combined staff of the two facilities added up to over 600 people.

In Bombay, though, French Motor Car Company had another very worthy rival in Fort Coach Factory. Established in 1877, the Fort Coach Factory was founded by a Parsee, Pestonji B. Press. With a background in art from Bombay's famous Sir Jamsetjee Jeejeebhoy (J.J.) School of Art, Press had an eye for aesthetics, and soon built up a very fine reputation for making exquisitely crafted horse carriages. With the advent of the motor car, Fort Coach Factory moved to specialize in automotive coachbuilding too, starting with making bodies for the French Brasier cars, imported in chassis-mechanical form.

The coachbuilder who was arguably the most successful in India, though, was Simpson & Co. from Madras. Established in 1840, Simpson & Co. eventually was on special appointment to none other than King Edward VII and the Nizam of Hyderabad, having made fabulous carriages, both the horse-drawn and elephant-drawn kinds. Into the motoring era, other than distributing and selling cars starting with steam-driven ones, Simpson & Co. built hundreds of car bodies based on chassis from 'mid-market' carmakers such as Darracq to the more prestigious Daimler, Delaunay-Belleville, Napier and Rolls-Royce.

Yet Simpson never plunged into full-fledged manufacturing of cars, let alone assembling, unlike several other coachbuilders-turned-carmakers such as Holden in Australia and Vanden Plas in the United Kingdom. Holden, founded by James Alexander Holden in 1856 as a saddlery, became a coachbuilder by 1914 and a full-fledged assembler of models from General Motors eventually. In 1931, Holden became a part of the General Motors Empire, but the brand still remains Australia's most important, though they ceased making cars a few years ago. Vanden Plas' history also goes back to the horse-drawn carriage era, then to coachbuilding of cars, to series manufacturing of bodies and eventually becoming a brand within the British Motor Corporation from 1957.

Simpson & Co., instead, took the route to becoming a manufacturer of diesel engines and trucks following India's Independence, and today specializes in manufacturing and supplying a family of diesel engines for truck, tractor, forklift, marine and genset (generator) applications. Sadly, Steuart & Co., French Motor Car Company and Fort Coach Factory did not survive the move away from coach-built cars to series production automobiles as the major carmakers set up assembly lines in India on their own or with local partners.

It may be interesting to note that, as per the *World Census of Automotive Vehicles* on 1 January 1923, a census report unearthed by Hungarian automotive historian and researcher Dr Pál Négyesi, there were as many as 34,289 passenger cars, 3240 trucks and 12,133 motorcycles in India by then.[1]

It was also during the same period, sometime in the 1920s, that a Calcutta-based entrepreneur, Bipin Behari Das, made an all-Indian car. Named Swadeshi—echoing Mahatma Gandhi's self-reliance sentiments—the car was made from locally available materials, and seems to have been lashed together in a garage with minimal facilities. Whether it was grounds-up all indigenous or whether it was based on existing mechanicals is not known. What is known is that nothing came of it, and that the car remained just a one-off, and was given to the Calcutta municipal corporation for its use.

Made in India

Thus, it so happened that the first set of 'made in India' (maybe more appropriate to call them 'assembled in India') cars were American automobiles. Though Ford Motor Company was first off the block in incorporating Ford India on 31 July 1926, the company took a while to set up its first assembly plant in Bombay, in the suburb of Bhandup, in 1931, followed a few months later by similar facilities in the port cities of Calcutta and Madras too.

Ford Canada had the distribution rights for the British colonies
and had set up assembly facilities in Africa as early as 1923 and in
Australia in 1925. In 1926, the first year of Ford's direct operations in
India, 4152 Model Ts were sold over the calendar year, accounting for
a third of all Fords sold in South and South East Asia that year, and
representing an almost 13 per cent improvement over the preceding
year, when Ford was selling through distributors. Of course, all of these
were direct imports. By 1930, the number of Fords sold in India had
gone up to 5107 (all imported), by 1935 to 5444 (by now, mostly
assembled), and then to 7011 by 1940. From 1940–46, coinciding with
much of the Second World War years, Ford assembled and delivered
as many as 1,14,485 defence vehicles to the Allied forces in India from
its three assembly plants!

Before Ford got going though, in 1928, two assembly plants were
up and rolling in India, both by rival American carmakers: General
Motors and Graham-Paige. Founded as recently as 1927 by brothers
Joseph and Robert Graham and their Canadian partner Ray Austin,
by taking over Paige-Detroit Motor Company, Graham-Paige went
international rapidly. Of the several assembly facilities that Graham-
Paige set up across the globe, one was in Calcutta, when wealthy
barrister Sushil Chandra Chaudhury decided to invest in a car
assembly facility.

Chaudhury's nephew Anil Kumar Mitra had studied automobile
engineering in the United States, and then worked with Ford, before
signing up with fledgling carmaker Graham-Paige and heading back
home to Calcutta to set up the assembly facilities at 2 Rowland Road,
where the Chaudhurys already had a tyre service centre, International
Tyre & Motor Company. Initially, Graham-Paige was very successful,
selling very well as taxis because of the car's rather compact turning
circle, but the investment was considerable and, within two years,
International Tyre & Motor was bankrupted. Also, the supply of kits
may have been affected by the Great Depression.

General Motors (GM), on the contrary, had a very successful run in
India. Though its assembly facilities at Sewri, neighbouring the Bombay
Port, were inaugurated in December 1928, series assembly began in

earnest in 1929, with several of the many GM brands, including Buick, Chevrolet, Oakland, Oldsmobile and Pontiac, rolling off the lines at the same time. By the time GM overtook Ford (which was in 1931) as world's number one carmaker, the Indian market too was contributing to the GM's global lead, and reflecting in the increasing popularity of Chevrolets and Buicks on the subcontinent.

By 1933, the Indian subcontinent was 'home' to 1,21,400 four-wheelers (62,600 cars, 30,992 buses and 7748 trucks), markedly more than the entire vehicle parc of Japan (1,01,968), incidentally, as per the *Automotive World News Bulletin* No. 469. Of the 33.57 million vehicles in circulation across the globe then, the United States accounted for more than 72 per cent, at 24.32 million! The French vehicle parc was a distant second at 1.85 million, ahead of the United Kingdom's 1.62 million. The only other countries ahead of India then were Germany with 6,16,200, Italy (3,23,336), Union of South Africa (1,56,850) and Sweden (1,46,947).

It may be worth noting that despite the not unimpressive figure for (an undivided) India, the country fell into the category of nations where the vehicle-to-people ratio was less than one per 250 people, when the world average was one for every sixty persons, with the American average at one for every five!

Yet, the eighth most important automobile market in the 1930s did not seem to have been particularly attractive to carmakers to warrant an assembly facility. Just a couple more assembly set-ups came up in the 1930s, that of Addison in Madras, to assemble British Wolseleys, a logical move as Addison was already the dealer for the Wolseleys, Morris and Riley, amongst others, as well as Morris Industries in Bombay, to assemble Morris cars.

Apparently, the Birla family built a car in Calcutta during these years, with the intention of putting it into production. The prototype car was registered in Calcutta, and its registration address was 8 Royal Exchange Place, which later became the registered address of Hindustan Motors. This Birla car, though, seemed to have remained a one-off.

The failure of the first Indian car-assembling venture, that of International Tyre & Motor to make the Graham-Paige cars, may have been a deterrent for many of the Indian entrepreneurs looking to invest in the car manufacturing business in the 1930s. The Great Depression, too, by wiping out two-thirds of the carmakers across the globe, may have also played a role.

It would also be interesting to note that it was in 1930 that Japan's fledgling car industry had made a very modest start with the manufacture of all of 500-odd units!

One theory on why car-assembling ventures failed in India is that Indian business houses just didn't have the confidence to take on such capital-intensive projects with the British 'masters' around, and that it was the changes in the political environment that finally induced Indian businessmen to seriously start thinking of automobile production. By 1940, the writing was on the wall—the beginning of the end of British imperialism and the dawn of a new order and a new era in Indian industry.

Made by Indians

Business houses like the Birlas and the Walchands, both close to the Indian National Congress party, were the first movers to perceive business opportunities in automobiles. Walchand Hirachand Doshi, born to a Gujarati Jain family based in Maharashtra's Sholapur town, was an enterprising young matriculate who cut his teeth in the railway construction business, but saw opportunities in shipping and then the construction of aircrafts.

In fact, Hindustan Aircraft in Bangalore (which later became Hindustan Aeronautics Limited, HAL) was born out of a chance meeting between an American aircraft executive and Walchand Hirachand on a flight to the US in 1939. Walchand's visit was for a possible collaboration with one of the American Big Three for the manufacture of cars. His first stop was at GM, the biggest of the Big Three, but then GM already had its assembly set up in Bombay, which was on full throttle.

An audience with Henry Ford, it seems, went well, but Ford asked him to speak to the Ford Motors' Canadian division, which was handling the British Commonwealth markets, including India. Ford also, by then, had three successful assembly operations going on in India, so Walchand Hirachand then knocked at the doors of Chrysler Corporation, a company that, in comparison to the other two giants, was almost an upstart.

Brought in to manage an ailing American carmaker called Maxwell Motor, Walter Percy Chrysler launched the first Chrysler-badged car, the Chrysler Six, in 1924. With quality products and the founding of the Plymouth brand for the entry-level segment, the DeSoto for the mid-range, and by buying Dodge Brothers Company, Chrysler soon had a full range of vehicles to offer. The strategy worked so well that, by 1936, Chrysler was in second place, behind GM, on the US sales charts, ahead of erstwhile leader Ford Motors! Ford, with its single model-to-suit-all-needs strategy, had slipped to third place in the US marketplace, with a market share of 22 per cent. Chrysler had 25 per cent of the market, GM 43 per cent. Between the American Big Three, they had 90 per cent of the world's biggest market. As well as more than half the world market!

The United States still ruled the car business worldwide. In 1938, the US produced more than 2.5 million of the world total of 4 million cars produced that year. Great Britain, which had become the number two carmaker in the world, overtaking France in 1929 for the first time, thanks to a larger 'captive' market in its colonies, had made all of 4,45,000 cars that year, accounting for 9 per cent of world production. In the meantime, the Japanese industry had come a long way from its very modest 1930 start to a total production of 24,000 units in 1938.

As Walchand Hirachand was not taking the Japanese route of developing an auto industry with products developed in-house, then what better than to tie-up with an international giant? Thus, Chrysler Corporation and Walchand Hirachand signed up in 1940.

The Second World War intervened, and car production was set aside for the war effort. Chrysler Corporation's contribution included the manufacturing of the famous Sherman tanks, and Dodge made the engines for the Boeing B-29 Superfortress and military trucks.

Walchand Hirachand, in the meantime, incorporated his car company, Premier Automobiles Limited (PAL), in 1941. After that, he had to wait patiently, as the War came to an end, and car production in the United States recommenced in 1946.

It was a somewhat similar story with the Birlas. Patriarch Ghanshyam Das Birla was very close to Mahatma Gandhi and a great supporter of the Quit India movement. He realized that there was considerable potential in setting up an automotive assembly plant near a port. Hindustan Motors was incorporated in 1942 and established at the tiny Gujarat port town of Okha. The War and the consequent diversion of efforts into the production of war material had all the car majors of Europe busy. Thus, Birla and Hindustan Motors had to wait.

With the possibility of India's Independence around the corner and an altogether new regime in power, Birla and Walchand Hirachand decided to wait things out. Other industrial groups also saw opportunities, and automotive enthusiast J.R.D. Tata decided to get the Tata Group to incorporate Tata Engineering & Locomotive Company Limited (TELCO) in 1945, with plans to make locomotives and vehicles. In Ludhiana, a company called Mahindra & Mohammed was incorporated in 1945 to trade in steel.

Independence and a new impetus

With India's Independence from British rule came the Partition of the country into India and Pakistan. The Partition of India caused the greatest transmigration in the history of humankind, with more than 12 million people crossing the borders between India and West Pakistan and East Pakistan.

It was only after things stabilized that the business of making automobiles was under consideration once again. By 1948, Mahindra & Mohammed had become Mahindra & Mahindra, as business partner Sir Malik Ghulam Mohammed left for Pakistan to become Pakistan's first finance minister. Hindustan Motors migrated to West Bengal in 1948 and set up a factory in a town called Uttarpara, some 15 km north of Calcutta.

Premier Automobiles was first off the block getting its factory in the Bombay suburb of Kurla up and running by 1949, when the first set of Dodge, Plymouth and DeSoto-badged cars rolled off the lines, along with the first batch of trucks with Dodge, Fargo and DeSoto branding (Fargo being the brand for trucks sold by the Plymouth dealers).

The same year, the assembly lines began rolling at Hindustan Motors as the company cleverly signed two deals, one with American carmaker Studebaker and the other with British manufacturer Morris Motors. One of the older American carmakers, Studebaker had a storied history. Starting with horse carriages in 1852, Studebaker migrated to making cars in 1902, initially making electric ones before moving to petrol-engine automobiles. During the Second World War, even though Studebaker was well implicated in the war effort, making amphibious vehicles, many of which found their way to India, they were also preparing for the anticipated post-War market. Thus, in 1946, Studebaker was ready with a brand new range of cars, which it launched with the famous slogan, 'First by far with a post-war car'. This may have attracted Hindustan Motors to ink an assembly deal with Studebaker.

The Studebakers, though, in typical American fashion, were big six-cylinder-engine cars, expensive to buy and even more expensive to run. A smaller car, which would appeal to the emerging middle class was what Hindustan Motors needed. As a complement to the Studebakers, Hindustan Motors decided to tie up with British carmaker Morris Motors, which had been selling its inexpensive 'middle-class' models in India successfully.

Founded by William Morris in 1910 and headquartered in Oxford, the first Morris car was a two-seater buggy from 1913. Producing reliable cars at bargain prices, Morris became Britain's number-one carmaker by 1925. After the Second World War, Morris reintroduced the Ten, a small car that it had first launched in 1939. Hindustan Motors began its Morris assembly operations with the Ten, launched in India as the Hindustan 10 in 1949.

Shortly thereafter, in 1950, Hindustan replaced the 10 with the 'Baby' Hindustan, which was the recently unveiled Morris Minor, and complemented that with the slightly bigger Hindustan Fourteen (the Morris Oxford). The Morris Minor retailed for Rs 8025 then. The Hindustan Fourteen went for Rs 10,085.

Hindustan Motors also imported and sold the Morris Six—an Oxford with a longer bonnet incorporating a bigger six-cylinder engine—at a pricier Rs 13,325. In comparison, the Studebaker Champions, the Deluxe Sedan and the Regal Deluxe Sedan, both also assembled by Hindustan Motors, retailed for a relatively reasonable Rs 11,910 and Rs 12,210.

In 1954, the Hindustan Fourteen was replaced by the Hindustan Landmaster, which was the Morris Oxford Series II. The Landmaster remained in production until 1957, when it was replaced by the Ambassador. The Ambassador was the Morris Oxford Series III, launched in 1956 in the UK, but was not introduced in India until 1957. In 1959, when the Oxford Series III was replaced by the all-new Farina-designed Series V, the tooling of the Series III was shipped to India . . . becoming the Ambassador, which remained in production until 2014.

Though Premier Automobiles had commenced activities before Hindustan Motors, its product planning was not as good. Until 1951, the cars that PAL was assembling were the Chrysler Corporation cars, the DeSoto Diplomat, the Dodge Kingsway and the Plymouth DeLuxe, all retailing for very similar prices: Rs 15,275, Rs 15,175 and Rs 15,075, respectively—thus cutting into each other's sales in their rather narrow market segment.

True, Premier had a lucrative truck-assembling activity, making Dodge, Fargo and DeSotos, but more important was the business of selling Fiat cars in India. Though Walchand Hirachand's first meeting with Chrysler Corporation is well-documented, how the Indian car assembler tied up with Fiat of Italy is not that well known. What is known, though, is that Premier had also approached Volkswagen among others. If inexpensive smaller cars had to be made, then the obvious collaborators had to be the European carmakers. Amongst them, Fiat already had the reputation of making some of the most popular of the smaller people's cars, specifically the legendary 500 Topolino, which, since 1936, had been one of the smallest and cheapest cars made out of Europe.

Initially, completely built up Fiat 500C Topolinos and 1100s were imported and sold for Rs 5400 and Rs 9725, respectively, with the former having the enviable reputation of being India's cheapest car then, the closest possible to a people's car. The Fiat 500C, though, had two serious shortcomings—it had just two doors and the four seats were enough to fit only two adults and two children, no more—features that were just not acceptable to chauffeur-driven, joint-family Indians.

Assembling and selling a bigger four-door car, like the HM (Hindustan Motors) models, was a more sensible alternative, so Premier inked a fresh deal with Fiat. At the outset, PAL assembled the two-door 500C starting 1951, but soon followed that up by introducing the all-new 1100 in 1954, a year after it had been launched in Italy. Until 1965, as Fiat in Italy kept updating the 1100 with cosmetic upgrades, the Premier-assembled Fiats in India too kept getting facelifts. In 1965, Premier introduced the Fiat 1100D, or Delight. This was the Italian Fiat 1100D from 1962, which was made in Italy until 1966. The tooling was shipped out to India soon thereafter, and, similar to the story of the Ambassador, the Fiat 1100D remained in production from 1966 . . . to 2000!

In the meantime, TELCO went into the business of manufacturing trucks in a factory in Jamshedpur, after it had got into a technical collaboration with Daimler-Benz, from Germany, in 1954. A prominent importer in Calcutta, Dewar's Garage also waded into the assembly business, bolting together and selling British brands such as Singers and Rovers. Mahindra & Mahindra inked a deal with Willys to assemble the Willys Jeep CJ3B, under licence in India, in a factory in north Bombay; this was sold as the brand 'Mahindra Jeep'. Even a few of the big American Kaisers were assembled at a facility in Bhandup, Bombay.

Madras, too, had its fair share of automotive assembling action. Raghunandan Saran, a Madras-based industrialist and a friend of India's first Prime Minister Jawaharlal Nehru, was advised by the latter to look at manufacturing cars. Saran set up an assembly plant to assemble Austin cars, naming the company Ashok Motors. Starting operations in 1948, Ashok Motors assembled and sold the Austin A40 from 1949. The Austin A30 was also considered but, apart from receiving a prototype in 1953, no progress was made on this, as Leyland trucks became the focus.

The advent of the Licence Raj

For the Indian automobile industry, 1951 was the landmark year, when the Industries (Development and Regulation) Act was instituted. The act required an entrepreneur to get a licence to set up a new unit, to expand it, or to change the product mix. The purpose of this system of licensing was to create a planned pattern of investment, to minimize resource waste, to counteract monopolies and the concentration of wealth and to maintain regional balances. All very good intentions, but then good intentions are one thing and execution (specifically in India) is another.

In the automotive sector, the execution meant that the right to make different kinds of automobiles was restricted to a handful of manufacturers. Mahindra & Mahindra were told to concentrate on just Jeeps. TELCO was given a licence to make only trucks. So was Ashok Motors, which had to give up its assembling of the Austins. Austin, in the meantime, had merged with Hindustan Motors' collaborator Morris and the Nuffield Organization in 1952 to form the British Motor Corporation (BMC). Similarly, Bombay-based Automotive Products of India (API), which commenced assembling the British Rootes Group products from Hillman, Humber, Singer and Sunbeam, since 1949, were given a licence to manufacture scooters, once the Rootes Group exited, selling the company to the Madras-based M.A. Chidambaram Group. So, in 1955, API switched to the manufacturing of Lambretta scooters (giving up the assembling of cars altogether), in collaboration with Innocenti of Italy.

If America could have its Big Three, India had its Little Three—Hindustan Motors, Premier Automobiles and a Madras-based assembler, Union Motor Company, which had set up an assembly line in 1949, after getting a licence to make cars. The government's thinking was that there should be at most one carmaker at each of India's three major ports.

Union Motors had tied up with British carmaker Standard Motor Company. Another pioneering British brand, Standard was founded in 1903 in Coventry by Reginald W. Maudslay. Standard made a very early impression on the royal families of India when it secured the order to supply cars for the Delhi Durbar of 1911, when King George V and Queen Mary travelled to Delhi for their coronation as emperor and empress of India. As many as sixty Standard cars and ten trucks were shipped to India.

From 1929, Standard was also supplying chassis-mechanicals to the Swallow Sidecar Company, which later became the Jaguar. After the Second World War, Standard acquired Triumph Motor Company in 1944 and the decision was taken to use the Triumph moniker for the sportier cars, and Standard for the regular saloons. The first post-War car that Standard launched was the Vanguard in 1948. Union Motors began its assembly operations with the Vanguard saloon in 1948, and then went on to introduce the smaller saloon, the Standard 8, followed by the 10 and, subsequently, the Pennant. Though the Vanguard was not exactly cheap at Rs 10,975, the 8 retailed at a relatively reasonable Rs 6500 in 1950.

At some point, the name of the company was changed from Union Motors to Standard Motors Product of India Limited (SMPIL), though Standard UK had no stake in the Indian company. Not unlike Hindustan Motors and Premier Automobiles, Standard Motors too narrowed operations to becoming a one-product manufacturer by 1962, when it launched the Triumph Herald, badged as a Standard Herald. Though the Standard badge was last used in 1963 in the United Kingdom, it carried on in India until 1987, with the Herald and its progenitor, the Gazel, being made until 1977.

Why did this product stagnation happen? A simple answer: government policies. With the Industrial Act of 1951 and the beginnings of what is now referred to as the 'Licence Raj', just three manufacturers in India—Hindustan, Premier and Standard—had licences to make cars. Then, in 1954, the government realized that there were some sixty-odd models of cars selling in a market which barely totalled up to 20,000 sales per year. Clearly, with competition from imported vehicles, the fledgling auto industry could not survive. The import of automobiles and components also was a serious drain on foreign exchange. With self-sufficiency as the mantra of Nehru and his government, the powers that be decided in 1954 that a high import tariff for automobiles and components was necessary to support localization and growth of the automobile industry. Consequently, both General Motors and Ford stopped their assembly operations that year.

With the eventual objective of complete localization, the three Indian carmakers decided that it would be prudent to concentrate on one specific model, for which they acquired the tooling from their respective collaborators. It also made sense to phase out the assembling of the slow-selling Studebakers and Chrysler Corporation cars, which is what Hindustan Motors and Premier Automobiles did, respectively, by the end of the 1950s.

From the beginning of the 1960s, it was a case of: 'You can have any car you please as long as it is a Hindustan Ambassador or a Fiat 1100 or a Standard Herald!' Most people opted for the first two as the Herald came in just a restrictive two-door form until the introduction of the Herald Mark III in 1968, which was a four-door development, unique to India. Yet, the Ambassador and the Fiat 1100 remained the dominant models, accounting for almost 90 per cent of the Indian car market in the 1960s and 1970s—an oligopolistic situation symptomatic of crony-capitalism, which led to industrial stagnation and constrained economic growth for the country.

Yet, less than a decade after the Industrial (Development and Regulation) Act of 1951 was enacted, the year when the 'Licence Raj' came into being, many of the who's who in the corridors of power began to question whether the system actually benefited the people. One school of thought was that passenger cars per se should be a low priority item for industrial growth and progress, that two-wheelers, buses and commercial vehicles were significantly more important than cars, a product available only to the very rich at that point of time. At the same time, politicians expressed concern about the prices of the cars that were in production. At a price of Rs 12,000 for the Hindustan Ambassador (Rs 11,554 plus taxes), the car represented forty years of an average Indian salary then!

Even though the Fiat 1100 Select was marginally cheaper at Rs 10,566 plus taxes, and the Standard Ten retailed at around Rs 10,000 (Rs 9988 ex-factory), they were all very expensive luxuries for the Indian masses. Localization had just about begun, but it was still a long way from a situation where the import of components was no longer a drain on foreign exchange, which had become very scarce by the late 1950s.

In search of the people's car

In 1959, with the country facing a serious foreign exchange crunch, the Nehru government looked at ways to cut imports. Swadeshi, localization, other than being a populist ideological buzzword, was also a necessity, so the government set up a committee in April 1959, under L.K. Jha, an additional secretary in the commerce ministry at that point of time, to look into the possibility of making a lower-cost 'people's car'.

The Jha Committee came to the conclusion that it would be possible to make an inexpensive people's car at a target price of around Rs 5000 to Rs 6000 (the equivalent of Rs 1.6 lakhs in 2018 values), which was about half the prevailing price of cars then. It also concluded that the demand for such a car could well be over 10,000 units per year. Submitted in February 1960, the report of the Jha Committee[2] recommended that the car should be small, yet roomy, sturdy and capable of carrying an average Indian family. The conclusions of the Jha Committee had the Indian government enthused enough for the then minister of industry to announce in Parliament, 'We will have the people's car, of the people, manufactured by the people, for the people of this country.'[3]

Despite such enthusiasm, the following year the government decided to create another committee (one has to remember that it was an epoch when one committee begat another), this time under the chairmanship of the retired chairman of the Railway Board, G. Pandey, to look into the feasibility of the 'people's car' project. The Pandey Committee concluded that it was indeed feasible and recommended that the car be made in collaboration with French carmaker Renault.[4] The fact that Renault was (French) government-owned may have influenced Pandey's recommendation.

Renault offered the Dauphine, a small rear-engine four-door saloon, which the French carmaker had launched in 1956. Not all that small, the Dauphine was not all that inexpensive. That did not seem to have deterred the Government of India, which began discussions with Renault. What did bring an end to those negotiations was the reaction of the then deputy chairman of the Planning Commission V.K. Krishnamachari, who believed that greater priority needed to be given to bicycles, scooters, buses and trucks. On 9 August 1962, the Minister for Steel and Mines C. Subramaniam stated in the Lok Sabha, 'The small car project cannot be moved up in any list of priorities. The priority in the field of automobiles for some time to come ought to be definitely and overwhelmingly in favour of the manufacturers of commercial vehicles which will provide the base for transport of goods and public transport.'[5]

The then chairman of Premier Automobiles, Lalchand Hirachand (the stepbrother of Walchand Hirachand), had also suggested to the Jha Committee—and later to the government—that the prices of cars would come down if production volume (which was restricted by the system of licensing) of the existing carmakers went up. He also mentioned that it would be unwise to launch a fourth project, a point of view echoed by the other existing carmakers. True, the numbers for the Indian marketplace were not that impressive: though the sales of cars had gone up from a very modest 14,688 in 1950 to 26,800 in 1958, achieving a volume of an additional 10,000 for a fourth carmaker looked ambitious.

With the war with China in 1962 and other matters of greater import coming up, even by 1964 no decision had been taken regarding the 'people's car' project. The government, at that point of time, still was not too clear whether the project would be a public-sector venture or a private enterprise. Then came the war with Pakistan in 1965, famine and the foreign exchange crisis of 1966–67, and the idea of the 'people's car' project was effectively shelved for the time being.

As the government was vacillating over whether the project was a priority or not, whether it ought to be executed by the public sector, or by private players, whether it should be completely indigenous or foreign, seventeen hopefuls had reportedly applied for licences.[6] Among them were the existing carmakers—Hindustan Motors, Premier Automobiles and Standard Motors.

Premier proposed to make the Fiat 600D, a small car launched in 1964, at a price of Rs 9000, with the promise that the price would come down if volumes went up to 40,000 cars per year. Hindustan, it seems, indigenously developed a small two-door car with a rather strange shape and an advanced 'front-wheel-drive' system (it is quite likely that the journalist from the period may have confused 'front-engine' with 'front-wheel-drive').

Standard Motors, the smallest of the three, resorted to a rather ingenious ploy. It took the 6CWT pick-up from Standard Triumph's UK line-up, a back-to-basics vehicle that shared most of its body panels with the Standard 10 that SMPIL was already assembling in India, and developed a shorter, smaller car, with the boot literally chopped short. The one prototype made was badged the Stanmobile.

A more serious proposal came from TELCO, which offered to produce a car made by its collaborator from Germany, Daimler-Benz; no, not a Mercedes-Benz model, but a DKW Junior. DKW was a German car and motorcycle manufacturer founded in 1917 by Jørgen Skafte Rasmussen, a Danish engineer. Originally standing for 'Dampf-Kraft-Wagen', or 'vehicles powered by steam', DKW was soon popularized by the slogan 'Das Kleine Wunder', or 'the little marvel', when it moved to making petrol-engine cars. It was also nicknamed 'Deutscher Kinder Wagen', or 'the German pram'! In 1932, DKW merged with Audi, Horch and Wanderer to form Auto Union.

Post-War, as Auto Union struggled to re-establish itself with just the DKW brand, Daimler-Benz took over in 1957.

Launched in 1959, under Daimler-Benz stewardship to make inexpensive cars for the mass market, the Junior was a two-door car, which at a tad under 4 metres, was actually a little longer than both the Fiat 1100 and the Standard Herald, but markedly lighter than either. Powered by a smaller 796cc two-stroke three-cylinder engine, the DKW would also have been more fuel-efficient. Most interesting was the price tag: TELCO said that the car would be priced at Rs 6950 ex-factory, which would have made the DKW significantly cheaper than the three cars being made in India then. TELCO proposed to supplement its truck-making facilities at Jamshedpur with an assembly line for the car, at an expenditure of Rs 14 crore for a capacity of 12,000 units per year.

Of course, TELCO did not get the green signal, and neither did most of the other applicants, which included the likes of international majors such as BMW, BMC, Citroën and Renault from France, Toyo Kogyo and Toyota from Japan, and Germany's Volkswagen. Incidentally, Auto Union had become a part of the Volkswagen Group in 1964, when Daimler-Benz sold it, and beginning 1965, DKWs were branded as Audi, a pre-War brand name revived by Volkswagen. What Volkswagen, in turn, offered to make in India is not known, but it may well have been the Beetle, which was the hottest selling car across the globe in the 1960s.

BMW apparently offered the 600, a slightly bigger four-seat in-house derivative of the Isetta bubble car, which it had been making under licence. The car was offered to Hindustan Vehicles Limited, a sister concern of Hindustan Motors. In fact, BMW even developed a special version for India taking into account the peculiarities of Indian weather conditions. Whether the BMW 600 with its odd design would have been acceptable in the Indian marketplace is a matter for conjecture.

Another German vehicle manufacturer, Tempo, which had inked a technical collaboration with Bajaj Tempo Ltd (which became Force Motors eventually) in the 1950s, had also developed a microcar along the lines of the BMW Isetta, but prettier. It then developed a second prototype that was more car-like, with two doors and the engine located at the rear, with the rear wheels farther apart. This was ready by either late 1956 or early 1957, two years before the Jha Committee and the plans for a 'people's car' took off, so nothing came of it. Instead, Bajaj Tempo brought out the Tempo Hanseat three-wheeled goods carrier and the Tempo car for India remained a footnote in automotive history, with the sole surviving prototype on display in a museum in Germany.

There was also an attempt to make the strange German Fuldamobil microcar in India, as it was licensed for manufacture in various countries—as the Nobel in Chile and the UK, the Bambi in Argentina, the Bambino in the Netherlands, the Fram King Fulda in Sweden, the Attica and Alta in Greece and the Hans Vahaar in India. There are photos of several Fuldamobils junked somewhere in India, thus a whole lot of bodies may have been imported, but barely a couple are known to have survived.

The models offered by the other carmakers are not known, and we can only speculate on what they may have been. BMC may have offered either the Mini or the Austin/Morris 1100. From Citroën, the guess would be that the 2CV would be on offer, being its cheapest car, other than the fact that the 2CV epitomized the concept of a 'people's car', more so than any of the others. Into the 1960s, Renault may have offered the 4L, the small and very successful front-wheel-drive model that had replaced the 4CV. Toyo Kogyo, the Japanese carmaker known today as Mazda Motor, may have offered the P360 Carol for the Indian small car project, given that the price mentioned was a most reasonable Rs 6700. Controversial political heavyweight Krishna Menon, though, was pushing the case for Toyota. As the incumbent defence minister, Menon suggested that the people's car be made by one of the ordnance factories.

The indigenous efforts

There were several indigenous attempts, too. One was a creative effort by a certain Shankarrao Kulkarni from the small town of Ichalkaranji, near Kolhapur, in Maharashtra. Another one was from HAL, the company created by Walchand Hirachand but then taken over by the government. The HAL initiative was the work of P.M. Reddy, a general manager at HAL, who had developed a car in-house in 1964. A photograph of the car, though, would seem to indicate that the design was rather derivative, as bits and pieces seem to have come from some other cars.

Shankarrao Kulkarni of Ichalkaranji developed a tiny car, which he called Meera, sometime in the 1960s, though in some reports it was claimed that the first prototype was made in 1949. This is doubtful as the design is more typical of the models from the late 1950s or early 1960s. Karl Bhote, an automotive enthusiast and expert on Indian automotive history specializing in period registration numbers, believes that the number plate on the prototype Meera indicates that the car could have been made any time after 1962 and before 1972. Cedric Sabine, who looks after the Indian section of the number plate histories club, Europlate, reconfirms similar dates.

The Meera was significantly smaller than those made by India's Small Three, with the engine located at the rear. According to a leaflet on the Meera, the car had been developed by Shankarrao Kulkarni who was 'very famous in engine designing'. Apparently, Kulkarni had 'an industrial tour in European countries, in Germany, and visited many motor industries as well as exhibitions'.

Incidentally, Shankarrao Kulkarni worked for industrialist Kirloskar and had as many as ten to fifteen people (one of them being a certain Vasudev Deshpande) working on different aggregates of the car. Components came from parts manufacturers such as Ceat Tyres, who supplied the tyres, Lucas provided electrical parts, and the glass bits came from Ogale Glassworks. Kulkarni's grandson, Hemant Kulkarni, has been reported to have said that his grandfather had studied till just standard seven, but in automotive history there have been several cases of cars designed by people who were not engineers.

Kulkarni, it seems, made six prototypes (or six evolutions of the prototype?) over the years, the last in 1970, or later. By then the styling had evolved to a rather distinctive sharp-edged boxy look, which may have been inspired by a Pininfarina concept car, the Autobianchi A112 Giovani, which dates from 1973! These compact four-seat cars featured three doors: two at the front like all two-door cars, plus an additional one on the left side of the car to give access to the rear bench seat. This idea may have come from the BMW 600, which, for rear seat access, had a single door on the right side of the car (as in Germany one drives on the right side of the road, so the kerb is on the right side, unlike India, where we drive on the left side of the road).

With its overall length at a little under 3 metres, and both width and height at about 1.3 metres, tiny 10-inch wheels, along with motive power from a two-cylinder engine developing a claimed 14bhp, the Meera was (in dimensions and specifications) surprisingly similar to several German bubble cars of the 1950s, most specifically the Goggomobil.

Even though the design of the body does not match that of the Goggomobil, in overall profile the Meera could very well have been inspired by it. It is quite possible that in Kulkarni's extensive travels through Europe, especially Germany, he had seen the Goggomobil, one of Germany's bestselling microcars during the 1950s and 1960s. It is also quite possible that Kulkarni may have come across a Goggomobil or two in India.

The Goggomobil was made by Hans Glas GmbH. A manufacturer of sowing and farming machinery traditionally, Hans Glas from Dingolfing, in Germany, had turned to car and scooter manufacturing after the Second World War. Under the stewardship of Andreas Glas, in addition to a Vespa-inspired scooter named Glas Goggo, a range of cars was developed; the tiny microcars that Hans Glas GmbH launched carried the Goggomobil branding. The Glas branding was used for the bigger vehicles.

Made from 1955 to 1969, the 2.9-metre-long Goggomobil featured a 14bhp 293cc two-cylinder engine located at the rear. The two-door four-seat car saw success not just in Germany and several other European countries, but was also exported to the US (with a bigger and more powerful 392cc engine developing 20bhp and named the T400). In Australia, the Goggomobil was produced under licence, and a pretty little sports two-seater was made in Sydney by an Australian company called Buckle Motors.

Collector Harit Trivedi, who has an extensive collection of automotive literature, came across documentation which indicates that the Goggomobil was one of the cars under consideration for India's 'people's car'. A sales leaflet, which Trivedi acquired in 2012 explains that a certain Bombay-based company, Associated Corporation of Industries (India) Private Limited (ACI) had as 'far back as July 1959 submitted to the Government of India a manufacturing programme' for the Goggomobil. Featuring the US-spec engine (which gave the car a top speed of 100 kmph), the Goggomobil was going to be priced at 'about Rs 5000, ex-factory, when progressively manufactured in India, excluding taxes' claimed the sales leaflet.

Along with the India-specific leaflet, Harit also picked up some two dozen sales brochures of the Goggomobil range—comprising the 682cc Goggomobil Royal (which was also sold as the Glas Isar T700), the convertible and coupé versions of the Goggomobil and the van. Whether these were also under consideration for manufacture is not known, but the Goggomobil T300 or T400 saloon surely was: Harit also came across three photographs of a Goggomobil with a temporary Delhi registration plate. One of the photos is of the car on the street, another with Morarji Desai (India's home minister during the early 1960s), and yet another—and the most telling—one with Indian Prime Minister then, Jawaharlal Nehru.

The Goggomobil was 'shown around' to the most important people in the Indian government, ACI appointed dealers in Delhi, Calcutta and Madras, and set up headquartering operations in Bombay. We can also safely speculate that some lobbying must have been resorted to, but obviously, nothing came of it. Whether that one right-hand-drive Goggomobil that came into India went back to Germany, or just disappeared, or morphed into some 'indigenous' proposal is not known.

All we know is that Hans Glas GmbH became a part of BMW in 1966 when the latter acquired the former, as it needed to expand production capacities. ACI did not get the licence to make the people's car, nor did Shankarrao Kulkarni, nor TELCO, nor HAL, nor, for that matter, any of the international majors.

That privilege was accorded to a certain Madan Mohan Rao. As well as a certain Sanjay Gandhi.

Of filial connections

On 13 November 1968, the minister of state for industrial development, Raghunath Reddi, announced in the Lok Sabha that his ministry had received a proposal to make an inexpensive people's car from Sanjay Gandhi, the son of the then Prime Minister of India, Indira Gandhi. The proposal from the twenty-one-year-old Sanjay Gandhi was for a small car that could reach a top speed of 85 kmph, run more than 18 km per litre, yet, cost Rs 6000 only. Reddi also mentioned that the government had received proposals from thirteen other carmakers, entrepreneurs and engineers.

Until November 1970, there was talk that the people's car would be made by the public sector, and the Union cabinet held discussions with several of the international majors, of which the most noteworthy was Renault, as the state-owned French major offered to cover the cost of foreign exchange. Yet the government decided that the investment involved was considerable and that it would best serve the interest of the nation to have the people's car made by the private sector. On 31 November 1970, the minister of industries, Dinesh Singh, handed over a letter of intent to Sanjay Gandhi to make the people's car. The decision, apparently, had been taken at a cabinet meeting, presided over by none other than the prime minister herself, Indira Gandhi.

Sure enough, controversy flared. The first point that came up was regarding Sanjay Gandhi's qualifications: What unusual abilities did he have to be awarded such an exclusive licence, other than being the prime minister's son?

Sanjay Gandhi was a diehard car fan. Prominent journalist and writer Vinod Mehta, who wrote a book on Sanjay Gandhi in 1978,[7] believes that it was his father Feroze Gandhi's obsession with tending to his immaculately maintained Morris, which must have had a profound influence on the impressionable young boy, giving rise to his passion for automobiles. That whenever Sanjay spent time with his father—who was estranged from his mother when Sanjay was still very young—he observed his father polishing, cleaning, repairing his car constantly. Apparently, at a very young age, Sanjay expressed his desire to make cars the vocation of his life, an ambition that even his grandfather believed his grandson had immense talent for.

Sanjay was not good at school and he was reluctant to pursue further studies. Thus, his mother, given her connections, managed to finagle a very prestigious three-year apprenticeship for the young boy at no less a car manufacturer than Rolls-Royce Motors, starting September 1964. The apprenticeship at Rolls-Royce was designed to train technicians for semi-skilled and skilled jobs at the carmaker's demanding assembly line. It was not the equivalent of an engineering degree, yet talented apprentices could find themselves in the prestigious design and engineering department of Rolls-Royce once their tenure was complete.

Sanjay Gandhi did not manage to stick out the three years of the apprenticeship—he left at the end of two years, as he believed that he had learnt all that he needed to learn, that there was nothing more that he would gain by staying on at Rolls-Royce.

Whilst in the United Kingdom, Sanjay also made newspaper headlines for the wrong reasons. In December 1966, he was arrested for driving without a valid licence. He also managed to have a couple of smash-ups with his Jaguar XK120 (showing good taste, but bad driving). Not exactly very popular with his fellow apprentices, it seems that Sanjay was not missed when he left Rolls-Royce to head back to India.

Back in India, Sanjay got down to his automotive obsession—to design and develop a small car for the masses, to provide the cheapest set of wheels to the nation. Sometime in 1967, Sanjay rented a shed in Motia Khan, a semi-industrial complex in the heart of Old Delhi, adjacent to one of the biggest wholesale markets of Asia, the Sadar Bazaar. Here he set up a small workshop, where he employed some artisans including 'denters' (metal-body workers), car mechanics, lathe machinists, welders, painters, electricians and a hands-on man who would oversee the entire operation. As he added to his team, he moved to bigger premises at Gulabi Bagh.

Work began on the development of 'Sanjay's car'. The usual process of designing and developing a car in those pre-computer days started with sketches and renderings, which were then converted into detailed scale drawings, from which 1:4 or 1:5 scale models would be developed. Once the shape and style had been finalized, full-size scale drawings would follow, along with packaging studies to ascertain the habitability of the car. Then, wooden forming bucks would be made, from which the metal panels for the body of the prototype would be beaten out. The chassis would be fabricated using jigs and fixtures. Whether Sanjay's project followed such a process is doubtful, given the garage-like set-up that the young man had.

When, in November 1968, Sanjay Gandhi submitted his proposal to the Indian government, he did not have any car to show. Whether extensive paper drawings and presentations were made, to make his case, is not known either, but it looks most unlikely. The project report[8] that Sanjay Gandhi submitted to the government for scrutiny envisaged a two-door car powered by a two-stroke two-cylinder rear-mounted engine developing 14bhp, with 'tyres similar in size to scooter rickshaw' which sounds suspiciously similar in specifications to that of the Goggomobil. The project report also claimed that no foreign collaboration or import of machinery, raw material or components was necessary.

Two years later, when Sanjay Gandhi was granted his letter of intent, his car was still not ready. It is worth noting though that letters of intent were granted to ten others too, one of them being the aforementioned Madan Mohan Rao. At the same time, the government put very stringent requirements: foreign collaborations, consultancies and import of capital goods and components were not to be allowed. Before the letter of intent was converted into a licence, prototypes also had to be developed and would need to be tested and approved. Given the kind of hold Sanjay was reputed to have had over his mother and Indira's tendency to take rather unilateral decisions, it is possible that these conditions were imposed at the insistence of Sanjay—with the sole purpose of eliminating competition. This, as we will see later, worked as a double-edged sword.

Madan Mohan Rao's letter of intent, along with those of the other contenders, lapsed because they could not fulfil the conditions imposed by the government. Sanjay Gandhi presented his prototype small car in November 1972. The car was named Maruti, one of many names of the Hindu monkey god, Hanuman. A little over a year earlier, on 4 June 1971, Maruti Motors Limited had been incorporated.

Sanjay's Maruti

The unveiling of Maruti was quite an event. The people's car, of the people, manufactured by the people, for the people of this country had finally arrived. The price though, in the meantime, had jumped up to Rs 11,300, some two-thirds more than the original proposed price of Rs 6693, and this was attributed to an 'increase in raw material costs'.[9]

India's first go at an indigenous people's car was not unattractive. The shape, to say the least, was rather rudimentary and boxy, with hardly any finesse in the design, yet it was not exactly ugly. Adopting a two-box look, the car was rounded from the front, with a look that borrowed quite a bit from the 1959 Mini, but with a shorter bonnet, and ended with an abrupt, almost vertical rear. The flat front windscreen had minimal rake, and the design was not particularly aerodynamic in its form. The beltline kicked up into an interesting hump at shoulder point.

The car used a whole host of proprietary parts from other popular cars of that period, specifically from the older generation Fiats and the Ambassador. Door handles came from the Fiat 1100 of the 1950s; door locks, quarter glass frames, dashboard metres, headlamp assemblies, all came from the Ambassador. Delhi-based restorer Tutu Dhawan, who was familiar with the car as he had one until the 1990s in his garage, believes that the floor plan of the car was derived from that of an Ambassador's, modified to suit the shorter wheelbase. The front suspension system, featuring wishbones with torsion bar, was also strikingly similar to that of the Ambassador. The car did not have a grille at the front, as the air-cooled engine was at the rear. The sloping, rounded front featured headlamps that came from the Ambassador, and the chromium-plated steel rings were from the Enfield Bullet.

The car was a two-door four-seater, with the front two seats featuring folding backrests, facilitating ingress to the rear bench seat. Getting in and out for the elderly, though, was not that comfortable. Yet, passenger volume, given that the car was significantly smaller than what was selling in India then, was impressive. Small 10-inch wheels saved space inside.

Thin wrap-around front and rear chrome-plated bumpers made from mild steel provided visual relief to a form that was essentially featureless. The body sides were almost flat, with very slight contours defined by parallel swage lines, to give some strength. The two doors had flat, winding glass panes, but the windows at the rear sides were fixed, though they featured folding quarter glasses aft. Seats had well-sprung cushions, with rexine doing the job for the headliner. Ordinary rubber mats covered the thinly insulated floor. There was no sound-deadening or insulating material, essentially to keep costs down. The promise was to sell the car much cheaper than the Ambassador, the Fiat 1100 (which had become the Premier President) and the Standard Herald.

On paper, the concept of the vehicle was rather original. The shape and packaging took a lot from the Mini school of thought in featuring a 'two-box' look that was still new in the 1960s. Yet the styling was already dated for its time as automotive design trends by the end of the 1960s was towards the sharper-edged origami look. In terms of mechanical configuration, too, Sanjay Gandhi chose something that was becoming rapidly outmoded. Most carmakers, including Fiat, Renault and Volkswagen, who had been the greatest exponents of the rear-engine cause, were moving towards front-engine front-wheel-drive layouts, yet Sanjay chose to go the old-fashioned way.

True, in some ways, the rear-engine layout was easier and cheaper to make and that thinking may have influenced him. It just may be possible that he had access to such a mechanical configuration when he was developing his car, as Dhawan suspects, conjecturing that the entire rear mechanical elements came from an existing automobile. Harit Trivedi believes that the Maruti may have been derived from the Goggomobil; indeed, from the front, the Maruti does have more than a striking resemblance to the Goggomobil.

The engine of the Maruti, though, was a horizontally opposed twin, very similar to that of a BMW motorcycle, and in that sense different from the in-line two-cylinder of the Goggomobil. Dhawan also points out that all the stampings and markings on the engine had been sanded out.

The location of the engine, gearbox and differential were all along the rear axle of the Maruti, whereas most of the rear-engine cars, including the Goggomobil, had the power pack 'overhung' at the rear, aft of the rear axle. Also Sanjay's Maruti was impressively wide— Dhawan estimates it at significantly more than 1.4 metres, whereas the Goggomobil was fairly narrow, at under 1.3 metres.

Either way, it seems that Sanjay Gandhi and his merry bunch of mechanics designed the car without any external help or advice. As the Opposition questioned the government's decision and accused the prime minister of nepotism, it was decided by the government that Sanjay Gandhi's Maruti Motors would get its licence only after the Maruti prototype passed certain types of tests. A committee consisting of the representatives of the DGTD (Director General of Technical Development), the VRDE (Vehicle Research and Development Establishment) and the ministry of heavy industries and public enterprises (with representatives from Maruti Motors present) prescribed that the car should run for 30,000 km, and after a reliability test of 10,000 km, a view should be taken regarding the licence, as was reported in the *Illustrated Weekly of India*.

The prototype—it seems—did complete 10,000 km and the test report showed 'satisfactory' performance on important counts. The earlier letter of intent was converted into an industrial licence by the ministry of heavy industries after the VRDE had been informed. On 30 March 1974, VRDE issued Maruti a clearance certificate. Though the prototype did cover 10,000 km, it did not cover the recommended 30,000 km, it seems. In fact, testing and development of prototypes is perhaps the single most important aspect of designing and developing an all-new car for series production. Most major carmakers test and run scores of cars over millions of kilometres, always learning, modifying and reworking the smallest of details before signing off the definitive design. Maruti Motors did not do that with the original Maruti.

Limitations and underdevelopment

In all fairness, Maruti Motors had very limited resources. It began with an authorized capital of Rs 2.5 crore, which went up to Rs 10 crore by June 1972. The total paid-up capital by September 1974 was just Rs 1.8 crore, whereas the value of the net assets of the company as of 31 March 1974 was Rs 4.5 crore. In 1972, Maruti Motors began appointing dealers, from whom deposits were taken. Rs 2.18 crore was collected from seventy-three dealers.[10]

Yet Maruti Motors' investments were not that substantial. The 296.7 acres of land was controversially acquired for just Rs 36 lakh, with farmers unceremoniously evicted, thanks to the efforts of the Haryana government, led by Chief Minister Bansi Lal, who was bending over backwards to please the Gandhi family. Looking at photographs of the factory from that period, it is obvious that machinery and equipment were minimal. With no conveyor belts for the assembly line, the bodies of the cars were pushed manually from one workstation to another on trolleys.

Vinod Mehta, in his book on Sanjay Gandhi[11] quotes from the *Sunday Times* (of London) report on the Maruti factory from April 1977: 'The body shop where the workers apparently hand-stitched the little Maruti bodies is a joke. So also is the engine shop, the pattern shop and the foundry, and the whole place with three ground level fireplaces looks like a dirty indoor barbecue.'

Mehta estimates that total investment could not have topped Rs 6 crore—for a project that needed at least ten times as much. When the government had discussed with Renault and other international majors for a public-sector 'people's car' project, the costs were estimated at Rs 57 crore.

Underfunding though was not the main problem. The bigger problem was that of Sanjay Gandhi's attitude. With an incomplete Rolls-Royce apprenticeship, Sanjay believed that he knew all that he needed to know about manufacturing cars. In 1971, Sanjay Gandhi went to Europe and toured several car manufacturing ventures and came away convinced that there was nothing that he did not already know about the auto business.

When the first Maruti prototype was unveiled (in November 1972), Sanjay promised that the first commercial production cars would roll out just five months later, by April 1973. In 1974, after Maruti had received its VRDE certification, the car was supposed to be at 'the threshold of production'.

In 25 May 1975, veteran editor Khushwant Singh wrote about his visit to the Maruti factory,[12] where he went for a short spin in one of the pre-production cars: 'I take the wheel. Sanjay sits beside me. The gear is on the floor. As I release the clutch, it lurches forward. Although it has only two cylinders and 8.3 horse-power, it responds to the pressure of the accelerator like a more powerful car. Its steering is also more sensitive to the touch and makes the wheels turn with greater alacrity than the steering-wheel of any car I've driven. Despite its minuscule size, it holds the road very well and attains its maximum speed of 110 km per hour without overstretching itself. I take the 60-degree bends at 60 kilometres per hour with the greatest of ease. My fear that it has too low a clearance for the rough Indian roads is soon dispelled. Sanjay takes over himself and drives it at breakneck speed over bush, brier and mound.'

A great fan and defender of Sanjay Gandhi, Khushwant Singh did question, 'How the Maruti will last remains to be seen.' He also succinctly pointed out that the car was no more a people's car, 'because it will cost Rs 25,000 (ex-factory is Rs 16,500; in Haryana Rs 21,000). Nevertheless, it will be Rs 5000 to 10,000 less than any of the three Indian cars in the market.'

Overall, Khushwant Singh was very positive: 'Soon little Marutis should be seen on the roads of Haryana and Delhi; and a month or two later they will be running between Kalimpong and Kanyakumari.'

That did not happen at all, not with Sanjay Gandhi's Maruti.

And then came the Emergency

Emergency was imposed in June 1975, and Sanjay Gandhi had other matters to attend to. In the meantime, to generate some business another entity, Maruti Heavy Vehicles was incorporated, to make bus bodies and roadrollers. During Emergency, business was good for Maruti Heavy Vehicles, but with Emergency coming to an end, business collapsed. With the Janata Party coalition voted to power, a series of inquiries against the Gandhi family and Maruti ensued. When, on 6 March 1978, the High Court of Punjab and Haryana ordered the winding up of Maruti Motors,[13] not more than forty Marutis, at most, had been completed.

In January 1980, the Congress party came back to power, and Indira Gandhi was back in the driving seat. Apparently, Sanjay was very excited about the possibility of reviving Maruti. Fate, though, had other plans. On 23 June 1980, Sanjay Gandhi crashed whilst flying a Pitts aircraft, and was killed instantly.

India's first small car project had a lot of promise, and given the kind of proximity it had to the powers that be, this venture should never have failed. Making a car, though, is not that easy. Making a body and giving it wheels was the easier part of the job as most of the bits and pieces came from the other automobiles manufactured in India or elsewhere. Putting that into series production was another matter.

There was also this little matter of the power pack. For the pre-production prototypes, Sanjay resorted to using imported motorcycle engines, which were mated to a four-speed gearbox, which also must have been sourced from somewhere. All very well for pre-production cars, but what about production cars? That is when the project struck a roadblock, specifically the power pack bit. The understanding was that the Indian 'people's car' was to be made indigenously, with all major and minor components of the vehicle produced in the country. It was on this premise that Sanjay Gandhi was the only one to receive a new licence to manufacture cars.

Sanjay and his inept team did not have the ability, nor the know-how to duplicate the engine for series production. Sanjay did get a German consultant who reportedly brought in a couple of engines, but the consultant soon realized that neither Sanjay nor his team had the ability to copy and bring into production the power pack.

Several senior people in the Indian automobile industry have opined that the conditions imposed by the letter of intent, that of indigenous design and locally sourced equipment, made it well-nigh impossible for Maruti to succeed. Though Maruti could not import any machinery, it could have had recourse to the sophisticated machine tools which Hindustan Machine Tools was manufacturing then. Maruti could have also got machinery from Eastern European countries such as Czechoslovakia (which had a relatively modern car industry then, manufacturing the Skoda and the Tatra) against rupee payment under the Stock & Trade arrangement, which India had with Eastern Bloc countries.

In the 11 March 1979 issue of the *Illustrated Weekly of India*, T.A. Pai, the minister of heavy industries from 1973, wrote a rather defensive article on Sanjay Gandhi and the Maruti mess.[14] He said: 'The disbelief that we could do it in India on our own is the usual belief prevailing in the country and in the Government and the financial institutions which has always resulted in many of our people not being able to utilize their ideas, their ingenuity and their resourcefulness for development in the country.'

Without doubt, Sanjay Gandhi, or for that matter, anyone with automotive knowledge had every right to experiment and every right to try developing a car for the people. Given the right opportunity and appropriate resources, this author believes that several brilliant Indians could have developed an indigenous people's car, which would have worked. By the 1960s, the automobile industry across the globe was very advanced, no doubt; yet, there were several budding young carmakers from many countries across the world, including Japan, who were just beginning to cut their teeth in the car-making business, developing brand new cars in-house.

The problem with Maruti was Sanjay Gandhi. A two-year apprenticeship was insufficient, a simple fact that Sanjay Gandhi, his mother and all her cohorts refused to acknowledge. Sanjay's competence was no more than that of a decent mechanic at best, and designing and developing a car calls for excellent engineering ability, great design skills, very thorough testing and developmental integrity, plus ample resources and very deep pockets. Sanjay's arrogance, overconfidence and hubris did not help matters either.

T.A. Pai also believes that Sanjay was eventually not serious about the project: 'Once Emergency was declared, the project did not make any progress as he shifted his activities to other fields.'[15]

An all-powerful Sanjay Gandhi, during the Emergency years could have used his position to have his car readied for series production. Instead, Sanjay was more bothered about dealing with his detractors. Pai points out that those who were opposed to the Maruti project got into serious difficulties when Emergency was imposed. 'If Sanjay could have pursued the car successfully, Emergency would not have possibly come,' opined Pai.[16] Failure may have driven Sanjay Gandhi to pressurize his mother into taking the extreme steps that she took, with disastrous consequences to the country.

Yet, India recovered and got back her democracy, Indira recovered and got back her prime ministership, and Maruti recovered—or more appropriately, was reincarnated—and India got back its 'people's car'.

4

A Car for the People

The death of Sanjay Gandhi on 23 June 1980, after the Pitts aircraft crashed, left Indira Gandhi totally devastated. Though she had lost her favourite son, it was still possible to keep his dream alive. So, soon after Sanjay's death, Indira Gandhi called Arun Nehru, the son of her second cousin, and a professional manager heading Calcutta-based paint company Jenson & Nicholson, and asked his opinion as to how the 'people's car' idea could be revived.

Arun Nehru went through all the papers and documents and concluded that the idea of a 'people's car' was still viable, and that it would be possible to revive Maruti. But the only way the project could work would be if the car was developed or made in collaboration with an international major using foreign technology. To be viable though, production capacity needed to be, at the least, 1,00,000 cars per year.

Soon thereafter, the assets of Maruti Motors Limited were acquired by the government, and a 100 per cent government-owned Maruti Udyog Limited, was incorporated on 24 February 1981. It is quite possible that 'if Maruti hadn't been nationalized, the liquidation proceedings would have brought many skeletons tumbling out of the cupboard, and might have even resulted in the prosecution of the guilty individuals', said a report on Maruti.[1] Writers Dilip Cherian and Mohan Ram added: 'Moreover, Indira Gandhi's sentiments in completing her son's dreams cannot be forgotten. The government's decision appears to have had more to do with maternal psychology than with hard-headed economics.'

However, the raison d'être that the government gave (in that same article) was: 'Looking at the present state of the car industry in the country, Government felt that it would be desirable to set up a public sector undertaking under the Central government for the manufacture of passenger cars, commercial vehicles. The purpose of nationalization was modernising the automobile industry, effecting more economical use of scarce fuel and ensuring a higher production of vehicles.'

So, within a little over a decade, from the buzzwords of 'Swadeshi', self-sufficiency, indigenous technology and the saving of precious foreign exchange, the government made a 180-degree U-turn. Foreign technology had become a must, as well as the need for a joint venture partner; the issue of foreign exchange no longer important (except for a rider that the joint venture partner needed to promise a buy-back possibility of vehicles). So the 'people's car', to be manufactured by the people for the people of this country, was going to come from some other people, from some distant land.

The objectives had changed, the means to get to those objectives had also changed, but not the name. The new company, very importantly, still used the Maruti moniker, a tribute to the memory of Sanjay Gandhi. Even if Sanjay's Maruti had not succeeded, a Maruti would be made one day.

Importing a product and a factory to establish a vast national car project was not new. Countries like Spain, Yugoslavia and Poland had based their national car industries on imported Fiat technology. The USSR, too, followed suit after an attempt at indigenously developing an automobile industry with home-grown products (such as the Moskvitch and the Volga) did not quite succeed. The mighty Russians went to little Italy's Fiat, for technology and expertise, transplanting the Fiat 124 and its manufacturing facilities to the city of Togliattigrad, in the south-western part of Russia. Between 1969, when production commenced, and 1979, over 5 million Lada (as the car was branded) had already sold, before the car became an even bigger sales success internationally as one of the cheapest automobiles on sale in the developed markets of Europe, Canada and Australia, earning the Soviet Union much-needed foreign exchange.

Though countries like Japan and South Korea had followed (or were still following, in the case of the latter) an altogether different route for their nascent automobile industries, for Indira Gandhi and the mandarins in Delhi, Arun Nehru's suggestion of a people's car 'acquired' from an existing carmaker seemed to be the safest route.

To take that route, the first essential was to identify the product and a foreign carmaker who would willingly part with technology and participate in the making of India's 'people's car'. Even before that though, a core team to head the project needed to be established.

The choice to head the project fell on V. Krishnamurthy, who had earlier turned around the unwieldy public-sector company Bharat Heavy Electricals Limited (BHEL). Krishnamurthy was appointed as the vice chairman-cum-managing director. For the chairman's post, Indira Gandhi zeroed in on Sumant Moolgaokar, the legendary chairman of TELCO. Getting the head of a very successful private truck-making venture to be non-executive chairman to India's people's car project made very good sense and gave the project much-needed credibility.

Krishnamurthy, in turn, hand-picked D.S. Gupta, an Indian Institute of Management, Ahmedabad (IIM-A) alumnus who had worked under him at BHEL as staff officer. Soon thereafter, R.C. Bhargava, who had been the director for commercial affairs at BHEL on a deputation from the Indian Administrative Services (IAS), joined the team. With the core triumvirate at Maruti Udyog in place, work began in earnest to identify companies for partnership and products that would be appropriate.

Though two of the triumvirate had excellent experience managing giant enterprises and, more importantly, dealing with the government and its many bureaucracies, with one of them a former bureaucrat, and the third was a bright young post-grad from India's premier management institute, none of them had a clue about the world of cars.

The world of cars in the early 1980s, though, was a very intricate politico-industrial complex. The oil crises of 1973 and 1979, as well as the revolution in Iran, had changed the automotive world order drastically. It was in 1980 that the United States' position as the automotive world's top dog ended. Japan became the leading car manufacturing nation in 1980, producing over 7 million of the approximately 30 million cars produced globally;[2] the US, in second place, made 6.38 million, while the UK, which used to be the world's second-biggest carmaker until 1960, had dropped to seventh place, manufacturing less than a million cars. Continental Europe produced more than 11 million cars, with Germany and France producing a little over 3.5 million and a little less than 3 million, respectively; Fiat made most of the 1.45 million cars manufactured in Italy, and Spain produced over a million cars.[3]

For perspective's sake, it may be worth noting that, in 1980, India and South Korea made 30,538 and 55,000 cars, respectively; China's auto manufacture that year was negligible.

The search for a partner

With Europe looking like the automotive centre of the world, the Maruti triumvirate decided that it made better sense to look at collaborating with a European carmaker than an American, given that two of the Big Three were bleeding badly with one needing a government-backed bailout. The American carmakers also tended to make mostly big gas-guzzlers, cars that were just the opposite of a frugal 'people's car'.

That though was not an easy task, as very few of the European majors were keen to work with the rider that the Indian government had imposed: that the joint venture partner, as well as taking a 40 per cent stake in the automotive venture had to buy back 50 per cent of production. After doing the rounds—negotiating with French carmakers Renault and Peugeot/Citroën, Italian giant Fiat, as well as Alfa Alfa Romeo, and the floundering English carmaker British Leyland—it was Volkswagen, which turned out to be the most enthusiastic of all the European carmakers.

To tackle the issue of foreign exchange, Volkswagen also offered to set up an engine manufacturing plant, from which it proposed to buy back power trains. This offer seemed to be the best and Maruti had almost narrowed down to the German carmaker when it got a message that Volkswagen was not interested any more, as the then chairman Toni Schmucker, had shot the idea down, believing that investing in India was a waste of time and resources.[4] This sudden shift was based on his belief that China had great potential, and would make for a better choice.

It was at that point that Maruti looked at Japan and its automobile industry. It was the only alternative left. When Krishnamurthy, Bhargava and Gupta visited the Tokyo Motor Show, they came across the kei-jidosha cars, this special breed of Japanese small cars, which had tax benefits, as they were space and fuel-efficient vehicles. All of them had engines just under 550cc, and were just short of 3.2 metres in length, cars which were much smaller than what they had seen in Europe, and much cheaper too, at about Rs 30,000 then.

The team initially met most of the Japanese carmakers, but the choice quickly narrowed down to the smaller cars from Daihatsu (which, by then, was a part of the Toyota Group), Mitsubishi, Nissan and Subaru. Discussion and negotiations with the Japanese did not go all that smoothly—there was enough intrigue, confusion and misunderstandings. A telex meant for Escorts (the tractor and motorcycle manufacturer, which was also keen on embarking on a car project) accidentally came through to Maruti, on reading which it became obvious that Daihatsu did not take the Maruti project seriously. When all seemed to have failed, and suitors had turned betrayers, a knight in white armour arrived in the form of an erstwhile recalcitrant Suzuki. A senior director with Suzuki Motor Corporation, who happened to be in India to sign up with TVS for a joint venture to make motorcycles, read an article[5] on the Maruti project on a flight, and decided to swing by Delhi to meet the trio from Maruti.

For Suzuki, a joint venture with Maruti Udyog seemed like a great opportunity. As it turned out, Maruti became for Suzuki Motor Corporation the most important deal in its history as a carmaker, a history, which had not been that remarkable until then. The basis for choosing Suzuki included a combination of commercial reasons regarding terms of the joint venture and pricing.

Sought as an almost last resort, Suzuki was one of the few carmakers that seemed to take the Maruti project seriously. It was willing to take a 26 per cent stake (not very willingly, one may add, as the company insisted that the investment should not exceed US$25 million; an option of taking up to 40 per cent was categorically refused). Most importantly, the CKD (completely knocked down) price of the Suzuki car was the cheapest at the equivalent of Rs 30,000, which meant that the target price of Rs 50,000 could be met, if import duties and so on could be tweaked markedly. This was not an issue, though, as the government was ready to do just about anything necessary, short of directly subsidizing, to make sure that the Maruti project would work.

With import duties and excise rates reduced significantly, what India was going to get was a car that was markedly cheaper than the choice then. Both the Hindustan Ambassador and the Premier Padmini cost over Rs 80,000 then. The Sipani Dolphin, a Suzuki SS80/Maruti 800-sized fiberglass-bodied two-door car which fledgling carmaker R.K. Sipani had launched in 1982, was a car which cost around Rs 70,000 then, some 40 per cent more than the Suzuki's target price of Rs 50,000-odd. Around the time when Maruti had been nationalized, in 1981, Sipani's three-wheeler manufacturing company Sipani Automotive Industries Limited also diversified into making cars—as the total investment was less than Rs 58 lakhs, it came under the radar of the licensing system for industry. Thus, Sipani was making cars (under licence) from specialist British carmaker Reliant Motor Company.

Krishnamurthy, Bhargava and Gupta met with Osamu Suzuki in March 1982 and on 2 October 1982, the deal was signed. There was, though, one very important caveat: that the first car had to roll out by 1983, and at a price of Rs 50,000. A tall order indeed, but with the full support of the government in terms of special waivers, lower taxes and import duties, the impossible became possible.

So, it came to pass that on 14 December 1983, on the thirty-seventh birth anniversary of the late Sanjay Gandhi, his mother,

Indira Gandhi, the then Prime Minister of India, ceremoniously handed over the key of the very first Maruti 800 to a certain Harpal Singh from Delhi.

Less than a year later, Indira Gandhi was dead, killed by her own guards. Whereas, Maruti Udyog Limited lived on, and became the nation's pride, the maker of the first Indian 'people's car'. Over the years, it also became the single most important outpost of the Suzuki empire.

Little car, very big impact

When Indira Gandhi handed over to Harpal Singh the very first Maruti 800 in December 1983, there were some 1,35,000 others in the queue waiting to take delivery of India's new marvel. Maruti Udyog, before production began, imported, displayed and held a series of roadshows of the three vehicles, which it was planning to make: the car, the van from the Suzuki range of models known as the Carry, and the pickup truck version of the van. Ten of each of the models were imported, and displayed in every important town and city in India.

Indians went crazy. Thousands thronged to take a close look at these little wonders, these brightly painted sculptures in metal that were so much more modern and smarter than the ancient Premiers and Ambassadors that the masses had got bored to the eyeballs with.

Maruti Udyog launched a scheme to take advance bookings of Rs 10,000 for each vehicle, some 20 per cent of the planned value of the vehicles. The Indian public went bananas: some 1,35,000 vehicles were booked, with the fledgling carmaker collecting Rs 135 crore, almost two-thirds of its planned investment of about Rs 200 crore for the entire project; this contributed, in part, to the fact that Maruti Udyog became a profitable carmaker from the start of its operations, from the interest earned from these bookings.

Of the 1,35,000 Marutis booked, very few were for the pick-up version, as it was petrol-driven, whereas the commercial vehicle market, historically, has always had a clear preference for diesel-powered vehicles. About 20,000-odd opted for the van version, called

Maruti Van initially (the Omni later), despite the fact that the van was markedly more practical than the car. More than four-fifths of the punters preferred the car, despite the identical pricing of Rs 45,000 ex-factory for the Maruti 800 and the Van. The bookings were put through a randomly generated lottery system, which ensured that the allocation system was fair.

The Maruti Van was launched exactly a year after the Maruti 800, on 14 December 1984; the star act, though, continued to be the latter, even if Maruti Udyog managed to deliver just 852 cars across the major Indian cities until March-end 1984.

These cars, initially in either post-office red or plain white, were absolute attention grabbers everywhere. Everyone wanted a Maruti 800, there was a massive premium on the cars (as much as what the car cost!), yet India's new small car was a great leveller, with owners ranging from shopkeepers to movie stars. For a short while in India's history, a car democratized the huge gap between the rich and the middle class, becoming a cult vehicle for all and sundry.

During the next financial year, from April 1984 to March 1985, Maruti Udyog was able to crank out 20,356 Maruti 800s and 2016 Maruti Vans. Yet the history of India's first people's car had not really begun. Harpal Singh and the 52,000-odd others after him who acquired the Maruti 800 until mid-1986 were not buying India's first 'people's car'. It was touted as one, true, and many make the mistake of acknowledging it as such, but it was just an interim model, a teaser, a preamble to the real McCoy that followed.

With the wisdom of hindsight, it can be said that it was a smart move on the part of the Maruti management to move to the latest version before committing to the not inconsiderable investment for an entire car project. The Suzuki SS80, which was launched as the Maruti 800 on 24 December 1983, was already a four-year-old design and its replacement in Japan was going to be unveiled the year after, in September 1984. Surprisingly, Suzuki Motor had not explained that to the Maruti management when negotiating and deciding on the models and the model mix, in sharp contrast to the offer that Peugeot had made for the yet-to-be-launched 205.

Suzuki's intentions were to sell off the toolings of a car that it was about to phase out.

In all ignorance and innocence, Maruti Udyog launched the Suzuki SS80, with the first batch of cars coming in semi-knocked-down (SKD) state, the bodies complete and painted, only the power train needing to be put in, the glasses and wheels attached and the seats and dashboard mounted within. Cars made almost completely in Japan, for the people of India.

As Maruti Udyog went about localizing the Maruti 800, little did it know that it would be a wasted effort. Around mid-1984, the Maruti management realized that the SS80 was soon going to be replaced by an all-new car. Logically, it made sense to invest in the toolings of a newer car. Much against the wishes of Suzuki Motor and that of Osamu Suzuki himself, Dr Krishnamurthy fought for and managed to convince both Suzuki (and the Government of India) that Maruti too should switch over to the new model.

'It wasn't just a matter of getting the very latest in terms of technology, but also the very principle of technology transfer and being a fair and just joint venture partner that as soon as Suzuki had a new model, it ought to be offered to us at Maruti Udyog,' pointed out Krishnamurthy, when interviewed by the author. 'Yes, Suzuki's intention was to sell off a car that they were soon phasing out. And if we had carried on with the manufacturing of the SS80 we would have been accused of having been party to such a deal.'

Either way, the 'new' Maruti 800 not only became a car which was more accessible to the hoi polloi, but also a status symbol, as well as a symbol of freedom for the 'fairer' sex, being an automobile that was easier to drive and manage. Small was not puny any more, lightweight was not weak, and many preconceived notions of the automobile changed. Before, the bigger, heavier and the more elaborate a car was, the better it was considered. Now, lightweight, smallness in size and easy to drive were attributes that became popular amongst the people. The Maruti 800 became the harbinger of a new India.

India's love affair with the Maruti 800 continued as Maruti Udyog drew up plans to replace the SS80 with the SB308, which, in Maruti's nomenclature, became the MB308. The latter was launched in August 1986, after some 52,000-plus of the first-generation Maruti 800s (on the SS80 model) had been made, with Maruti Udyog assuring the customers whose bookings were still pending, that their priority would not be affected.

Localization plans also shifted to the second-generation car, creating a situation whereby the first-generation Maruti 800 became an 'orphan' in the supply of spare parts, making the maintenance of a car from the early years an expensive proposition.

Soon after the second-generation 800 was launched, Maruti Udyog decided to call for a second round of bookings, in September 1986. The newer car seemed to have even more fans—1,57,000 people booked for the new Maruti 800, setting it on the road to becoming India's first real 'people's car'.

During the first year of the MB308, the financial year April 1986 to March 1987, Maruti sold more than 50,000 units (to be exact 52,344 cars) of the 800, a first for any car in India. For the first time, Maruti Udyog's sales of vehicles totalled more than that of the rest of the passenger car industry's put together. Maruti sold 74,511 of the 800, the Van and the Gypsy four-wheel-drive vehicle (which had been introduced in December 1985), in an industry total of 1,25,894 cars sold during 1986–87, accounting for almost 60 per cent of the Indian car market, and marking the beginning of total dominance by this public-sector car company.

It took Maruti Udyog a little over eleven years to produce a million cars but less than four years to make its next million cars—by 1998; of these, the 800 comprised a significant proportion. By February 1997, Maruti Udyog had produced its millionth Maruti 800. The two millionth mark was crossed in April 2003. The history of the Maruti 800 was thus also the history of Maruti Udyog the carmaker.

Liberalization and the rest

After the famous economic 'liberalization' of 1991, international car majors began looking at India seriously and PSA Peugeot Citroën

was the first to enter into an (ill-fated) joint venture with Premier
Automobiles. South Korean carmaker Daewoo followed, inking a
joint venture agreement with DCM, taking over from Toyota, DCM's
erstwhile partner in manufacturing light trucks. GM tied up with
Hindustan Motors and Honda entered into a tie-up with Shriram
Industrial Enterprises Ltd.

It was not until 1998–99 though that Maruti saw serious
competition in the form of the Santro from the other South Korean
carmaker, Hyundai Motors India Limited, the Matiz from Daewoo
and, later, the indigenously developed Indica from Tata Motors. The
coming competition though seemed to have caused a drop in Maruti
Udyog's sales from 3,27,240 to 3,09,544 for 1997–98, which until
then had been going from strength to strength. By 1996–97, Maruti's
market share had risen to an impressive 79.6 per cent of India's
passenger car market; in the financial year 1997–98, Maruti's market
share was a staggering 82.7 per cent.

Interestingly enough, clones of the Maruti 800 were also produced
in other parts of the world, including the country across the border.
The Suzuki SB308 was sold in Pakistan as the Mehran. Across the
other border, in China, the SB308 was produced by several Chinese
carmakers, with badges reading (in Mandarin!): Chang'an SC 7080,
Jiangbei Alto JJ 7080, Jiangnan JNJ 7080 Alto, or Xian Alto QCJ
7080. When Zotye took over Jiangnan, the car was badged a Zotye
JN Auto. A version of the JN Auto was also assembled in Tunisia for
the African markets until 2005, and to confuse the issue further, was
badged a Peugeot JN Mini!

What was to Japan an interim fifth-generation model (with a
planned obsolescence of five years) of a line that was into its fourteenth
generation by 2020, it became the people's car for not just India, but
also, to an extent, Pakistan and China. Amusingly enough, the 800
was never intended by its designers to be a people's car—it was just
another competitively priced kei-jidosha car, one which was meeting a
Japanese-specific market requirement, but thanks to the strange twists
of fate, it became the car which put the world's second most populated
nation on wheels.

This begets the question: Could any other similar car with similar pricing and specifications have become India's first people's car? R.C. Bhargava expressed his doubts to the author: 'It's not just a question of the right product. The right partner and people involved are no less important.' Bhargava has always maintained that Osamu Suzuki and the senior management at Suzuki Motor were no less crucial in the success story of Maruti Udyog and the Maruti 800.

Of course, detractors will point out that the success story of the Maruti 800 and Maruti Udyog, the carmaker, had very little to do with the collaborator or Mr Suzuki, but more to do with the clear mandate from the Government of India that this project had to succeed at any cost. 'Every rule of the book that could be bent to make the project work was bent . . . every rule-bending resorted to,' said an industry veteran—who wishes to remain anonymous—to this author.

'To start with, licence was given to just one other insignificant carmaker, Sipani Automobiles,' says that industry veteran, 'then import duties were reduced drastically, as was excise. Almost complete cars were allowed to be imported initially. Maruti was always behind on its localization commitments, yet the government turned a blind eye to that. Lower excise for fuel-efficient vehicles was just an excuse to justify minimal taxation. And then when Rajiv Gandhi came to power and decided to "broadband" licensing, which was supposed to allow other four-wheeler manufacturers to make cars too, their joint venture proposals were never given a green signal, so that Maruti could be continuously protected. After all that if you cannot succeed, then you need to be incredibly incompetent!'

Krishnamurthy concurs, mentioning to the author, 'Yes, any other similarly priced small car from Japan would have succeeded for sure. Of course, working with Suzuki was easier as versus giants like Mitsubishi, but the initial success of the Maruti 800 and Maruti Udyog is mainly thanks to the Indian management.'

Yet, there is no denying that Maruti Udyog was a favoured child and the Maruti 800 had a charmed early life. Maitreya Doshi, the managing director of Premier Limited, pointed out to the author that the government largesse in terms of tax and excise benefits gave Maruti 'at the least a 15 per cent cost advantage over the others'. That was so for the first—crucial—decade of the company's existence.

Existing carmakers such as Hindustan Motors, Premier Automobiles and Standard Motors, all had the opportunity to work out new collaboration deals to bring in cars and designs that could have competed with the 800. Yet they chose to bring in outdated designs with outmoded technology, launching cars like the Hindustan Contessa (based on a Vauxhall design from 1972), Premier 118NE (a Fiat design, via Fiat's then Spanish subsidiary Seat, from 1966) and the Standard 2000 (a Rover from 1976, powered by an engine which went back to the 1950s). Of these, the 118NE, at its launch, created quite a buzz, with some 1,08,000 cars booked and Rs 118 crore garnered by the carmaker, but quality issues saw the waiting list dwindling rapidly.

It was only by the mid to late 1990s, after the 'liberalization' of 1991, that Maruti Udyog had serious competition. Yet, not only did the 800 survive, it thrived despite a crowd of very worthy competitors launching several fine small cars, from the Fiat Uno to the Tata Indica.

When Premier Automobiles tied up with Fiat of Italy to announce the launch of the Fiat Uno, some 2,90,662 punters put down almost Rs 600 crore as booking deposit (creating a record, which remains unsurpassed). Everyone believed that the days of the Maruti 800 were numbered. Trade union militant Datta Samant though decided to 'intervene' and history took a very different turn as Premier Automobiles' two joint ventures—one with Fiat and the other with Peugeot—came apart, allowing the 800 to remain the king of the hill.

Tata's Indica, Hyundai's Santro and Daewoo's Matiz also looked like serious threats when they were unveiled in early 1998. Alas, they priced themselves out of the 800's segment. It was not until the 800's intended successor, the Alto, came along (in September 2000) that the 800 finally had competition. Yet, it took the Alto another five long years to topple the 800, to begin a new chapter in India's 'people's car' history.

A car for India

When Tata Motors' launched the Indica in 1998, it looked like the car that would be the real people's car, made by the Indian people for the people of India.

Ratan Tata felt that the Maruti 800 was too small, as was the Zen, which was supposed to replace the 800, a more modern Japanese kei car, also an entire generation more up to date than the 800. Though the Zen was bigger than the 800, most of the increase in length was ahead of the front wheels to accommodate the bigger engine the car had as compared to the 'donor' Suzuki model, the Cervo Mode, with passenger space marginally bigger than that of the 800. Tata and his team decided that more appropriate for the Indian marketplace would be a bigger car with significantly greater space for passengers. Yet, pricing and running cost had to remain close to that of the bestselling 800. Thus, the project objective became for a small car as big as a Maruti Zen to provide the space of an Ambassador.

The Ambassador was legendary in the kind of space and comfort the car provided for its passengers, the single most important reason why it was still selling in significant numbers in the 1990s. To provide that kind of space though in a car the overall size of a Maruti Zen; how was that going to be managed? More challenging was the price benchmark—that of matching the bestselling Maruti 800.

To develop a 'world-class' car, TELCO signed up Italian design consultancy I.DE.A, as well as French engine specialist Le Moteur Moderne (LMM). LMM had been involved in the development of Peugeot's TU3 version of the TU engine family, and they helped Tata Motors improve the refinement of the engine that they had developed. The first set of prototype engines and transmissions were sent to I.DE.A's facilities in Turin in April 1997 and the first two prototypes were assembled by June, the occasion celebrated by the toasting and spraying of champagne.

By the end of 1997, well over 400 engineers and designers from TELCO's Engineering Research Centre were on the project, apart from hundreds of others who were working on getting the manufacturing facilities ready. Eventually almost 700 engineers were involved in the development of India's first all-Indian car. It took thirty-one months to complete the project, which involved the design and development of 3885 components, with as many as 740 dies and over 4000 fixtures specially made for the manufacturing of the car, accounting for Rs 74 crore in tooling and Rs 1420 crore in setting up the plant. In the process, Tata's capital cost per car worked out to Rs 1,13,000 versus Rs 1,14,000 for the Maruti Zen, which was, in 1997, not only a four-year-old car, but markedly smaller than what Tata was about to unveil in January 1998.

15 January 1998 was a red-letter day in the history of Tata Motors and India's automotive history. On that day, at New Delhi's Pragati Maidan expo grounds, several significant new cars were launched, but the car which really grabbed the headlines was the Tata Indica, India's first home-grown 'people's car'. Even if all knew that the new Tata car 'that would be as big as a Maruti Zen, yet provide the space of an Ambassador, at a price of a Maruti 800', was going to be called the Indica (like in *India*+*Ca*r), they still had not seen the car.

Thus, the unveiling of the car became a much-awaited moment. Sure enough, expectations ran high, and at the unveiling, which had thousands of journalists, politicians and spectators crowding the huge Tata stand at Hall 11 of Pragati Maidan, the car did not disappoint. Here was a car that did deliver on the promise of space and size . . . and in a package that was indeed very good-looking.

Less than three months later, Tata was at the Geneva Motor Show. In fact, it was the first time that Tata, the brand new carmaker, was at the Geneva show. Though it was not the first Indian car marque in Geneva (Mahindra had preceded it some years earlier), it was significant in presenting an all-Indian car for the first time to a worldwide audience. The Indica was unveiled. There was a lot of interest. Ratan Tata was very much there at the show, his speech, as modest, even humble, as ever. There were huge crowds thronging the stand. Tata's new car seemed to make a good impression on the international press. A greater impression, though, may have been made by reigning Miss World, Hyderabad girl Diana Hayden, who was there to unveil the Indica.

The Indica was launched in the Indian marketplace by the end of 1998 as Tata had promised, and initial bookings (about 1,15,000) and expectations were huge for a car that, though priced higher than the Maruti 800, was still markedly cheaper than the smaller Maruti Zen. Sadly, early teething problems blunted somewhat the enthusiasm for the Indica. To the credit of Tata Motors, it did realize the shortcomings of the Indica and began addressing them.

The Indica eventually became the basic platform for Tata's passenger car range. Four years after the unveiling of the Indica, at the Auto Expo of 2002, Tata Motors launched the Indigo, a three-box saloon derivative based on the Indica. Two years later, the Indigo Marina, an estate derived out of the Indigo, followed. In the financial year April 2006–March 2007, Tata Motors managed to sell as many as 1,44,690 Indicas.

The Korean riposte

The Tata Indica was not the only star in January 1998, at New Delhi's Pragati Maidan expo grounds. As well as India's first two-seater sports convertible, the San Storm (more about it in Chapter 6), two other small cars had caught the fancy of the hundreds of thousands of visitors to India's fourth motor show, Auto Expo 1998. One was a very cute little car called the d'Arts; the other was another small car, the Santro, which was being shown again, after being unveiled in India at the Delhi International Motor Show a year earlier, in January 1997. Both these were cars presented by two South Korean carmakers. The Indian public was just getting to know one of the two manufacturers, as the large and rather expensive Cielo, assembled by Daewoo at a brand new factory near Delhi, had started selling in modest numbers across the bigger cities.

Daewoo or Hyundai (the other Korean carmaker, which had unveiled the Santro) then were far from being household names in a country which had grown up on a diet of European and American cars, with a smattering of Japanese brands such as Toyota, Honda, Nissan and Mitsubishi, most of which had been brought in by consulates and returning expatriates. Yet, these two Korean carmakers seemed to have ambitions way beyond the European or Japanese carmakers when setting up fledgling Indian operations.

In the meantime, French giant Peugeot had tied up with Premier Automobiles to make the relatively expensive Peugeot 309, Ford was assembling the rather expensive Escort with Mahindra & Mahindra, and General Motors was making the very expensive Astra launched by its German subsidiary then, Opel. Honda was planning to make the relatively expensive mid-sized car, the City, Hindustan was planning to assemble the no less expensive Mitsubishi Lancer, and Toyota was bringing in an unappetizing multipurpose vehicle, the Qualis. None was really aiming for the main segment in the marketplace, where all the action seemed to be—that of small inexpensive hatchbacks, potential 'people's cars'.

Except for Fiat, which, with Premier Automobiles, had unveiled the Uno two years earlier, no one else seemed to have any plans to take on redoubtable market leader Maruti Udyog. As Fiat and Premier seemed to be floundering with labour problems at their factory in Mumbai, along came Tata Motors (TELCO had, in the meantime, been renamed Tata Motors) with the Indica. Matching Tata and Maruti, spec for spec, price for price, came these two unknown Korean upstarts, Daewoo and Hyundai, with their two new small cars.

The unsuspecting Indian public had no clue about Hyundai's history or, for that matter, of Daewoo's, when the Santro and the d'Arts had been on show to the enthusiastic public at the 1998 edition of the Auto Expo. Nor was it aware that by 1998, Daewoo and Hyundai were, respectively, the fifteenth and sixteenth biggest carmakers in the world, having produced 7,27,000 and 7,04,000 cars, respectively.

What the Indian public could see and make out was the commitment of the Koreans. It was Daewoo which had made the first move into India, investing in a huge plant near New Delhi. But when the management insisted that the Daewoo Cielo was a 'brand new' design, the first seeds of suspicion were sowed, as most motoring journalists knew that the Cielo was just a heavily cosmetically facelifted Opel Astra from the earlier generation.

With the d'Arts, which was renamed the Matiz at the time of its launch, Daewoo was taking a leaf out of the Hyundai strategy and launching a car, which, though it had Suzuki mechanicals under the skin, was an all-new design by Italian design house, Italdesign. The Matiz was Daewoo's take on a small car, a 'people's car' for markets other than South Korea, which preferred bigger saloons. As the international market, specifically that of Europe had become important—and the Europeans had a penchant for small cars—Daewoo realized that it needed a small car for Europe, which could work as a 'people's car' for markets like India.

The biggest problem with the Matiz, though, was its introductory price—it was far too high for a car which was not very much bigger than a Maruti 800 and featured a similar power train. People did not wish to pay Maruti Zen prices for a car which had an engine that was essentially the same as that of the 800. In fact, the Matiz was actually a redesigned Suzuki kei car, the Alto from one generation after the SB308 (the 800), which Daewoo had been making under licence, badged the Daewoo Tico. Thus, what Daewoo did was to update Suzuki's 'people's car' to Daewoo's car for the people.

Despite the huge factory that Daewoo had set up in India, its localization programme was too slow and it could not reduce prices without losing a significant amount of money. Daewoo had grown too rapidly in the 1980s and 1990s, fuelled (and over-leveraged), no doubt by its very ambitious owner Kim Woo-Choong (who had written a book at the height of his success story, titled *Every Street is Paved with Gold!*), so much so that it was in big trouble thanks to the Asian financial crisis of the late 1990s.

Hyundai, though, was made of sterner stuff.

By the time the South Korean carmaker came to India, it had decent in-house capabilities. It had had the humbling experience of succeeding and almost failing in the world's most competitive market, North America, and it had had the experience of setting up a plant in a foreign country with great expectations and seeing it fail within four years, when Hyundai had to close down its Canadian assembly operations at Bromont, near Quebec, in 1994.

The opening of the Indian car market proved to be a heaven-sent opportunity for Hyundai. With liberalization, several Indian business houses had approached Hyundai, and the Korean company's executives, in turn, made several trips and surveys in India, engaging in detailed discussions with potential collaborators. When they saw that it was possible to come into India with a wholly owned subsidiary, they chose to do so. Not only was their subsidiary in India 100 per cent, their commitment too was 100 per cent.

Hyundai Motor India was registered on 6 May 1996. Hyundai was clear, that like its gigantic factory at Ulsan, in South Korea, the factory in India had to be near a major port. It decided to locate the plant at Sriperumbudur, near Chennai. The 'ground-breaking' ceremony for the plant was on 10 December 1996, and then the process began to transplant the recently mothballed Canadian plant of Hyundai Motors to India, lock, stock, barrel, paint, and press shops.

By early 1997, they had hired B.V.R. Subbu as director, marketing and sales, who had been a star at TELCO, and at one time Ratan Tata's blue-eyed boy, and who would be the main architect in overseeing the Hyundai success story in India. The initial plan was to bring in the Hyundai Accent, the mid-sized saloon model, following the template that Daewoo had set in India—come in with the more expensive car and, as localization progresses, bring in the smaller car later, a top-down approach to entering a new car market.

Subbu explained to this author that he did not agree with that strategy: 'It appeared quite clearly that the small car segment should be the starting point and we could graduate later into the higher-price segment.' What the market needed was a 'people's car'. Subbu believed that it made much better sense to go straight for the jugular, the main segment of the market, that of small hatchback cars—cars like the Maruti 800 and the Zen, which accounted for some three-quarters of the total car market in India then. Hyundai had just (1977) launched the Atos, the company's first small city car, and that, to Subbu, seemed to be the most obvious choice for India. Hyundai's senior management agreed.

There was one problem though with Hyundai's in-house product: it was aesthetically most unappealing.

The car had been put through a customer clinic in India where people had been asked their opinion regarding the car. Though most thought that the car had many virtues in terms of space and comfort, all disliked the looks of the car. Hyundai's first small car, designed in South Korea, was an aesthetic disaster. Inspired by the 'tall boy' design of the very successful Suzuki WagonR, which had become one of Japan's bestselling cars in the 1990s, the Hyundai Atos was a rather gawky-looking tall car with an upright backside. Though that liberated a whole lot of inside space within the rather compact dimensions, it gave the look of a car which was going to keel over at the slightest provocation. Subbu was convinced that the car, as it was, would not sell. The Hyundai management also came to the same realization.

Hyundai, though, could not go back to the drawing board and redesign the Atos into a completely new car for India. So the best compromise was to rework the rear portion of the car and somewhat ameliorate the design, which, of course, called for new dies and tooling for the rear tailgate, the hatch, that is, the rear roof section and the rear fenders, the rear bumper and the rear lamp assemblies. It is to Hyundai's credit that it realized the importance of making these changes, to incur the cost of additional dies and toolings for a product which had been launched only recently.

At the Auto Expo of 1998, Hyundai unveiled its small car on 13 January, christening it the Santro, instead of the Atos. The Atos moniker, in the meantime, had changed to Atoz for the UK market as Hyundai's marketing folks realized that the British public would not give a toss for the Atos; so the car became the Atoz—a car which would take you from point A to Z.

For India, a newer, better-looking car deserved a different name, hence, the Santro. Hyundai also seemed to be in a rush to get to the market—it had realized the importance of being a first mover. On 27 May 1998, the pilot production of the Santro began at the plant—within a record seventeen months since 'ground-breaking', and four months since it had shown the car to the public at Delhi. By 23 September 1998, the first batch of Santros for customers was in showrooms across India, beating the other two stars from the Auto Expo to the marketplace.

Priced between the Maruti 800 and the Maruti Zen, the Santro did not exactly set the sale charts afire at the beginning. The expectations were more modest for this car, a car which looked rather practical but did not quite have the sheer elegance of the Tata Indica or the lovable cuteness of the Daewoo Matiz. Yet, there was no denying its functional quality, including a spacious interior, which seemed to match the markedly bigger Fiat Uno. The 999cc four-cylinder engine was smooth and linear in its power delivery, the engine note refined and unobtrusive, with low-end driveability seemingly better than that of the Maruti Zen. The body though rolled when cornering hard, road holding seemed to be good enough, and ride comfort was quite decent. The air conditioning was very effective and the top-end version came packed with features such as power steering, electric power windows for the front pair, an audio system, a rear screen wash-and-wipe system, and body-coloured bumpers with fog lamps. Here was a car for the people, but with the appropriate bits and baubles.

At a price markedly lower than the Zen, the Santro seemed to make very good sense, even if the car did not spark love at first sight. No one at that point of time had really heard of Hyundai. Koreans were new to car making and thus, people were unsure. Were they good enough to compete with the likes of the Europeans and the Japanese? There were just too many questions, too many doubts.

That is when the role of marketing and a brilliant advertising campaign came into play, a clear first in the Indian automobile scenario. Hyundai Motor hired advertising agency Saatchi & Saatchi to think up a campaign and a way to break into the Indian marketplace. Saatchi & Saatchi brought in the concept of a brand ambassador for Hyundai's first car. Not just any brand ambassador, but one of Bollywood's, and India's, biggest rising stars then, film actor Shah Rukh Khan.

In a series of television commercials starting April 1998—before the Santro had been launched—Hyundai began to address the many doubts and issues surrounding the brand, the car, the abilities of the Koreans and the commitment of the carmaker to India.

In the first phase of the advertising campaign, from April 1998 to June 1998, Shah Rukh Khan was chased by a Hyundai executive who was trying to convince the Indian actor to endorse the product. The very first advertisement introduced the brand and the company with a very subtle statement from Mr Kim: we settle only for the best. Then the teaser advertisements which followed had Mr Kim trying to convince Shah Rukh Khan that Hyundai was serious about India— that it already had in place dealers, suppliers, workers, and so on— about quality issues and the brand Santro.[6]

In the second phase of the advertising campaign, which ran from July to September 1998, Khan was shown asking the kind of questions a typical Indian consumer would ask: Who or what is Hyundai? How can Santro be good enough for Indian roads? Will Hyundai be able to match customer requirements and provide proper aftersales services? At the end, Khan pronounced: 'I am convinced', and in the process convinced more and more Indian consumers that the Hyundai Santro could indeed be the 'complete family car' that they were looking for, a car, which had more space and features than the people's car of the period, the Maruti 800.

This very high-profile celebrity association with some innovative media buying, along with aggressive press coverage, created enough hype for the Santro, and sales took off, contrary to expectations. Priced at a competitive Rs 2,89,000 against the Maruti Zen's Rs 3,45,000, consumers flocked to the showrooms on 23 September 1998, when the Santro went on sale. Instead of a booking system, the Santro was available against full payment.

At the same time, Subbu's marketing team had already set up an extensive dealer network, with proper aftersales facilities. Whilst considering potential dealers, Hyundai looked at educational background, details of income, taxes paid and the kind of investment they could make. An important prerequisite for dealership was a fully functional workshop with properly trained people.

Moreover, Hyundai's marketing blitz was backed by very deep resources and good manufacturing fundamentals. Hyundai Motor's investment of Rs 2300 crore by 1998 was already the single largest investment by an automobile company in India until then. More importantly, the plant was not another assembly operation for knocked-down kits, but an extensively integrated manufacturing facility. The Santros which were rolling out of the factory were cars which were being manufactured by the plant, unlike the assembly operations of Daewoo for the Matiz, or the way Maruti had begun the roll out most of their models until then, by assembling completely or semi-knocked-down.

Of course, volume was necessary to meet the localization targets, so Hyundai set up its new factory with an initial installed capacity of 1,00,000 cars per annum. At the same time, Hyundai brought along the Korean developmental philosophy right from the start: cars needed to be exported, too, and, from the third year onwards, a target was set to export up to 40 per cent of production and 10,000 sets of transmission gears.

The virtues of a clean car

For exports, the cars needed to be technically up to date, and so Hyundai brought engine technology to match European requirements for emissions. With pollution becoming an issue in India, specifically in Delhi, the Supreme Court took matters in hand. Hyundai was ready with cars that met the emission requirements, which the Supreme Court believed should be introduced, standards set by the Euro II norms, or Bharat Stage II as it was named in India. Hyundai went to town to stress that its cars met Bharat Stage II ahead of the rest of the Indian industry, thereby hinting that these cars were technically more modern than those from the competition.

It was the Shah Rukh Khan campaign though, which worked brilliantly. By August 1999, Hyundai had managed to shift 42,283 cars, and by the financial year ending 31 March 1999, Hyundai Motor India had already become India's second largest carmaker, after Maruti Udyog.

By 27 April 2000, the 1,00,000th Hyundai rolled out of the Chennai factory, and by 12 June of the same year, the 1,00,000th

One of the strangest cars ever made, the Swan Car, intrigued and frightened the people of Calcutta when it was first seen.

The unusual Swan Car of Calcutta, with the 'baby' Cygnet.

Courtesy: Gautam Sen

One of rarest cars ever made, the Farman A6B, which belonged to the princely family of Idar.

Courtesy: Gautam Sen Archives

This unique Delahaye 175 Coupé, with exquisite Figoni et Falaschi bodywork, was newly acquired by the Maharaja of Mysore. Later owned by Elton John, this car is now in the Petersen Automotive Museum in Los Angeles.

No less rare is this Figoni et Falaschi-bodied Talbot-Lago, from 1938, with its then owner, Stella de Kapurthala; the maharani poses with her prized possession and wedding gift for a concours d'elegance event in Paris.

Arguably the most beautiful car in India today, the 1939 Delahaye 135MS, also bodied by Figoni et Falaschi; now in the long-term ownership of Dalip Singh, from Jodhpur.

Perhaps one of the fastest cars during the 1930s, this specially modified, extremely rare Bentley 8 Litre is one of the several exceptional cars to have survived in India today.

One of the most astounding line-ups of cars ever—two Duesenbergs, two Mercedes-Benz SS and an experimental Rolls-Royce—in the ownership of one family, the Mitters of Calcutta, circa 1930s.

The same experimental Rolls-Royce, the 17EX, with an erstwhile stablemate, a Mercedes-Benz SS, both of which used to belong to the Maharaja of Kashmir, photographed at Pebble Beach for the special Cars of the Maharajas class, in 2012.

Another exceptional car in India, the last Rolls-Royce Phantom II Continental, with svelte J. Gurney Nutting coachwork; also in the long-term ownership of the Jetha family.

Another rarity, this remarkably well-restored Imperial Crown Southampton, from 1961, is one of several distinctive cars owned by inveterate collector Viveck Goenka.

Arguably one of the most unusual conversions of a Rolls-Royce ever, the cricket-team car, in the collection of the Udaipur princely family of Arvind Singh Mewar.

A period advertisement of one of India's oldest coachbuilding firms, Steuart & Co., from Calcutta.

One of the earliest Fiats assembled in India by Premier Automobiles, this Fiat 500C Topolino is also a part of the Viveck Goenka collection.

Courtesy: Makarand Baokar

An Indian-assembled Chevrolet Fleetmaster, now owned by the Nieddu family in Jodhpur.

Courtesy: Makarand Baokar

Another rare car; despite being produced in India, this four-door variant of the Standard Herald came too late and could not save the model from being phased out.

Courtesy: Heritage Transport Museum

The SAIL Badal three-wheeler was perhaps the first indigenously developed personal-use vehicle in India which was successfully commercialized—but sold in very modest numbers—in the 1970s.

Indian Prime Minister Jawaharlal Nehru
examining the German Goggomobil,
which was under consideration for
manufacture in India.

One of Sanjay Gandhi's ill-fated Marutis, under
construction at the factory.

Sanjay Gandhi
being interviewed
within the confines
of a Maruti.

Another oddity which
was planned for
manufacture in India,
this rare Fuldamobil-
based Scootacar is from
the year 1972 and now
resides in the Gedee Car
Museum, Coimbatore.

The car that won the Delhi–Bombay Reliability Trials in 1904–05, a De Dietrich driven by M.L. Sorel.

A Citroën Traction Avant, which used to be the daily driver for Calcutta resident Minnie Pan, was also raced by her during the weekends when racing was a regular scene in the City of Joy.

An SS100 Jaguar—probably the only one that ever came to India—in action in Calcutta.

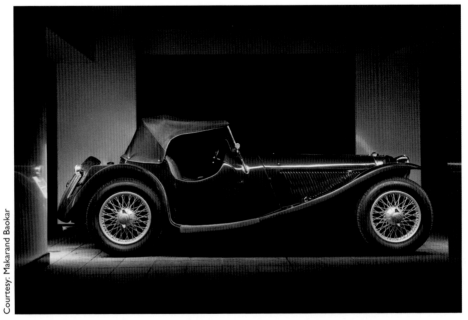

The same SS100 Jaguar, now restored and owned by popular Bollywood actor Jackie Shroff.

Amongst the unusual racing machines competing in Calcutta was this startling Lancia Astura-based racer, in action during the 1950s.

The same Lancia Astura racer has been restored and is taken out occasionally for events by current owner and collector Harit Trivedi.

One of the first Indians to race competitively abroad since India's Independence, Kinny Lal, seen here with a modified Standard Herald at one of the Calcutta races.

Englishman Peter Heilborn won many races with this Jaguar XK120 in Juhu, Bombay.

Polish rallying legend Sobiesław Zasada's Porsche 911 RS during the 1977 London–Sydney Marathon in India, when he was still leading the rally.

One of India's better-known racing families, the Bhathenas, with three-time Indian rallying national champion, Farad, at the centre, his father, Darayus, and brother, Zoru, on his right, his sister, Navaz, on his left, and his uncle, Bomi Mehta, accompanying them.

Gave Cursetjee's fibreglass-bodied Cobra sports coupés, based on Standard Heralds.

Another aborted sports-car project for India—the De La Chapelle Roadster.

The epoxy mock-up of the San Storm coupé prototype, with the author posing with the owners of San Engineering, Shubhash and Milind Thakker.

The prototype San Storm coupé and cabriolet, photographed in late 1997 at Le Mans, France, a few days before the cars were flown out to New Delhi for the official unveiling at the 1998 Auto Expo.

SCOOTERS INDIA LIMITED PRESENTS THE VIJAI deluxe

We are pleased to announce that you can now book your Vijai Deluxe from our authorised dealers:

How to book your Vijai:

1. Deposit Rs. 500/- in a Post Office Savings Bank Account pledged to Hindustan Petroleum Corporation Ltd., Bombay.
2. Show the passbook to our Dealers two days prior to the date of commencement of bookings and get an application form.
3. Present the Application Form duly filled, and the passbook at 10.00 A.M. on the commencement date and onwards.
4. Obtain the Acknowledgement Form from our Dealers.

Scooters India Limited
Post Bag. No. 1 Sarojininagar
Lucknow-226008

HINDUSTAN PETROLEUM CORPORATION LIMITED
DEALERS FOR BOMBAY CITY
Bookings for **Vijai Deluxe Scooters** will start
from 10 a.m. on March 10 onwards at:

Car Care Centre
45, Nepean Sea Road
Bombay 400 026.

Auto Care Centre
Jn. of Swami Vivekananda Road
and Turner Road
Bandra, Bombay 400 050.

Courtesy: Dr Anjan Chatterjee

The advertisement announcing the booking for the Vijai Deluxe, the Scooters India-made Innocenti Lambretta, which the Indian government introduced in the 1970s.

Well-known 'Bikerni' Sonia Jain has set out to record the highest number of motorcycle models one can ride.

Ridhi Nahata believes that riding a motorcycle is a symbol of independence and emancipation for women in India.

One of the early aficionados of motorcycling was Natasha Alpaiwalla, who set up a baking business to finance her first two-wheeler; she hopes to pass on her passion for biking to her daughter, Tanaya.

Santro rolled out (Hyundai had launched the mid-sized Accent model, too, in the meantime). A little over a month later, the first batch of 760 Santros and Accents were shipped out for the company's first 'serious' export out of India (nineteen Santros had been shipped to Nepal in 1999 as the first tentative toe testing).

A year later, on 11 July 2001, Hyundai unveiled a 'newer' look Santro, with a mild facelift. By then, the carmaker had made its 2,00,000th car in India. The 3,00,000th car rolled out a year later, on 26 June 2002, and the 4,00,000th on 8 May 2003.

It was on 22 May 2003 when an important event happened: Hyundai Motor India unveiled the Hyundai Santro Xing. The Santro Xing was an extensively reworked facelift of the Santro, with the front end completely redesigned into a markedly better-looking car: Hyundai's ugly duckling had after five years, become an almost-pretty cygnet.

More importantly, the redesign was not just for the Indian market, but was developed for all markets internationally. The Atos/Atoz had met with, at best, modest success in Europe, and sales in South Korea's domestic market were rather poor as Koreans preferred bigger saloons (the executive-sized Sonata had become South Korea's bestseller). Hyundai thus decided that instead of two production bases, the Atos/Santro would be best served in terms of scales of operations, by being made out of one factory, Hyundai's Chennai plant, to serve both its single biggest market, India, and for sales in Europe and the rest of the world.

The Santro Xing became Hyundai's global small car, and exports began in significant numbers, the Xing badged as the Atos Prime in Europe and most markets, Amica in the UK, Dodge Atos in Mexico, Inokom Atos in Malaysia and as the Kia Visto in Indonesia and South Korea. The first batch of 1500 Santro Xings left for Europe on 12 August 2003.

For India, the positioning changed. Initially, the Santro was positioned as an upgrade for Maruti 800 users, a complete family car for those who wanted more space and desired to move to a bigger car. The Santro Xing was positioned to appeal to first-time car buyers.

Again, a very innovative advertisement campaign played an important role in the transition from an upgrade to becoming an essential, the bread-and-butter car. A series of teaser ads on television had brand ambassador Shah Rukh Khan surrendering the keys of a Hyundai Santro to Mr Kim, with the audience wondering whether Shah Rukh's contract with Hyundai Motor had come to an end, as the speculation was that Hyundai was going in for a new brand ambassador. Instead, Mr Kim returned to a pleasantly surprised Shah Rukh with a new Santro, handing over the key to the actor. Sure enough, Shah Rukh grabbed the key and zoomed away in the Santro Xing, with Mr Kim left stranded on the road . . .[7]

With the launch of the Santro Xing, Hyundai took the car and the brand into the smaller towns, as well as opening over a thousand new service points across the country. Hyundai Motors backed that by tying up with Indian Oil Corporation and Bharat Petroleum Corporation to position trained technicians at the petrol pumps belonging to these two oil majors, extending service and repair facilities across the length and breadth of India.

By the end of 2003, Hyundai had made its first half-millionth car in India and by end October 2004, had exported its first 1,00,000th vehicle—mostly Santros—out of India. The next 1,00,000th car for the international market was exported in less than another year (by 18 October 2005). By 13 March 2006, Hyundai Motor India had rolled out its millionth car from its plant in Chennai. By November 2006— less than a decade since its launch—Hyundai Motors India had made over a million Santros.

Interestingly, Hyundai reached its millionth Santro some three years earlier than the Maruti 800. Moreover, it did not have the protective 'umbrella' of governmental largesse.

Without doubt, the product was intrinsically good, even if the styling was not. The Santro was very reliable, it was a very practical car and it represented great value for money. Hyundai also had its basics in place, in terms of localization and volumes (aided by exports). Servicing quality improved significantly with a dealership expansion programme in 2007–08. The number of dealers went up from 187 in

2006 to 320 by 2010. There was no doubt that the way the car was marketed and the way B.V.R. Subbu and Hyundai played their media cards, contributed significantly to the Santro's success.

Even as late as 2007, when Shah Rukh Khan was hosting the very popular television show *Kaun Banega Crorepati*, during the 26 March episode, things took a dramatic turn towards the end. Shah Rukh announced that one of the nine contestants who had made it to the hot seat would be getting a Hyundai Santro, adding that the remaining eight would get consolation prizes. The consolation prize was a box, but within that box was a set of keys . . . to a Hyundai Santro, for each of the eight . . .

The audience—and of course the participants—were stunned, and overjoyed. The media, the next day, went to town, and like how!

Hyundai's success story is remarkable when one remembers that by the late 1990s, Hyundai was short of air on American territory, struggling for one last gasp. Instead of retreating, as many others had done, the company made massive investments in new design and technology, other than addressing quality issues on a war footing.

It also bought out Korean rival Kia, which, like Daewoo, was floundering soon after the Asian financial crisis of the late 1990s. Over the next decade or so, it integrated its design and sourcing activities with Kia's, though it has retained the distinctive branding differences between the two. Hyundai brought Kia into India in 2019, and going by the initial results, Kia too has been making impressive inroads into the Indian marketplace.

Hyundai's biggest rival in the 1990s, Daewoo, collapsed by 2000, and the car division was eventually taken over by erstwhile collaborator General Motors, which, in the irony of things, had been denied a majority stake in the 1970s by the South Korean government. GM Korea is now South Korea's second-biggest carmaker after Hyundai-Kia and most of the lower priced Chevrolets for worldwide consumption came from its facilities in Korea. The Korean-made cars, though, were still selling as Daewoos in Korea. In India, GM India dropped the Opel brand eventually, to replace it with Chevrolet and, amusingly, most of the Chevrolets sold in India were models sourced from GM Korea.

Then, in 2017, GM India stopped selling cars in India altogether, exiting the country for the second time since 1954.

In another strange twist of history, a bankrupt Daewoo's truck division was acquired by Tata Motors in 2002 and renamed Tata Daewoo, with the trucks selling in Korea and several other markets as a Daewoo, or Tata Daewoo.

The other Korean carmaker, SsangYong, had a convoluted history too, being taken over by Daewoo for a brief period, followed by Chinese ownership when Chinese carmaker SAIC took over SsangYong for a few years, before putting the latter into receivership in 2009. Then, in February 2011, it was the turn of Mahindra & Mahindra to win over SsangYong for 522.5 billion won (Rs 2200 crore).

Playing the Alto

The unveiling of the Tata Indica, the Hyundai Santro and the ill-fated Daewoo Matiz in 1998 at New Delhi's Auto Expo, had India's then dominant carmaker, Maruti Udyog Limited, galvanized into some serious action—this, despite the fact that in the financial year 1997–98, Maruti's market share was already at a staggering 82.7 per cent. The management at Maruti Udyog realized that the good times were not going to last and they needed to do something, to react and take on the imminent onslaught.

Before that though, Maruti Udyog needed to get its own house in order. On 2 June 1992, Suzuki increased its stake in Maruti Udyog from 40 per cent to 50 per cent. With that, Maruti Udyog ceased to be a national car company, which, in principle, was fine with most, except for several industry experts, including Dr V. Krishnamurthy, who believed that Maruti Udyog was as good as gifted away to Suzuki Motor.

Suzuki paid just Rs 269 per share, a valuation which most, in retrospect, will agree was woefully below what it ought to have been. Moreover, there was the issue of principles. Considering Maruti Udyog had been created in the first instance as India's national car project, it was very important to retain that aspect. Krishnamurthy's suggestion (as spelled out to the author) was, 'Yes, Maruti Udyog needed to be privatized, but not by selling out to Suzuki, but by the government selling off 20 per cent of its 60 per cent stake to financial institutions, vendors, dealers and employees, so that it would be a board-managed company.'

What Krishnamurthy had in mind was a carmaker, not unlike Renault and Volkswagen in France and Germany, respectively, both of which were very successful government-owned but board-managed companies. Both saw progressive privatization, without any single family or shareholder taking full control . . . things, though, panned out differently for Volkswagen, which finally had the company landing under the Porsche family's control, after some astute stock market play-outs. In a way, Krishnamurthy's suggestion was somewhat similar to what happened in China over the last two decades, where all the carmakers used to be joint ventures with the local or Chinese government, without a single multinational having a controlling stake. (This has been changing since 2018.)

Of course, Osamu Suzuki, by then, had realized that Maruti Udyog was the ultimate 'cash cow' Suzuki Motor could have had and he was rather insistent on increasing Suzuki's stake to over 50 per cent, which is what R.C. Bhargava, as the managing director then, pushed for too. This is what was 'gifted' to Suzuki. Virtually nobody protested; with the first waft of real liberalization in the air, nobody dared question this decision, as it would have been seen as a non-progressive anti-liberalization sentiment and out of place with the emerging winds of change.

The financial year 1999–2000 was a good year for Maruti Udyog: for the first time it made more than 4,00,000 cars. But overall car sales were down the following financial year, a 12 per cent drop, thanks to a recession. Maruti had unsold inventories and, for the first time in its history, it went on to post a loss of Rs 269.4 crore. This was followed by Maruti's first serious labour dispute.

All these problems galvanized Suzuki and Maruti into drastic cost-cutting measures, including offering a lucrative voluntary retirement scheme to workers and some managers. At the same time,

Maruti embarked on an extensive model renewal programme. The mainstay of Maruti's product line-up until then had always been the 800, introduced, as we know, as long back as August 1986. The Omni, introduced as the Van in 1984, was a success story too, but the Gypsy (1985) and the Maruti 1000 (from 1990) had always been modest sellers.

The launch of the Alto, though, on 27 September 2000 was the move that signalled the crossing into the second phase of Maruti Udyog's rapid expansion programme. The Alto was Maruti's third try at making a 'people's car'. The first had been a huge success, as we know, but it was ageing. The second, the Zen, was a failure and had been recently bettered and battered by both the Tata Indica and the Hyundai Santro. Maruti needed an all-new people's car to take the fight back to the two new wannabes.

Though received well, the initial sales were slow, and the Maruti Alto was not exactly setting any sales charts afire. Maruti Udyog needed to do something. And then it did what it had been saying it would not do: it slashed prices.

The year 2004 became pivotal for Maruti. With further price cuts for the Alto, sales began to move north. In May 2004, for the first time, the Alto outsold the Maruti 800—10,373 versus 10,016—and dethroned the champion of the best part of two decades. In six more months that year the Alto outsold the 800; yet, for the full year, the 800 was still India's bestseller at 1,32,706 sold, as against the Alto's 1,12,048.

For the financial year ending March 2005, Maruti Udyog crossed the half-a-million-car mark for the first time, making as many as 5,40,415 cars that year, most of that thanks to the Alto and the 800, the new champ and the outgoing one. In fiscal 2004–05, the Alto became India's bestselling car at 1,26,233, the 800 trailing at a close 1,16,262.

During the financial year 2007–08, the Alto sold a record-breaking 2,27,193 units; most significantly, the Alto found its first millionth domestic buyer in November 2008 (after manufacturing its first millionth Alto in February 2008), a little over eight years since its launch. The first millionth 800 had taken eleven years.

The Alto's next millionth customer came in less than four years, as the second millionth Alto rolled out of Maruti's factory in May 2012. On the way, the Alto blitz ripped through the Indian marketplace, with sales topping an amazing 3,46,840 during the financial year 2010–11, an average of close to 29,000 cars every month!

In calendar year 2010, the Alto sold a tad over 3,00,000 cars in India. That was when it was crowned the world's bestselling small car, a feat that it repeated in 2011, when 3,11,367 Altos were sold that year. That same year, Volkswagen's small car, the Gol, had found 2,93,454 buyers in Brazil and Fiat's Uno had sold as many as 2,73,537 units in the same country. But for 2012, the market slowed down for the Alto, with just 2,86,833 changing hands in India, even as the overall market grew by 14 percentage points (to a record 2.65 million).

A Swift change to a cult car

While all this was happening, Maruti launched the Swift in 2005, which marked a turning point in the carmaker's history. Until then, Maruti had been launching competent, reliable, workaday cars, which made sensible buys, cars, which were essentially everyday runabouts, nice, but not necessarily very desirable. It also became obvious that what could be the people's favourite in another country may not be popular in the Indian market—the WagonR was a case in point. Japan's bestseller was criticized for its looks and it took a while to get the market to accept it.

The Swift was quite unlike any other Suzuki. It was stylish, funky, with attitude, and the advertisement campaign, which ushered in the car's launch did wonders in making the car desirable—changing the image of Maruti (as well as Suzuki) with the targeted audience a younger, smarter set.

As ex-Maruti executive Avik Chattopadhyay explained to this author: 'The Swift has been much more than just a car for Maruti. It has been much more than yet another milestone. It was the symbol of transition. Of Maruti Udyog to Maruti Suzuki. Of India into a market and economic force at the world stage. Of the Indian customer as young, ambitious, aspirational and proud to be Indian.'

'The vehicle actually had a "greater purpose" for the entire organization,' added Chattopadhyay. 'Of emerging from a traumatic entry into the new millennium, after the company had lost market share. It also went through its first labour strike, and lost image due to no new products and delay in meeting emission standards. It had to reinstil confidence and pride within the organization, and it had to reformat the "Maruti" image before the newly emerging middle class.'

The brilliant campaign worked. With the success of the Swift, the average age of Maruti's customers came down from thirty-eight to thirty-two. The launches of several subsequent models—the SX4, the Dzire, the A-Star and the Ritz—helped bolster this newer, younger image.

Maruti Udyog Ltd, the nation's pride two decades ago, the maker of the first Indian 'people's car', has, over the years, become the single most important outpost of the Suzuki Empire, and will, in the years to come, remain the main driver of the Indian automobile industry. In more ways than one, the story of Maruti has been the story of the Indian automobile industry of the last four decades. It took Maruti Udyog Limited eleven years to produce a million cars. It took another four years for it to make its next million cars (by 1998).

It then had to wait another dozen-odd years for Maruti Suzuki India Limited to make a million cars in a year. That was during the financial year 2009–10, when, in a first, an Indian carmaker manufactured a million cars in a year. Since then it has been doing well over a million every year with sales of over 1.86 million vehicles during the financial year 2018–19.

Most noteworthy is the fact that since it became a subsidiary of Suzuki Motor Corporation (SMC) in 2008, Maruti helped Suzuki get to the top ten amongst major international car manufacturers. Until 2007, sales of cars in India and exports from Maruti contributed to over a quarter of SMC's sales worldwide. Since then, Maruti's sales have zoomed, as traditional car markets across the globe—where Suzuki has always had a significant presence—imploded, taking Maruti Suzuki's share in Suzuki Motor's global sales figures to over 60 per cent, and propelling Suzuki to the ninth spot among car majors in the world. Maybe we need to rephrase the popular American statement from the last century: what is good for GM is good for America, to what is good for Maruti Suzuki is indeed very, very good for Suzuki Motor Corporation.

And then came the Nano

In the meantime, as Hyundai, Maruti and Suzuki were consolidating their positions in India and internationally (even as Suzuki was losing ground rapidly in the United States and China as sales collapsed for them in these two very important markets), Tata Motors was on a very ambitious trajectory. For Tata Motors, 10 January 2008 became another important date, one, which, in retrospect, they may wish to mark more as a black-letter day, than otherwise.

On that day, the tenth day of January 2008, Tata Motors unveiled the Tata Nano, the car touted as the ultimate 'people's car', the car that was expected to be the wheels of choice for millions of Indians.

In a very impressive unveiling at the Auto Expo, in Pragati Maidan's Hall 11, a hologram image of Ratan Tata spoke. 'Today's story started some years ago when I observed families riding on two-wheelers, the father driving a scooter, his young kid standing in front of him, his wife sitting behind him holding a baby, and I asked myself whether one could conceive of a safe, affordable, all-weather form of transport for such a family,' continued Tata. 'A vehicle that could be affordable and low cost enough to be within everyone's reach, a people's car, built to meet all safety standards, designed to meet or exceed emission norms and be low in pollution and high in fuel efficiency. This then was the dream we set ourselves to achieve. Many said this dream could not be achieved. Some scoffed at what we would produce, perhaps a vehicle comprising two scooters attached together or perhaps an unsafe rudimentary vehicle, a poor excuse for a car. Let me assure you and also assure our critics that the car we have designed and we will be presenting to you today will indeed meet all the current safety requirements of a modern-day car.'[8]

'Anyway I have said enough, ladies and gentlemen,' concluded Tata, 'now I give you the new car from Tata Motors, the people's car that everyone has been waiting for.'

Then in a halo of lights, with the theme music from Stanley Kubrick's 1968 classic, *2001: A Space Odyssey*, blaring in the background, as bits and pieces of the much-anticipated car flashed on the screen behind, an iridescent silver white egg-like ball of metal emerged from the shadows, rolled on to centre stage, and Ratan Tata himself stepped out. Within seconds two other cars—a red one with black bumpers and a bright-yellow one—were driven on to the stage and parked, flanking the silver on either side.

Thunderous applause, and then, mayhem, as photographers, journalists, the audience, everyone scrambled for a closer look at the three cars. In the midst of that excitement, Tata quipped, 'Since it is high-tech and small, we called it "Nano",' adding, 'the car will be priced at Rs 1 lakh. A promise is a promise!'

Until late that evening, Hall 11 at Pragati Maidan remained crowded, jam-packed. Outside, the eager crowds reminded you of a cricket stadium before a one-day match. Hundreds of security men formed uncompromising barricades with thick ropes.

It was not just on 10 January that the crowds were crazy—on subsequent days of the Auto Expo, the hall that everyone was heading for was the one that had the 'lakhtakia' car. Despite the fact that there were more than 2000 exhibitors from over twenty-five countries displaying everything from automobiles to accessories at the Auto Expo, thousands upon thousands came essentially to get a glimpse of the Tata Nano. By 16 January, the last day of Delhi's ninth motor show, some 1.8 million people had thronged the Expo, comfortably beating the Paris motor show's draw of a million and a half, and perhaps eclipsing that of the Bangkok motor show too. The people came in their thousands, from Delhi, Haryana and UP—riding cars, buses, the Metro, and even tractors and tongas. They filled Bhairon Marg and Mathura Road, and set off traffic snarls that stopped Delhi at several places.

For what everybody had gathered to see at Hall No. 11 in Pragati Maidan was not just another small car, but to see hope emerge on wheels.

For this 'lakhtakia' car, in Hindi meaning 'the 1-lakh rupee' car—as the man on the street had already named it—had enabled millions to dream of a life beyond the motorbike, of a life that would be safer and more comfortable for themselves and his (or her) near and dear ones.

The morning after the launch, newspaper headlines about the 'lakhtakia' car screamed for attention—from a nicely said 'Small Wonder' to a more dramatic '1 lakh car drives 1 billion dreams'. Since the 1983 launch of the Maruti 800, no other car in the history of India had garnered as much newsprint space or as much airtime in India as the Tata Nano had. Every television news channel in India and some of the most important news channels across the world—whether it was CNN, BBC or TF1 in France—all had the Tata Nano as headline news on the evening of 10 January. The cheapest car ever in the history of the automobile had captured the imagination of the people, not just in India, but across the globe.

While India's press went hyperbolic, the press across the globe was not necessarily that enthusiastic, though most did admit that the Nano was a very significant car. 'Many were surprised by the Nano's natty styling, confounding pre-launch predictions that a car at that price would be little more than "a super-charged autorickshaw" or "two motorcycles joined at the hip",' wrote Peter Foster and Pallavi Malhotra.[9]

The excitement over the Nano spilled over to the Internet too. On 10 January 2008, the day the Nano was unveiled, the Tata Motors website saw nearly 7.9 million hits, while the Tata Nano website saw 4 million hits in thirty hours, making these sites among the busiest in the world!

Some of the reactions on the Internet were indeed amusing, such as the one by a person who signed himself/herself as VCHAGZ: 'This car would be great for Americans, till you get crushed by a reckless SUV or cargo van . . .'

'This is the greatest achievement in the history of the automobile. How much to FedEx it to the US?' was the reaction of a certain Albert Kunze.

Undoubtedly, Ratan Tata and his team had orchestrated an extraordinary unveiling on 10 January 2008, an event which had not only captured the imagination of the teeming masses of India, but that of people across the globe. This was obvious when the Tata Nano was shown for the first time to the international media and audience at the Geneva Motor Show, less than two months later.

Amongst the many articles written on the Tata Nano, was the design analysis of the Nano in the June 2008 issue of the American car magazine *Automobile* titled 'Tata Nano: A Design Analysis', by design expert Robert Cumberford (who has designed several cars himself). He commenced by saying: 'Here it is at last, the $2500 car that Ratan Tata proposed several years ago, perhaps the most significant new car since the Ford Model T was introduced 100 years ago.' France's leading automotive website, *leblogauto.com*, voted the Tata Nano the Car of the Year for 2008! Ben Oliver of British car magazine *CAR* said: '. . . the Nano is a staggeringly important, clever, exciting new thing.'

Stéphane Meunier, the editorial director of *Motorpress France*, opined to the author by email on 10 March 2008: 'For me, the Nano is less of an alternative amongst automobiles: it is more of an ambassador for India, an ambassador that announces the new India of IT, steel, automobile, of the fact that Jaguar and Land Rover are part of the same group. The Nano is the Indian UFO that has caught the fancy of the media.'

Veteran Indian journalist and writer Rahul Singh pointed out to this author (also by email, on 24 March 2008): 'I have a list of defining moments when India, instead of being considered a perpetual basket case, started being looked at positively by the developed world. One, our nuclear tests. Two, at the risk of sounding flippant, our successes on the stage of beauty, that is, Sushmita Sen and Aishwarya Rai. Three, our stunning achievements in the Information Technology area. But if you were to ask me if there was one single event that really defined India's entry into the consciousness of the people who matter internationally, it has to be the launch of Tata's Nano. Nothing else so captured the world's imagination.'

It was similar to a story that another prominent journalist, columnist and writer, Anil Dharker, related to the author on 23 September 2008: 'The French Riviera is full of "old villages". These are perfectly preserved remnants of older settlements adjoining the fashionable towns of Cannes, Nice and Antibes. For reasons unknown, most of them are uphill so there's a price to pay for doing something less touristy (Although truth be told, it's only tourists who go up to see these places).

'One morning we were trudging up a steep hill that was to take us to Eze. We heard the puttering of a lawn-mower type engine and turned around to see a motorized trolley laden with large bottles of Coke and other soft drinks. Guiding the trolley was a grizzled old Frenchman, who saw us, stopped and said, "You are from India, no? You know Tata company? I am going to buy a Nano. The first car I will ever have." His smile was as bright as the sun shining overhead. It struck me then that the Nano wasn't just an Indian phenomenon. It was an international one, a revolutionary idea that could have a world-wide impact in the years to come.'

In retrospect, Dharker, Singh, Meunier, Cumberford, all seem to have spoken too soon, as had many others. What went wrong despite the unprecedented acclaim and praise?

Of course with praise comes pride. Pride is, more often than not, followed by a mighty fall. With the unprecedented media coverage, the people involved just lost their perspective. Along with that, a pronounced amount of hubris had begun to set in amongst the engineers and the managers of Tata Motors as one triumph seemed to beget another.

What went wrong with the Nano?

On 17 July 2009, Ashok Raghunath Vichare of Mumbai became the very first owner of a Tata Nano. Ratan Tata, in a ceremony at a Tata dealer outlet in South Mumbai, Concorde Motors, handed over the keys to Nano number one to Vichare. For Vichare, it was not just his 'fifteen-minutes-of-fame' moment, but the moment when he became the proud owner of his very first car. Like Harpal Singh of the first Maruti 800 fame, Vichare was not just acquiring a slice of history, but was enacting it, a little over a quarter century after India's first proper go at a car-for-the-people rolled off the assembly lines in Gurgaon.

The best-laid plans, of mice and men, often go awry. Since Vichare received the keys to the very first Tata Nano, on 17 July 2009, less than 2,80,000 Nanos found buyers until the cessation of production ten years later, in April 2019. Incidentally, planned capacity at the Tata Motors plant was 2,50,000 Nanos *per* year!

At the car's launch, no one ever imagined that the Tata Nano would not succeed in its main market, in India. It is possible that the Nano will go down as one of the major marketing disasters of the twenty-first century. It is also possible that in some years' time the Nano will be seen as a cult car, a collectible.

In the meantime, the failure of the Tata Nano will be the subject of business school case studies and PhD theses, as students and experts delve deep into dissecting what went wrong.

It is very easy to explain what went wrong. For all those who dreamt of owning their first set of (four) wheels, to acquire an automobile, which had been labelled the 'world's cheapest' car, was the very last amongst aspirational bucket lists. Even if that car made a lot of sense, in terms of cost of ownership, running costs and practicality.

Of course, the label of the 'world's cheapest' was not the only shortcoming. Several other factors seem to have contributed to the Nano's lack of success. The first big problem was the series of fires when a couple of Nanos combusted thanks to the short circuit on the switch in the indicator stalk, which controlled the headlamps and the windscreen wipers. That, for sure, frightened away a whole lot of customers, even after the issue had been addressed, and there were no further incidents.

When certain very difficult price targets had been set—to build the car with the Rs 75,000 out-of-the-door price point, so as to meet the Rs 1 lakh customer price—some compromises in quality were bound to happen, and something was going to give eventually. Several Tata Motors engineers expressed this in confidence to the author. Apparently, meeting the price and component cost targets had become such an obsession within the company, that quality took a back seat.

Even if the wait for the car was getting a little too long, Tata still managed to have the car ready for launch by April 2009. Starting from 9 April 2009, Tata Motors began taking advance bookings for the Nano, and, by the time bookings had ended on 25 April 2009, as many as 2,06,703 cars had been booked by eager punters.

Some of the shortcomings were 'addressable', but Tata Motors was rather slow to address them. The so-called virtues of 'convenience and the practicality of the Nano' came in for early criticism, especially since the launch of the Maruti Alto 800. One of the very first shortcomings of the Nano, which was pointed out at the time of its launch, was the lack of a rear 'hatch' or boot opening. In fact, at the time of the launch, this aspect was acknowledged by Ratan Tata himself, and Tata spokespeople mentioned that they would be looking at a redesign. It took more than five years for this to be fixed.

The first test drives also showed that the car needed power steering, at least as an option for those who had already become used to power steering. It took five long years before power steering was offered. The interiors, too, had come up for criticism early on, and the improved dashboard arrived too late, by June 2013. At the car's launch, there was talk of several future developments: a diesel engine variant, an option of a five-speed gearbox, a CVT (continuously variable) type automatic transmission option and a more powerful three-cylinder engine version with disc brakes. Except for a robotized automatic, none of the others saw the light of day.

The time it took to develop the Nano—some six to seven years—is not that unimpressive when one considers that it was a clean-sheet back-to-basics design, which started from first principles. The time it took to iron out or address some of the obvious shortcomings, though, was just too long.

Even as late as 2012, when American TV show host Jay Leno ordered and was delivered a specially done up Nano in the USA, it may have been possible to ameliorate the situation. Yet Tata Motors never did get around to capitalizing on this image-rebuilding opportunity. Like Jay Leno, many enthusiasts and Westerners appreciate the Nano's back-to-basics approach, an attribute, which is lost on most Indian car buyers, especially the first-time buyers. Even as most Indian customers are attracted by bells and whistles, Europeans see a virtue in the Gandhian belief of 'less is more'.

Looking back, looking ahead . . .

As much as the unveiling of the Tata Nano hoisted India and Tata Motors on to the world map, the failure of the Nano also marked a turning point in the growing maturity of the Indian population. The limited success of two of the Nano-inspired products, the Hyundai Eon and the Renault Kwid, confirmed the prognosis: the most affordable is not necessarily the most popular.

Renault though, may argue that the Kwid is a success story. Unveiled in May 2015, the Renault Kwid seemed to be a runaway success at the beginning, with sales topping 1,05,000 during 2016, and the car reaching seventh place amongst the Indian bestsellers in certain months. By June 2019, more than 3,00,000 of the Kwids had been sold in India, a rate which was significantly better than that of the Nano. Yet, the figures were far from the market leaders, the Maruti Alto 800, the Swift and the Dzire, all of which were selling close to 20,000 units each, every month.

Renault insists that the Kwid is an excellent example of 'make in India', which it is, even if the sales figures have never been quite what the French giant would have liked them to be. What the Kwid proves, though, is that international efforts at designing and developing a product are much better than chauvinistic national projects. A car for India, by people who are strictly Indians, is not necessarily the best recipe for the best product. The Kwid was designed by a predominantly Indian team, which was led by an experienced Frenchman Gérard Detourbet, who brought with him an international core team. This international team brought to the table their various experiences, expertise and best practices from across the globe.

The Kwid is a very international product—albeit with three different levels of safety standards in its design—which has seen success in Brazil, and is expected to succeed in its electric avatar in China, where it was launched in 2019, with Renault, Nissan and Venucia (a China-only Nissan sub-brand) branding.

At the end, the consumer does not care whether a car is all-Indian in concept and execution. In fact, it may have concerns if that is so. What they look for is the best, for the price. For the best, it would be much better to have the inputs of the best engineers and designers, whatever their nationality may be.

Over the years, as the Indian market has matured and the consumer has become much more demanding, the automotive industry has come a long way since the country became a sovereign independent nation. Against sales of 14,688 cars in 1950, Indians bought more than 5.17 million cars, SUVs, multi-utility vehicles and commercial vehicles in 2018—a growth of 350 times in less than seven decades.

This is just the beginning. As of 2019, just twenty-eight people in a thousand had a car in India, as compared to the developed countries' average of well over 400 cars per thousand inhabitants.[10] Maybe India will never get to that. For the sake of the environment, let us hope it does not. Yet, there is a long way to go in fulfilling the human desire for mobility, travel, freedom and (very importantly, in India) status. Thus, every Indian should have the right and the opportunity to experience the satisfaction of owning and using an automobile.

As one of the top five car manufacturing nations in the world, India already has a very important place amongst the leading motoring nations. The difference is that countries like China and South Korea do not have the automotive history and culture which India has. Moreover, that automotive history and culture is not just the cars which were imported, but all those that have been made in India.

India's own automotive history

Following the definition of FIVA—every vehicle, which is more than thirty years old, is considered a historic vehicle—cars such as the Hindustan Contessa, the Premier 118NEs, the Standard 2000s, even the early Maruti 800s, are all historic. Thus, the choice of historic vehicles in India today runs to not just thousands, but tens of thousands of automobiles of all shapes, sizes and colours, all of which have contributed to shaping the country, our history, our culture.

Thus, it is worth looking back and understanding how the industry evolved. For the first three decades of India's nascent car industry, it was mostly under governmental regulation, as India chose the planned economy route towards growth. Given the circumstances and the international environment then, it must have seemed the best choice, so that the most could be made of limited resources.

It was the choice which several other democratic nations made, too, countries like Japan and South Korea included. In Japan, though, the automobile industry was a priority sector, initially for commercial vehicles and two-wheelers, but soon thereafter, for cars too. For two-wheelers, governmental regulation was non-existent, and a free-for-all followed, with just four extremely strong manufacturers surviving— and dominating the world even today.

South Korea, too, followed a planned economy system. The first step in the automotive arena was providing the necessary protection, followed by a Japanese-style government-backed export-led growth, encouraging a select group of five carmakers. Most of these carmakers were part of the chaebol system of a conglomerate of many companies clustered around one family-owned parent company, not unlike the oligopolistic system that the Indian economy evolved into.

A more recent example is that of the Chinese auto industry, which emerged as the world's biggest a few years ago—another very good example of planned growth, with intensive state intervention.

Thus, a planned economy was not the problem of the fledgling Indian car industry. The problem was the very low priority that the car industry was accorded by the Indian government, and the planning which followed as a consequence of socialistic thinking, in the form of a Licence Raj, which, in turn, curtailed the industry's growth potential, whilst benefiting certain oligopolistic groups. This situation remained so for the best part of two decades after India's Independence.

True, there were several attempts at a rethink and several proposals and suggestions for a people's car, but it was only in the fourth Five-

Year Plan period that the car industry was accorded some importance and that too for essentially serving nepotistic ambitions, when Sanjay Gandhi received the licence to make his idea of a people's car.

As we know, India's first attempt at a 'car for the people, by the people and of the people' was a disaster. The second attempt at a 'people's car' for India, mainly came through thanks to filial reasons—that of Indira Gandhi's desire to rehabilitate her son Sanjay's reputation and 'legacy' even though it was couched in policy terms as an attempt at 'modernizing the automobile industry, effecting more economical use of scarce fuel and ensuring a higher production of vehicles'. The approach this time was, of course, more professional, the attitude more thorough, and misguided delusions of abilities did not have a role to play any more. The car, though, the Maruti 800 was, of course, for the people and by the (taxpaying) people of India, though it was not of the people of India.

However, with the Maruti 800, the scenario changed, and this little 800cc car finally became the engine of growth for the Indian automobile industry, some four decades after India's Independence.

Yet, even after the successful launch of the Maruti 800, the government's short-sightedness persisted, with blatant protectionism favouring Maruti Udyog and discouraging others from embarking on alternate people's car projects. It was the financial crisis of 1991, which changed all that. The government did a complete about-turn and opened up the Indian economy, with the automobile industry 'liberalized' fully for the first time. Not because the government thought that it made good economic sense for the nation, but because the International Monetary Fund (IMF), which was bailing India out of its foreign exchange crisis, insisted on a set of rather radical 'reforms'.

Thus, from a very controlled industry, the Indian car segment became the showpiece of an open economy with very limited restrictions, an almost laissez-faire regime, which translated to a spate of joint ventures between Indian carmakers or industrialists and multinational auto majors, and most of them, as cooperative ventures, failed eventually.

The one exception to these was the wholly owned subsidiary set up by Hyundai Motors, with more than 100 per cent commitment to the market reflected in terms of significant investments, extensive localization and in redesigning its first product to suit the Indian market preference. Hyundai not only quickly got to the second rank amongst the carmakers in India, but also started making money fairly early on.

Looking at the Indian auto industry, it would seem as if joint ventures in a free market economy do not work, at least not in India. (It will be interesting to see how they pan out in the long-term in China, where, until 2018, all the multinationals were into joint ventures. With the regulations changing in China, the situation will surely change.)

The other lesson is that designing, or at the least tailoring, a product for India is a very important ingredient for success—both the Tata Indica and the Hyundai Santro are good examples of this hypothesis.

The third lesson was that a car which had been successful in other markets, may not necessarily succeed in India, unless modified to Indian tastes and requirements, which was what was done to both the WagonR and the Zen Estilo. The Suzuki WagonR's Japanese success or the Renault/Dacia Logan's worldwide success did not translate to significant sales in India.

Of course, the most important lesson was the cascading effect that a reasonably priced people's car could have on the industry and the economy. Until the Maruti 800 came by, the Indian car market grew at a little more than the 'Hindu growth rate' (of 3.5 per cent or so for the Indian GDP), averaging 7 per cent between 1950 (when 14,688 cars were sold) and 1980 (with 30,989 cars sold that year). In the 1980s, with the Maruti 800 introduced midway through the decade, the growth rate spiralled upwards to 56 per cent per year with as many as 1,74,633 cars sold in 1990.

Into the 1990s, the growth rate of the car industry stabilized at 40 per cent per year, and then at a still impressive gallop of 34 per cent every year in the first decade of this millennium, to 7,00,925 cars sold in 2000 and over 2.37 million cars sold in 2010.

Driving these amazing growths were the 'millionaire' cars: the Maruti 800, the Hyundai Santro, the Tata Indica and the Maruti Alto, amongst others. It may be worth noting that the Maruti Van/Omni and the Mahindra Bolero have also been 'millionaire' vehicles.

Driving the popularity of most of these volume leaders was the governmental 'incentive' to encourage a section of the Indian automobile industry in the form of an excise differential. Introduced in 2006, this made the small cars (defined as cars less than 4 metres long and with engine capacities of less than 1200cc for petrol-fuelled cars and 1500cc for the diesel-fuelled) more attractive than the bigger ones. In the process, this resulted in a spurt in the demand for small cars, accompanied by the necessary industrial environment to make India a global manufacturing base for smaller cars, which, by 2012, represented over two-thirds of India's total car market.

Yet, as markets mature, they evolve to a level where the cheapest is not necessarily the bestselling. When the Maruti 800 came in, the Indian market was very young and more than eager to buy a cheap but cheerful car, which was significantly better in many ways than the existing offerings in the marketplace. As the range of models widened and the consumer matured, the cheapest was not necessarily the best option for many. The success of the Maruti Dzire and the Swift, both more expensive than the 800 Alto proves that the Indian car market has matured too, to a point where perceived value is a balance of functional utility, status and price, rather than price alone.

A maturity of the market though also means a tendency for bigger and bigger automobiles, which is not necessarily a trend that must be encouraged. Instead, it may be better to encourage the manufacturing of smaller cars, as they consume less fuel, are cleaner, and as cities get more and more congested, address the increasing issue of size and road encumbrance. So a telescopic taxation system with higher GST or cess penalizing vehicles that emit more: cleaner cars, whatever the technology that they use, ought to be taxed lower than cars emitting greater quantities of greenhouse gases. Thus, instead of providing and spending substantial money in supporting a technology—such as electric cars—the Government of India should encourage all technologies that reduce emissions and consumption of conventional fossil fuels.

For several decades now there has been an effort (by the automobile industry and Western society in general) as part of a global initiative to improve urban mobility in the form of small, space-efficient vehicles that are low in fuel consumption and emission and with limited road encumbrances, deemed more appropriate for in-city use.

With the concept of car sharing, the kind of automobiles in use is expected to change too. Thus, it is highly possible that some out-of-the-box designs could very well be the future of motoring for India's millions, and that the next 'millionaire' vehicle could very well be an automobile that is not quite a car but a quadricycle. These are vehicles, which are intrinsically four-wheeled motorcycles, which have the virtues of a two-wheeler (small size and limited road encumbrance, less fuel consumption and lesser pollution), yet the greater safety (almost), convenience and comfort of a car. The market potential for such vehicles is, therefore, tremendous and any move from a two- or three-wheeler to this segment is not only natural but also the next logical step.

In the Indian context, the idea of using the quadricycle segment as an entry point into the car industry could be revolutionary, specifically for motorcycle manufacturers such as Bajaj Auto, Hero MotoCorp and TVS Motor Company. So, will the future of the automobile be that of quadricycle-type vehicles, or short-butted saloons, or will a mini SUV rule India? Will Maruti and Hyundai continue to dominate or will Bajaj come by and mess up the pecking order altogether? Or, will there be another upstart, another agent of disruptive technology which may turn the order upside down?

Despite a history of over a century, the automobile industry—which time and again has been written off as a 'sunset' industry—has had some very strange twists and turns, ups and downs, ins and outs, as the rapid economic growth of emerging markets has changed the dynamics of this industry altogether. Amongst them, not only has India, as a market and as a culture, emerged, but is expected to play an important role way into this century.

5

A Love for Speed

At the advent of the automobile, very few saw it as a means of transport. For long-distance travel, there was the train, and for most of the wealthier people in Europe and America, the horse and carriage remained the most important reliable form of transport for travelling. In India and the rest of Asia, there were also bullock and camel carts, as well as elephants for transporting people and goods.

The automobile, in its infancy, was just a plaything, a device for sports, pleasure and entertainment. Also, very scary to many. Thus, there was a certain strong psychological resistance to the very early set of horseless carriages. They also aroused considerable disbelief as to their viability and endurance over long distances. The automobile was, above all, a sport, not a means of locomotion, and thus competition became one of its natural modes of expression, synonymous with modernity. Manufacturers wishing to prove the quality of their products and to test their technical innovations, as well as sportsmen adoring challenges, all willingly and enthusiastically participated in races and competitions to prove that these machines could be fast, reliable and exciting.

These races were not without danger, because there were victims, both amongst the competitors, as well as in the ranks of the spectators, watching these thunderous machines rolling by in a cacophony of mechanical clatter, smoke and explosions, the rush of the wind, teetering on narrow wheels, and the occasional one veering off into the crowd.

Automotive historians recognize the first automotive race to be the one organized by the French magazine *Le Petit Journal*, on 22 July 1894 from the city of Paris to Rouen, which is a distance of 137 km. There had been several documented instances of races organized for horseless carriages, but most had a couple of automobiles, at most a handful—all invariably steam-driven—participating. Whereas, on that balmy summer morning of 22 July, in the year 1894, the pioneers of the automobile industry—Panhard et Levassor, Peugeot, Serpollet, De Dion-Bouton, Benz and several other lesser-known ones—gathered together at Porte Maillot, in Paris. In total, twenty-one competitors took the start of the race, after qualifications eliminated most of the rest of the 106 entries originally registered.

Flag-off was at 8 a.m. A sizeable prize money of 5000 francs awaited the winner. The organizers warned that the winner would not automatically be the fastest. Other criteria such as manoeuvrability, the safety of the vehicle and the financial cost of transport would also be considerations. Conceived by one of the journalists working at *Le Petit Journal*, Pierre Giffard, who was convinced that the automobile was an invention of the future, one that would triumph over the horse and carriage, the Paris-Rouen race was designed to demonstrate his and his magazine's conviction to a sceptical public.

To make matters more difficult, the state of the roads was abominable. The wheels were shod with either steel or solid rubber (Michelin had yet not invented tyres), which barely dampened the shocks from the potholes and stones. Two of the cars gave up with broken axles. In the absence of a roof or windows, the driver and the passengers suffered dust from the roads, as well as the smoke and soot from the steam-driven vehicles.

Several cyclists followed the race to Rouen. In fact, these early cars were not any faster than many of the cyclists. A little after 2 p.m., the leading cars entered Vernon, in Normandy, some 70-odd km from Paris, to popular applause and excitement as women threw flowers at the competitors, and farmers offered fruits, and the competitors were forced to slow down. A pleasant surprise for the organizers was that the many horses on the road did not seem to be scared of the automobiles as the latter overtook them.

Despite taking a wrong turn, Count Jules Albert de Dion's car, a steam-driven De Dion-Bouton, a strange contraption of a four-wheeled tractor pulling a two-seater two-wheeled carriage, reached Rouen before the others, at 5.40 p.m., well over an hour before the cars were expected. The De Dion-Bouton covered the 170-odd km in six hours and forty-eight minutes, at an average speed of 19 kmph, and just five and ten minutes ahead of the two following Peugeots. A steam car had won over the petrol-engine ones.

Yet, that was not to be so. The jury of *Le Petit Journal* reminded everyone that speed was not the only criterion. After half an hour of deliberations, they decided to give the joint first prize to Albert Lemaître's Peugeot and the fourth-placed Panhard et Levassor, of Hippolyte Panhard. The second prize was awarded to a furious Count de Dion, as the jury found the concept impractical, for the driver had to have another person shovelling the coal.

The thousands of curious spectators at Rouen could not care less about the results, as they all crowded around the cars excitedly, many seeing one for the first time ever. Pierre Giffard, in an enthusiastic article titled 'Le concours de Petit Journal' (the competition of the Petit Journal), in *Le Petit Journal,* from 6 August 1894, wrote, 'The conclusion of all this is that in some years we will all have our mechanical vehicle to drive around and do our shopping, or our trips.'[1]

Even if Giffard's prediction took a few years—nay, decades—to materialize, the concept of competitive motorsport took off. The following years saw a proliferation of city-to-city races: Paris-Bordeaux on 11 and 12 June 1895, and Paris-Marseille-Paris from 24 November to 2 December 1896. In 1897, three major races took place: Marseille-Nice-La Turbie, Paris-Dieppe and Paris-Trouville.

With the races came accidents and casualties: Emile Levassor (of Panhard et Levassor fame), seriously injured during the Paris-Marseille-Paris race, died in early 1897. During the Paris-Dieppe race, the Marquis de Montaignac lost control of his vehicle whilst overtaking and fell into a ditch, dying three hours later. Many more accidents and deaths followed, yet that did not stop the races and the human desire to win whilst risking life and limb.

The first big races in the Grand Prix style were the Gordon Bennett Cup series, launched in 1900 for the carmakers (or the automobile club of the country), to test their performance. The regulations stipulated that all parts of the vehicle had to be made in the country of origin. In fact, the team represented the country, and not by manufacturer, unlike today. There was only one manufacturer per country and they had to be in specified colours: red for the Italians, blue for French, green for English, yellow for the Belgians and white for the Germans. It was Panhard et Levassor who won the first Gordon Bennett Cup for France, in 1901, Britain, with Napier, dominated in 1902, and Germany with Mercedes in 1903.

Indians get the competitive bug

It did not take very long for the motorsport bug to reach India. There has been speculation that the first competitive event in the realm of the automotive in India may have been in 1903, in Pune, though details are sketchy. Even if the very first automobile may have arrived elsewhere, it was the city of Calcutta which rapidly embraced the new-fangled toy for the rich, so much so that the first automotive association in India—the Automobile Association of Bengal—set the ball rolling for all the other automobile associations to follow. The Automobile Association of Bengal (AAB) also nudged the ball rolling for the very first bit of competitive activity early in the history of the automobile in India.

In the spring of 1904, the AAB organized a drive from Calcutta to Barrackpore, a small cantonment town used as a base for the military, just 40 km north of the capital of British India. Essentially, for like-minded gentlemen (and one lady), the eleven-car grid may not have sounded very impressive but it was eleven out of a total of sixty-odd cars registered in all of Bengal Presidency then, which of course made the turnout fairly significant.

It was not really a race, but more an amiable trundle to a distant suburb, with a debonair break for tea at the country house of Maharaja Bahadur Sir Jeetendro Mohun Tagore. For its time, though, it was quite a feat, considering the cars those days had to be hand-cranked, were hopelessly unreliable, had a ride that made sure that dentures fell out, and suffered a tyre puncture every other kilometre. The most powerful car developed a meagre 8.5bhp, but it was sport nonetheless as cars were not quite point-A to point-B transportation until then. It is quite possible that the Calcutta-Barrackpore run (or the Pune one before that) were the first 'motorsport' events in all of Asia.

It was an all-British event, even if the tea break was at the home of a native. Soon thereafter, Indians too began to participate in automotive events. By the end of the same year, 1904, India had its first important competitive event, with the Delhi-Bombay Reliability Trials. It was around September 1904 when The Motor Union of Western India (the regional automobile association then, based out of Bombay) announced the eight-day reliability trials.

The Maharaja Gaekwar of Baroda (Sayajirao Gaekwad III) was offering a splendid cup to the overall winner, and there were several other class prizes offered by the likes of the Raja of Kapurthala and others. Clearly, it was not a speed event, as the maximum speed throughout was restricted to 30mph (48 kmph). The result was only for amateurs, with each entry made by the owner of the car (disallowing factory entries). As many as thirty-three cars entered, and amongst them was Gordon Bennett Cup ace Selwyn F. Edge's giant Napier (Edge would later convince the Nizam of Hyderabad to purchase six Napiers through him). The Maharajas of Gwalior, Pudcottah and Nawanagar (Ranji) were amongst the participants, driving a De Dion-Bouton, a Gardner-Serpollet and a Lanchester, respectively.

The 883-mile (1421-km) run from Delhi to Bombay consisted of eight legs, with the flag-off on 26 December 1904. Cars participating included a whole host of French cars. The winner of the Gaekwar Cup for the most 'reliable' car though was a De Dietrich, a carmaker from the Alsace region, which at that point of time was German (though the de Dietrich family had been French for generations).

With the success of the Delhi-Bombay Reliability Trials, several more followed over the next few years, with the third one run on 2–5 February 1908, with the winner of the most powerful class, Class 5, a Rolls-Royce 40/50hp, a model that later came to be known as the Silver Ghost. It was from Bombay to Kolhapur and back, with the total length of the drive working out to 590 miles (950 km).

As many as twenty-five cars competed in these tough trials, as mentioned: 'This trial course presented many more difficulties than the Scottish one, owing to the intense heat of the climate and the terribly long and dangerous hills.'[2] In this trial, a trophy valued at Rs 1000 (which was a considerable sum of money then), was given away by the Maharaja of Cooch Behar.

Learning from the British, the concept of TT (tourist trophy) racing also came into India soon thereafter. It was a copy of the Isle of Man Tourist Trophy, a series of races (as the Gordon Bennett Eliminating Trial), which began in 1904 on the island between Great Britain and Ireland, as the Isle of Man did not have the same speed restrictions (of 20mph, or 32 kmph) as applicable in the United Kingdom. Though the first ones may have been on the Bhor Ghat between Mumbai and Pune, the *Brooklands Gazette* (which became the famous magazine *Motor Sport* soon after) claimed that the first road races held in western India—and the first Indian TT races—were on 8 March 1925, over a 51-mile (80-km) course between Thane and Lonavala.

Organized by the Bombay Motor Cycle and Car Club, an Indian named Palkiwala won the Senior class for motorcycles on an (American-made) Indian motorcycle. The Junior class for motorcycles was also won by an Indian, Ghandy, on an English Matchless. In the car category, in the class up to 3000cc, a Lancia won, the class up to 1600cc was won by an Alvis, and the class up to 1200cc was won by a really quick and much modified Austin Seven, raced by Ralph Ricardo, the Englishman who had been making cars in England, before developing the Morvi in India.

Noteworthy were the efforts of several Indians in the international motorsport scene. The Maharaja of Tikari, Gopal Saran Narain Singh, participated in the Alpine Trials, raced at the famous Brooklands circuit in England, as well as competing in France. In 1937, for the first time, an Indian named Shankar Vartak, from Pune, entered the by-now-legendary Isle of Man TT astride a Rudge multi-cylinder racing motorcycle. Unfamiliar with the track, and perhaps a bit intimidated by the tightness of the circuit, Vartak was too careful and too slow, so much so that he was considered a hindrance to the other much quicker riders. On the second lap, the clerk of the course black-flagged Vartak, and an Indian's first attempt at the Isle of Man TT ended ignominiously.

Efforts were made to send Vartak to the Isle of Man for the TT race once again, in 1939. With war clouds on the horizon, though, the plan was dropped. Into the late 1940s, it became too late for the ageing ace. In fact, with the Second World War and then the Independence of India and the turmoil that ensued, motorsport took a back seat.

Post-Independence, Indian motorsport was back once again. In 1949, a small advertisement in the 'personal' section of the *Statesman*,[3] the leading English-language newspaper in Calcutta, asked anyone interested in racing to turn up at Red Road on one Sunday afternoon. Red Road is one of Kolkata's well-known avenues, very much in the centre of the city, which is ruler-straight. Constructed as an airstrip during the Second World War for planes to land or take off in the eventuality that the Japanese Army advanced deeper into India, Red Road became a broad avenue after the War. It got the appellation Red Road, as during the summer months the Royal Poinciana trees lining the two sides of the road make it the reddest avenue in the world when in full blossom.

Racing in the city of joy

On that fateful Sunday, fifteen petrolheads turned up, and the Calcutta Motor Sports Club (CMSC) was born, with the wealthy enthusiast, the Maharaja of Burdwan, Uday Chand Mahtab, as a patron. At Red Road and in the central Maidan area of Calcutta, the drivers took part in trials to gauge ability, and finally, scratch races were organized, with races held every Sunday. In true tally-ho fashion, a hat was passed around for expenses, everything was done in a friendly, picnic atmosphere, and skills improved imperceptibly yet steadily.

Then, the CMSC finagled permission to use the Alipore Mint airfield, in the southern part of the city, and the heat was on. At the Alipore Mint airfield (which used to be a base for a couple of squadrons of Supermarine Spitfires during the Second World War), a track was marked out and people started turning out in droves, both in stock machinery and in specials—one-off cars knocked together from assorted parts, normally existing chassis-power train set-ups with lightweight bodyworks. Along with the cars came the spectators and hangers-on. Calcutta had its own Grand Prix, the first ever in India. For the record, Robbie Robertson won the first Calcutta Grand Prix in 1953. Tutu Imam driving a strangely modified Lagonda took the prize the next year. Eddie Isaacs—who raced an SS100 and which was with Jackie Shroff as of 2019—won in 1955 and again in 1957.

It was a cavalier exercise, though. People turned up in pretty much anything that they could knock together, oddities like a Land Rover-based single-seater and a contraption with a Jaguar engine in an Avon body, challenged serious racers, which included an Allard, a Lancia, MGs, Jaguars, a Bentley, a Lagonda, even Citroëns and Studebakers. Eventually, Calcutta had a serious racer in the form of a pre-War Alfa Romeo 8C 2300 Monza.

The cars were indeed interesting, some with fascinating histories. The Alfa Monza was far from new—chassis # 2311206 had been delivered new to Renato Balestrero in Genoa, Italy, way back in June 1933. Balestrero campaigned the car in several races and hill climbs and had to his credit one outright win at the Varese Campo dei Fiori hill climb. In 1934, the car recorded three sports car class wins at hill climbs in France, Germany and Austria. The car was also raced at the Monaco Grand Prix of 1934 but it failed to finish. In 1935, it had less success, other than a class win at the Kesselberg hill climb. The car was next sold to Giacomo de Rham, a Swiss living in Italy, in December 1935. Participating in the 1936 edition of the Mille Miglia, chassis # 2311206 finished a creditable seventh overall.

The car changed hands several times. By September 1937, the Alfa was in the ownership of Emilio Romano, who participated in the 1938 Mille Miglia, where it failed to finish. The body was then modified—'modernized' essentially—and the car raced at the Coppa di Natale on Christmas Day in 1938 at Asmara, the capital of Eritrea, which at that time was a part of Eastern Africa, and was under the occupation of fascist Italy. The car stayed there during the war years and was, at that point of time, owned by Mario Riccioni. The Monza was finally 'liberated' by British troops in 1942. A certain British Army officer, Lieutenant Marsden, picked up the car and brought it to India, when he was transferred to the subcontinent.

Marsden then sold it to a fellow officer, Jimmy Braid. It was then rumoured to have been acquired by a raja, who exchanged the Alfa for a Fiat 1100 (!) with American Howard Jackson. Though Jackson worked and lived in Jamshedpur, the car was garaged in Calcutta. Jackson was a regular on the Calcutta racing scene in an SS100 (probably the same one with Jackie Shroff). When he acquired the Alfa, though, the SS100 was disposed of to a fellow racer, in all likelihood, Eddie Isaac.

The other famous car in Calcutta was the Allard J2. Delivered new to Desmond Titterington in the United Kingdom on 1 September 1951, the Allard made its first public appearance on 19 April 1952 (after a running-in period), at the Mansbery hill climb in Northern Ireland, where it took two firsts, two seconds and fastest sports car climb of the day. Subsequently, the car participated in Phoenix Park, Dublin, and Dundrod in Northern Ireland. In two full seasons, this Allard managed fourteen podium finishes in twenty-four starts.

Even though just ninety-nine of these J2s were ever constructed, all between 1951 and 1953, the cars had done very well on the sports racing scene in the early 1950s. An outright win at Watkins Glen in the USA, a first-in-class at the 1950 Le Mans and at the Scottish Rest-and-be-Thankful race, outright wins at the Portuguese and Danish hill-climb championships, as well as being declared the fastest sports car at the Brighton Speed Trials and the fastest un-supercharged car at the Swiss Vue des Alps.

Titterington drove a Jaguar for Ecurie Ecosse several times, and then later on, a 300SLR for the Mercedes-Benz works team, which was made up of legends such as Stirling Moss, Juan Manuel Fangio, Peter Collins, John Cooper Fitch and Karl Kling at the Targa Florio, a legendary race in Sicily, Italy. Titterington eventually competed in Formula 1, too, in a Connaught in 1956 for one race.

The Allard, in the meantime, was sold to Jimmy Braid in summer 1954. Braid had the car shipped out to his home in Calcutta. On its arrival, the car was driven to the track to race immediately, as soon as it was unloaded from the ship. Braid then sold the car to the other Calcutta racer Allan Ramsay, who replaced his not-so-competitive Lancia with the Anglo-American hybrid.

Built mostly out of Ford parts, the Allard used a Mercury engine. On the straights at the Alipore track, the Allard was usually topping 160 kmph in top gear. Unsurprisingly, the Allard—with Ramsay at the wheel—held the lap record at the Alipore track with an average speed of 100.58 kmph during the late 1950s. Ramsay also went on to win the Calcutta Grand Prix in 1958 and in 1960 with the Allard. Later owned and raced by Peter Cowper, in the 1980s, the car was taken out of India, to the United Kingdom. Restored to its original glory, the Allard has been the subject of several articles in magazines such as *Classic & Sports Car*.[4]

The other Italian machinery starring in Calcutta during the 1950s was a dramatically modified Lancia—campaigned by Allan Ramsay before he switched to the Allard—which was based on the chassis of an Astura. Produced between 1931 and 1939, the Astura featured a narrow-angle V8.

Though the Astura was designed as a large, flagship product, and most Asturas which survive (including a very beautiful example in Mumbai) are mainly elegant and luxurious tourers and saloons, some were modified into racing specials. An overall tenth at the 1934 Mille Miglia, inspired the racing team of Carlo Pintacuda and Mario Nardilli to enter their modified Astura and win the 6000-km-long Giro Automobilistico d'Italia, ahead of an Alfa Romeo and another Astura that same year. On 8 July 1934, three Asturas participating in the 10 Hours of Spa, in Belgium, finished second, third and fourth, behind the race-winning Bugatti. Results like these must have inspired whoever it was, to subject an Astura to the metalworker's saw, and this very exciting Calcutta car emerged after such a surgery.

Legend says that the infamous British lady racer Fay Taylour (who was interned during the Second World War as a fascist sympathizer), came to India and drove the Lancia in a race in Calcutta. As did Jack Wilkes, a famed motorcycle rider from Calcutta (who is known to have raced in the 1952 edition of the Isle of Man TT, on a BSA, thirteen years after Shankar Vartak's failed attempt). The car was next campaigned by Allan Ramsay for some years. The latter, in turn, sold the Lancia in 1956, in all likelihood, when he acquired the Allard J2 from Jimmy Braid. The Lancia was then campaigned by Tutu Imam. At some point the Lancia's V8 blew up, and was therefore replaced by the 1.6-litre engine from a decrepit SS Jaguar 1 ½ Litre saloon.

No less fascinating were the 'home-grown' specials. Inspired by racing cars in Europe and elsewhere, the enthusiasts of Calcutta built a series of surprisingly quick one-off single-seaters, which were quite competitive despite the inexperience of their makers. One such special was the Ixion. Others were Rustam and Delilah.

As the cars got quicker, there was a problem, however, with the track. New constructions creeping up on the airfield meant that they had to use a smaller track each year, and finally they gave up on the Alipore Mint strip. The action then shifted back to Kanchrapara for a few years, and then to a dirt track in Barrackpore by the 1970s, and the grassroots feel of the early years returned.

The racing, though, got even stronger. Specials were getting serious, and some like Dickie Richards' Bijou, were indeed works of art, as was the gorgeous Cheetah, designed and made by Imperial Chemical Industries (ICI) boss, Mike Satow, and the dramatically low Q'marri.

Calcutta was not the only city with a racing passion—several other cities in India had caught the racing bug, too. Pune, Bombay and Bangalore followed with a very active motorsport scene during the 1950s and 1960s. The Pune-based Deccan Motor-Cycle Sports Club (DMCSC) started a series of motorcycle races at the Lohegaon airstrip, near Pune. AJS, BSA, CZ, Ariels, Jawas, Nortons, Royal Enfields and Velocettes competed in several classes: the 125, 250, 350 and 500cc. The idea of using an airstrip for racing acted as an incentive for the sport in Bombay and Bangalore too, with the use of Juhu and Yelahanka, respectively, with cars taking the upper hand in these cities. At Bombay's Juhu airstrip, Jaguar XK120s scrapped it out with cars like a Lancia Flaminia Zagato, a Mercedes-Benz 300SL roadster, a couple of Fiat Spiders and several MGs, as much as lesser machines went fender to fender in the other classes.

Yet, as cities like Calcutta, Bombay, Bangalore and Pune had situations which made them miss out a season or more of racing, as airstrips became unavailable, or the clubs had problems, the city of Madras did a terrific job of making the city India's Le Mans, a mecca for motorsport enthusiasts over the decades.

The very first race meet at Sholavaram, near Madras, was on 25 October 1953. By the 1970s, the racing action in India had shifted mainly to Sholavaram, away from Calcutta and the other cities of India. A converted airstrip just like many of the others, the Sholavaram racetrack was a classic T-shaped circuit of 2.2 km, with start and finish on the long straight at the top of the T.

Initially, the cars and motorcycles participating at the Sholavaram races were not as exotic as the ones at the Calcutta and Bombay races. Yet, as Sholavaram became more of a regular fixture, and as the races ceased taking place in Bombay and then Calcutta, most made Madras the one regular track that they would all participate in. Over the years, the most exotic and the quickest automobiles in India found themselves racing at Sholavaram's famous T-track. From Alfa Romeos to Formula 1 racing machines raced at Sholavaram, and with them came the stars of Indian racing: from the likes of the Maharajkumar of Gondal, to liquor baron and later Formula 1 team principal (as well as tax fugitive) Vijay Mallya.

If in the 1950s and 1960s, English, Scots, Australian and a couple of American names starred at Calcutta, Bombay and Bangalore, by the 1970s it was time for the Indians to come into the limelight. With the expatriates and the Anglo-Indians leaving—either heading back to

England or America or emigrating to newer pastures in Australia and New Zealand—more and more Indian names were to be seen amongst the racers. The Kumar brothers, Ravi and Rishi, Niaz Ali, Sajid Moujee, Shantanu Roychowdhury and Madhukar Birla were some of the newer stars in Calcutta. The one who was the best of the bunch, though, was Diwan Rahul 'Kinny' Lall.

Starting off in the soap box derby in Delhi, Kinny Lall (as he was popularly known) went across to Europe where he raced in Formula 3 and Formula 2 events, becoming the first Indian from the post-Independence era to seriously compete at top-level racing internationally. In 1968, Lall finished tenth at a race in Sweden, followed by a sixth place finish at a Formula 3 race in Finland. At the Swedish F2 race in Karlskoga, Lall finished ahead of future F1 Dutch legend Gijs van Lennep and Italian ace Giorgio Pianta, but immediately behind another future F1 legend, New Zealander Howden Ganley. It was a race where the pole position was taken by Swedish Ronnie Peterson, the future F1 vice-champion, twice. Coming back to India, Kinny Lall made the racing scene in Calcutta his own.

When women embraced racing

Calcutta, with its cosmopolitan and more liberal outlook, also had its share of very fast women racers. There was the young Minnie Dhingra, known as the 'Lady on the Lambretta', going handlebar to handlebar with the boys in their Ariels, BSAs, Hondas, Triumphs, Suzukis and Nortons. Then there was the young Leesa Lumsdaine, whose father raced a Bentley, whilst she competed in an SS II.

Most unforgettable, though, was the redoubtable Minnie Pan, one of Calcutta's many Chinese immigrants. She went bumper to bumper in her big and powerful Citroën 15-6 with the men in their specials. The Maharani of Cooch Behar also raced and even won a class at the Alipore track in the Q'marri 1000 Coupé.

Some of the diplomats who came in, as well as a couple of European business investors, also brought exotic sports cars, with which they went racing. That was how an Alfa Romeo Giulietta Zagato, which had finished sixth overall in the famous Targa Florio, found its way to Bombay. Subsequently raced by a Mrs Cassiandra at Yelahanka, the Alfa Zagato was also campaigned by the famous Italian enthusiast, Dr Cesare Rossi, who spent most of the later part of his life in Bombay after he had set up a bottling facility for the Italian Cinzano aperitif drink in India. Rossi seems to have raced the Alfa Zagato in Calcutta, as well as at Sholavaram, the racetrack at Madras.

A 'gentleman racer', Rossi raced the same cars he drove for his daily commutes. Amongst the cars that Rossi owned, one was a very rare Lancia Flaminia Zagato, from 1959. Not only was the Lancia raced regularly by Rossi, it is the car that still holds the record for the fastest time for the Mumbai to Pune run (driven by Rossi in 1964). However, in the late 1960s, when Rossi acquired a lightweight, and very potent, Ferrari 275 GTB/C, the Lancia found a new home with VCCB's Roni Khan.

Rossi's Ferrari, too, saw racing action. As did several other Italian machines such as Rossi's daily-use Alfa Romeo Giulia saloon, plus, another Alfa Romeo, a very rare 1900 Super Sprint coupé (with Carrozzeria Touring lightweight aluminium coachwork), even a large and unwieldy Maserati Indy, which was owned by the Maharajkumar of Gondal, Ghanadityasinhji Jadeja. In fact, in all likelihood, this Indy may be the only one (out of 367 4.7 Indys, from a grand total of 1102 made), which has ever been raced anywhere . . .

Ghanu's elder brother, Jyotendrasinhji Vikramsinhji, the Maharaja of Gondal, raced in a no less exotic and rare car, a Mercedes-Benz 300 SL Roadster. It seems that the 'maharaja', when visiting Germany in 1958 test drove a 300 SL Roadster, getting to easily touch 200 kmph on the autobahn. He was smitten, and so he ordered a Mercedes-Benz 300 SL Roadster. The car arrived in early 1959. A keen enthusiast, Jyotendrasinhji Vikramsinhji had no intention of keeping it as a boulevard cruiser. So he went racing in the 300 SL. By 1967 it had participated, and won, in more than fifteen races at Sholavaram, Bangalore and Pune. In 1967, he decided to give up his racing gloves, and the 300 SL Roadster was 'retired' for occasional use.

Ghanu also raced another rare car, a Jaguar XK150 3.8S, which was owned by the family. The 1960 XK150 is special in being an S version—a 252bhp derivative of the standard XK150—and just nineteen of these were ever built in right-hand-drive convertible form. How the car was acquired is a story in itself. The deal was made to buy the Jaguar XK 150S from the Maharaja of Dharampur, and the car was to be delivered by the morning of the practice session, a week before the race day, as it happened to be the eighteenth birthday of the maharajkumar. The car was given as a birthday gift to him from his father, the maharaja then, Vikramsingh. Ghanu did go on to win a race in the Jaguar, and his brother Jyotindrasingh, went on to win the other race in his Mercedes 300 SL Roadster.

Ghanu's next racer was even more special: a single-seater Formula 5000 racer, the Surtees TS11, from 1972. The only person to have won world championships on both two and four wheels, John Surtees also saw success as a racing car constructor once he retired from driving. In 1970, he created his own team, the Surtees Racing Organization and as a constructor made Formula 1, Formula 2 and Formula 5000 cars. In 1972, the Surtees Racing outfit developed the TS11, a Formula 5000 single-seater, which was based on the F1 TS9, and was a design that attempted to take forward the promise of the previous season's TS8 design. Two teams opted for the Surtees design and both saw considerable success, Gijs van Lennep (who had finished behind Kinny Lall in Sweden in 1968!) taking the UK series, and Sam Posey finishing second in the US series of the Formula 5000. The Gondal car is the one that Gijs van Lennep drove to win the UK championship, and is one of up to seven cars made.

In 1973, this car, car number 02, was campaigned by Clive Santo, and then in March 1974 the car was bought by Chris Oates and fitted with a 5.7-litre Chevy engine, and the car was used for sprint events during 1974–76. In January 1977, the car was bought by Mike Gue, who then sold it to Ghanu, who then went on to win the 'All India GP' at Sholavaram in 1978 and 1979, but retired with engine problems in 1980. Fitted with a new 5.7-litre engine from the United States, he won again in 1981 and won a preliminary race in 1982 despite the presence of Vijay Mallya's recently acquired Formula 1 car, an Ensign N177. The Surtees also won races in Calcutta and Bombay.

Mallya's Ensign N177 was the other extremely quick car, which blazed the tracks of Calcutta, Bombay and Sholavaram during the late 1970s and early 1980s. Acquired from Ensign's team owner Mo Nunn, Mallya bought two Ensigns (MN08 and 180B), with which he went on to win races in 1978 and 1979. Powered by the then ubiquitous Ford Cosworth DFV V8 engine, the Ensigns were campaigned by the likes of racing legends Clay Regazzoni, Jacky Ickx and Patrick Tambay.

Developing upwards of 470bhp, the Ensign may have been capable of a top speed of well over 250 km/h on the short straights of Sholavaram and the Barrackpore air force base circuit in the 1980s. The Ensign and the Surtees gave Indian enthusiasts the first taste of top-level speeds. Yet, the ones which had the crowds mesmerized in Sholavaram and Barrackpore were the bunch of riders who came from Europe, astride their lightning-fast Yamaha TZ350 racing motorcycles. These two-stroke buzz bombs, developing 60bhp from a 347cc twin-cylinder unit, had top speeds close to 290 km/h!

On the straights they were, in all likelihood, topping 270 km/h or more, as these 'balls of fire' screamed by, the riders tightly hunched, nay draped, over their compact machines, lapping the lesser machines and mortals, gladiators of a new age. The crowds, the thousands who thronged to Sholavaram and Barrackpore, lapped it all up. Sholavaram, in some years, was rumoured to have attracted as many as 70,000 ticket-paying spectators!

Surprisingly, though Indians had developed a passion for speed, the desire to break speed records seems to have been limited. The first recorded attempt at establishing a speed record was on 31 March 1953, when twenty-three-year-old Shankar Ramanan managed, at the Yelahanka airstrip, to get to an average speed of 114.64mph (184.49 km/h) for the 'flying quarter mile' and an average speed of 68.92mph (110.92 km/h) for the 'standing quarter mile' on a 1-litre Vincent Rapide. In a report in an automobile magazine from then, it was mentioned, 'It is a pity that motorcycle racing is confined to Calcutta and Bangalore.'⁵ For that matter, attempts at speed records too, seem to have been confined to just this one by Ramanan.

The art of rallying

What did catch on though was the sport of rallying. What may have triggered this passion for rallying could be the passing of the London-Sydney Marathon through India in 1968. Conceived in 1967, in a period of time when there was considerable despondency in Britain, the ambitious plan to run a rally of cars all the way from London to Sydney, in Australia, a distance of 16,694 km, caught the imagination of the people.

With prize money of £15,000 as an attraction, and the thought of driving across the Globe as a motivation, ninety-eight cars took the start in London, on 24 November 1968. Following a route that took the cars to Paris, then Turin, Belgrade, Istanbul, Sivas, Tehran, Kabul and then to Pakistan, the cars entered India on 1 December, exactly a week after flag-off.

With newspapers covering the progress of the cars on a daily basis, people in India were forewarned, and thousands lined up along the route as these cars thundered by, through Punjab, to Delhi, arriving at the wee hours of the morning of 1 December. After a few hours' rest in Delhi, the cars left once again, winding their way through Agra and Indore, with crowds cheering them on, reaching Bombay early morning of the 2 December.

A major part of the Indian spectators' excitement was that one of the cars was an Indian entry. Though car number 81, a Ford Lotus Cortina, driven by Dr Bomsi Wadia and his teammates, K. Tarmaster and Farokh Kaka, had 'dropped out' just before the Khyber Pass, the car was still following the rally, and flying the Indian 'flag'. The speeds that these cars were doing and the line-up that passed through—Ford Cortinas, Falcons, Fairmonts, BMC 1800s, several Volvos, Mercedes-Benzes, Saabs, Porsche 911s, BMWs, Citroëns, Vauxhalls, Moskvitchs, Simcas and Hillmans—was no less fascinating. Moreover, several of the drivers were already famous rally stars: Paddy Hopkirk, Rauno

Aatonen, Roger Clark, Simo Lampinen, Innes Ireland, Giancarlo Baghetti, Sobiesław Zasada, and others.

When the cars were shipped out of Bombay, on 5 December 1968, the Ford Lotus Cortina of Roger Clark and Ove Andersson was in the lead. In sixth place was the Hillman Hunter of eventual winner Andrew Cowan. The four days of short stages in Australia—from 14–18 December—though, changed the overall standings, with Cowan winning the marathon in his Hillman Hunter. Of the ninety-eight cars that took the start, fifty-six managed to make it to Sydney.

The London-Sydney Marathon really caught the imagination of all automotive enthusiasts in India, as well as created a new generation of car and motorsport fanatics. As marathon cross-country rallies became fashionable across the world, the United Nations underwrote the first Asian Highway Motor Rally, from April 1969, as a show of unity and peace in a part of the world which was being ravaged by the Vietnam War. Restricted to the south-east nations of Asia, from Vientiane (in Laos) to Singapore, 152 cars took the start, with 132 completing the run.

If the rest of the world could do it, India too could do it. So, in 1970, the Western India Automobile Association (WIAA), based out of Bombay, decided to organize a 7000-km-long All India Highway Motor Rally, based loosely on the Monte Carlo Rally. Completed over a week, it was part of the silver jubilee celebrations of India's Independence. Sanctioned by the Federation International Automobile (FIA), and backed by all motor sport clubs in India, the rally attracted 120 entries, with the run starting simultaneously from Madras, Calcutta, Delhi and Bombay, all heading towards Nagpur. This was the first time that big prize money was on offer.

With the success of the first trans-Asia rally, a second one was planned. The Second Asian Highway Motor Rally was going to go right through India; it would begin in Teheran, Iran on 7 November 1970, and end in Dacca (which was the capital of East Pakistan then) on 15 November, passing through Afghanistan, West Pakistan, India and Nepal.

Bombay-based motorsport enthusiasts Mohinder Lalwani and Nazir Hoosein wanted to participate. They roped in Suresh Naik as mechanic and convinced the late Ajaypat Singhania from the Raymond Group to come in as a sponsor. For a suitable car to compete with, they turned to bon vivant and fellow racing enthusiast Jehangir Nicholson for his recently imported Triumph Herald 13/60. As the rally was going to be a time-distance-speed (TSD) competition, speed was not an essential, so the car was modestly modified with a high-performance camshaft, a pair of twin-choke 40DCOE Weber carburettors and closer ratios for the gearbox.

Sixty-two cars from eight countries (India, Iran, Japan, Nepal, Pakistan, Singapore, Sweden and Thailand) took the start of the rally, which took drivers over one of the world's toughest routes, covering over 6800 kilometres. Sponsored by the UN Economic Commission for Asia and the Far East (ECAFE) to promote trade and tourism in Asia by publicizing improved road network across the continent, the rally was a bit of a disaster, as the crowds in India got too excited and started stoning the cars and aggressing the drivers.

Most of the run in India was reduced to a convoy of cars under police escort, with just forty-six cars eventually finishing the rally. Fortunately for Lalwani, Hoosein and Naik, they had managed to get into the lead early on (by the time they had reached Lahore), and before they had entered India. With the rest of the run becoming a procession, under police escort, the Indian trio of Lalwani, Hoosein and Naik was declared the winner! For the first time, an Indian team had won an international rally.

Into the 1970s, rallying became a very popular sport in India. Various clubs in different parts of India began organizing local two-to-three-day-long rallies, with special stages and transport sections. Indian cars, such as Premier Padminis and Hindustan Ambassadors were prepared for rally competitions, sporting safety items such as roll cages and special rally seats. The engines underwent modifications, with extra carburettors, shaved and re-profiled cylinder heads and the exhausts tuned into noisy, free-flow types for improved performance.

In the meantime, nine years after the great success of the London-Sydney Marathon, Australian advertising publicist Wylton Dickson decided to organize another such marathon, once a gain from London, with Sydney as the eventual destination, but this time shipping the cars from Chennai in India, to Malaysia, driving through Malaysia and Singapore, before shipping them once again to Australia. The total distance this time was 30,000 km, divided into thirty stages, with an average of a thousand kilometres every day, making this the longest car rally in history.

Sixty-nine cars took the start on 14 August 1977, in London, and Dr Bomsi Wadia was amongst them, in his good ole Ford Lotus Cortina. In all likelihood, Wadia's Cortina was the oldest car in the rally, as the rest were brand new, rally-prepared specials, some of which were official factory entries. Wadia's teammates this time around were rally veteran Adi Malgham and Suresh Naik, who had been part of the Double Barrel Team Alpha from the trans-Asian rally.

The winner of the first London-Sydney Marathon, Andrew Cowan was back, but this time behind the wheel of a Mercedes-Benz 280E. Several of the veterans of the first marathon were back too: Paddy Hopkirk, Giancarlo Baghetti and Sobiesław Zasada. Newer stars such as Australian Ross Dunkerton, French female rally star Marianne Hoepfner, Englishman Philip Young and German ace Joachim Warmbold were in the starting line-up.

Despite the length of the rally, as many as forty-seven cars made it to Sydney. Of the twenty-two that did not, Bomsi Wadia was, once again, one of them. Like the time before, Wadia made it to India, dropping out in Iran, in time to bring his car home to Bombay. The route to India was longer this time, as it meandered a bit, going east to Germany, coming back to Paris, then getting to Milan, then Yugoslavia, next Turkey, Iran, to Afghanistan, to Kabul, the North West Passage, into Pakistan over the Khyber Pass to Rawalpindi, Lahore, Jalandhar, and then to Delhi.

As the rallying ace Sobiesław Zasada was in the lead, his car, a Porsche 911 Carrera, was the first to be flagged off from Pakistan, and led the convoy all the way to Delhi. Though it has been more than four decades since Zasada and his navigator Wojciecj Schramm competed, ninety-year-old Zasada remembers clearly the run from the Pakistan border to Delhi. Relating his experience to Grzegorz Chmielewski in January 2020 (and translated by Aleksandra Kasztelewicz),[6] on behalf of this author, Zasada remembered, 'For the duration of the rally, other traffic was not allowed on the road. There was no way we could go astray because there were crowds of enthusiastic Indians standing along the road for almost the entire distance; they were no longer hundreds of thousands, but probably several millions!'

Zasada continued: 'We spent a few hours in the hotel in Delhi [it was probably the Hilton], and on 1 December, at 1.35 a.m., we set off on the competitive section to Bombay. The asphalt road was narrow, wavy. We were to arrive in Bombay on 1 December, at 18:00hrs, but we were much earlier.'

The passage of Zasada in his Porsche must have been the stuff of legends . . . The Polish rallying legend covered the 1400-odd kilometres through Jaipur, Ajmer, Udaipur, Ghodra, Baroda and thence to Bombay in less than twelve hours . . . averaging close to 120 kmph throughout, implying that there must have been moments when Zasada's Porsche may have been flying at 180–200 kmph! ('The top speed of the Porsche was about 230 kmph,' points out the rallying ace.)

Zasada was so quick, arriving at the time control in Bombay (near the Gateway of India), so well ahead of time, that the control set-up and the marshals were not there to note his arrival! 'We made up 4 hours 30 minutes on the route,' remembers Zasada, which implies that they were at the Gateway by 11.30 a.m. on 1 December.

After Bombay, the event curled south and east to Pune and Bangalore and then to Madras, with the cars ready to be shipped to Penang, in Malaysia. Until then Zasada was leading, but an accident in Australia caused considerable loss of time, with the Polish rally star finishing a sad thirteenth. Once again, the slower, but steadier Andrew Cowan (the marathon man) won London-Sydney, in a Mercedes, ahead of Tony Fowkes' Mercedes 280E, and the two Citroën CX2400s of Paddy Hopkirk and Claude Laurent.

Rallying in the Himalayas

With the second passage of the London-Sydney Marathon, the desire to host an international-class rallying event had become very strong. India had the terrain, the investments required to organize a rally was a fraction of that of Formula 1 or track racing, and the rallying world championship had grown to rival Formula 1 for popularity and driving skills. Whilst the likes of Jackie Stewart, Emerson Fittipaldi, James Hunt and Niki Lauda were the superstars of the world of Formula 1 racing, the names of Sandro Munari, Markku Alen, Bjorn Waldegard and Stig Blomqvist was as well known to enthusiasts following international motorsport. Moreover, the cars—the Lancia Stratos HF, the Fiat 131 Abarth and the Ford Escort RS 1800—seemed more realistic, more reachable, yet dreamlike in their shapes and abilities.

Inspired by the success and popularity of the London-Sydney Marathon, one of the winners of the Second Asian Highway Rally, Nazir Hoosein, founded the Himalayan Rally Association in 1978, with plans to develop a rally which could be a contender for a part of the World Rally Championship calendar. This was after Hoosein had met Bharat Bharadwaj, the chairman of the East African Safari Rally organization, when the latter was visiting Nazir Hoosein. Bharadwaj volunteered to help organize an international rally in India. With most of the championship rallies taking place in Europe and with just two in the African continent (Rallye Côte d'Ivoire and the gruelling East African Safari) and none in Asia, a world championship rally in India would be a logical option, to complete the calendar. Thus, was born the Himalayan Rally.

Hoosein and several of his enthusiast friends from Bombay, including Homi Commissariat, went across to Kenya to marshal at the rally there and understand the intricacies of the organizing of such an event. For the first Himalayan Rally, Bharadwaj and others from the East African Safari Rally team came across to help organize and operate the running of the event in India.

Billed as India's grand debut on the international motor rally circuit, the first Himalayan Rally attracted a glittering array of international stars, with Kenyan rally ace Joginder Singh topping the 'billings' as the one who had won the toughest rally in the world—the East African Safari—the maximum number of times (thrice) until then. Despite the build-up, the 'Flying Sikh', as Joginder Singh was nicknamed, could not make the start, which was on 18 October 1980, though he had arrived in Bombay with a Mercedes-Benz 450SLC.

Yet, the line-up was most impressive, with fellow Kenyan (of Indian origin) Shekhar Mehta, with three Safari Rally wins under his belt (he would go on to win a record five times eventually), coming in with an Opel Ascona 400. Other star starters to the rally included Wolfgang Stiller (in a Datsun 160J), Marianne Hoepfner (who had passed through India three years earlier for the London-Sydney) in a Toyota Celica, Peter Lippmann (Mercedes 450SLC), Philip Young in an old Morris Minor belonging to the Archbishop of Canterbury (!), as well as German rallying champion Achim Warmbold (Toyota Celica).

Even though the flag-off at Bombay's Brabourne Stadium was disappointing—barely 5000 of the 40,000 seats were occupied, and the unexplained absence of political and cinematic celebrities was glaringly obvious—there was tremendous countrywide interest generated for the rally. With a 5300-km run promised, from Bombay to Delhi and then onwards to the Himalayas, and back to Delhi, enthusiasts had the opportunity to spectate in various parts of the country.

What the organizers had not bargained for, though, was the unpredictability of the Indian political system. Despite the assurances of the Central government and the Prime Minister of India then, Indira Gandhi, opposition politician George Fernandes and his Lok Dal Party attacked the rally.[7] The threatened anti-rally demonstrations by Fernandes and his supporters disintegrated into ugly scenes of violence with rally participants getting stoned, and their cars damaged.

Ultimately, instead of the original 5333 km, the organizers were forced to reduce the rally route to less than 4000 km of which the final leg of 980 km saw the incredible sight of the cars travelling in convoys under heavy police escort. The ultimate irony lay in the fact that the cars barely traversed the treacherous Himalayan tracks, which the rally had been named after.

Shekhar Mehta was declared the winner of a rally that was hardly one, with French lady rallyist Marianne Hoepfner as runner-up. Third place went to German driver Wolfgang Stiller. The highest placed Indian was, interestingly, Dr Bomsi Wadia (with Suresh Naik once again as his co-driver), in a Toyota Celica, at thirteenth place. Fourteen of the top fifteen finishers were international drivers.

Even after Bharat Bharadwaj, the chairman of the Kenyan Safari explained that tourism was Kenya's number two industry, and that the Safari had 'largely been responsible for that' as it was covered by every major TV network and gave the rally and country enormous publicity, Fernandes remained adamant. Bharadwaj was quoted as saying: 'The Kenyan Safari costs around Rs 17 lakh each year, but recovers Rs 24 lakh from one single advertiser alone.'[8]

The damage, though, had been done. Despite the profound apologies, as well as the assurances, of the Prime Minister of India, Indira Gandhi at the prize distribution ceremony in Delhi on 23 October 1980 that next year it would be 'roses, roses, roses all the way',[9] most of the top rally stars chose to stay away from then on.

With just thirteen of the fifty-nine starting cars surviving the week of dust, rain, snow and rocks—including some hurled by anti-rally demonstrators—the top prize went to Ramesh Khoda of Kenya, driving a 1978 Datsun 160J, in the 1981 edition of the Himalayan Rally (8–14 November 1981). Once again a few cars were stoned during the flat stages of the 3780-km route by political activists protesting that the rally was an energy-wasting 'rich man's sport' irrelevant to India.

The years 1983–85 were another Kenyan winfest, with Jayant Shah, in a Nissan 240 RS, dominating these three editions of the Himalayan Rally, though in the last one he had quite a fight on his hands, fending off eventual runners-up Aussie Ross Dunkerton (Subaru) and German ace Flory Roothaert (also in a Nissan 240 RS).

For the years 1987 and 1988, Japanese rising star Kenjiro Shinozuka, in a Mitsubishi Starion in '87 and a Galant the next year, dominated. Dunkerton played 'second fiddle' to Shinozuka in '87, with Roothaert doing the same the next year. With the win at the Himalayan in '88, Shinozuka went on to win the Asia-Pacific Rally Championship that year, and would later make his name leading Paris-Dakar several times, before winning it in 1997.

With the disaster of the early years, Nazir Hoosein's dream of making the Himalayan Rally a part of the World Rally Championship never materialized. Instead, it became a part of the Asia-Pacific Rally Championship from 1986.

Less than two years later though, in 1988, India finally had its first world championship event in motorsport: the Indian round of the Rodil Trophy Stadium Motocross World Championship. What the car world could not achieve, the bike world managed, when the Jawaharlal Nehru Stadium in Pune played host to the first round of the world championship for stadium motocross (versus the traditional motocross on dirt tracks, and also known as supercross) on 17 January 1988.

A rugged and spectacular event featuring fast and tough motorcycles battling it out on a specially created dirt track within the confines of a stadium, supercross racing brought on a new motorsport lexicon such as whoop-de-doos, berms, camel jumps, table tops, kidney belts, and so on. The Pune event was the inaugural round of the 250cc championship, and an estimated 17,000 spectators enjoyed several hours of dirt, dusts, thrills and spills.

With the 8-metre-high 'table top' sending riders flying up in the air, soaring dramatically at 10 to 12 metres in the air, the crowd enjoyed every minute of the spectacle. While the stuntman-ship was breath taking, winning was also a matter of steely survival, as Sweden's Bo Hoegeberg (just twenty-two years old), riding a white Yamaha YZ250, won the first round of the Rodil Trophy, defeating the favourite, Jim 'Gentleman' Holley (just twenty) of the USA, as well as the defending champion, Lief Niklasson of Sweden. The second place was snatched by American Willy Musgrave on a red Honda CR250, while the crowd's favourite, Olivier Perrin, of France, made a spectacular recovery to finish third after falling off his canary yellow Suzuki RM250 at the start of the race. For the spectators, however, there was satisfaction in the fact that India's lone entry, seventeen-year-old Jagatweer Singh of Pune, completed the race and picked up the first Rodil Championship point for the country.

Supporting the main race were the 125cc and 250cc Indian Grand Prix races, which encouraged the local riders. With the Rodil Trophy race as the flagship event, India soon had a flourishing supercross/ motocross national championship, and more and more youngsters seemed to take to the sport. Yet, the very next year, 1989, was the last year the Rodil Trophy championship was held in India, dropping the curtain on India's only world championship motorsport happening, until India's first Formula 1 race on 30 October 2011.

In the meantime, circuit racing, specifically at Sholavaram, reigned supreme, as India had its spate of rallying championships and motocross racing. With the airstrip available every year since 1953 at Sholavaram, motor racing in Chennai became a part of the city's fabric. On the first two weekends of the month of February every year, thousands of motor-racing fans would bus, ride or drive their way to the track at Sholavaram, packing into makeshift bamboo stands with up to anywhere between 40,000 and 70,000 spectators, all gathered together for a weekend of speed, spills and thrills.

In the good years, entries across all the various categories of motorcycles and cars numbered over 800, and the state government would specifically ply buses, ferrying fans who travelled from all over India to and from the track. There was even a thriving black market for forged tickets!

There was no television those days and the only place enthusiasts could get their racing fix was at Sholavaram. It was just about the only place in India during the 1970s and 1980s, where every year aficionados could get to see exotic racing machines as well as rare sports cars blasting around a track, fender to fender. Suresh Kumar, in Calcutta managed to organize some racing at Barrackpore every other year, and even Nazir Hoosein managed a couple of years of racing at Juhu, in Bombay. But Sholavaram remained the one place where every year it would be possible to see the Surtees of Ghanu, the Formula 1 Ensign Vijay Mallya, or the Formula 2 Chevron B42 of Vicky Chandhok.

It was also a place where enthusiasts had the rare opportunity to see—and sometimes meet—India's many racing legends then. Mallya,

Ghanu, Chandhok, as well as Bullet Bose (Subhash Chandra Bose), Nazir Hoosein, Mohinder Lalwani, Kamlesh Patel, the Kumars from Calcutta, Niaz Ali, the Bhathena family, Rajesh Malhotra, and many others became household names, racing at Sholavaram.

Even if it was hobby racing in the raw, with temporary pits made of straw-roofed shelters, holes in the ground for toilets, and food stalls selling inexpensive street food, the amateurishness of it all made the racing that much more exciting.

For the sport to progress though, it needed a structured series, which provided the base for talented racing drivers to build a professional career. The Formula Maruti single-seaters designed by S. Karivardhan, provided the competitive springboard for the likes of India's first Formula 1 drivers, Narain Karthikeyan and Karun Chandhok. Honing their early skills in the series' basic single-seater cars, these two, as well as the others who followed, brought about a level of professionalism into Indian motorsport.

Madras Motor Sport Club, which organized the races at Sholavaram decided to invest in a purpose-built racetrack, believing that the move in 1990, to the all-new FIA Grade 2 Madras Motor Race Track at Irungattukottai, would be an important step forward for Indian motorsport. In terms of safety and the honing of skills, the new racetrack was a heaven-sent, but it robbed the sport of the lure, which drew tens of thousands of spectators to Sholavaram those two weekends every February.

Veteran Indu Chandhok believes that the fault with the new track was in its design. 'At Sholavaram, you could see the entire track from the grandstand. At Irungattukottai the most exciting part of the track cannot be seen from the stands. Also, the racing is much closer, with less overtaking, less spectacular.'

'We definitely lost that mystique part, or the crowd-pulling part of the sport,' adds his son, Vicky Chandhok, whilst explaining to the author. 'But what we gained is proper motorsport now. Drivers can make careers. We have to acknowledge the fact that the change was for the better ultimately. Yes, we lost spectators. But we gained a lot in the sport.'

For the third generation Karun Chandhok (Vicky's son, Indu's grandson), the track at Irungattukottai was what he grew up with, and was the one which gave him, and the likes of Narain Karthikeyan, the skills to make it into Formula 1 eventually. Thus, when in 2005, Narain Karthikeyan made his Formula 1 debut with the Jordan team, it marked the coming of age of Indian motorsport.

Five years later, with Karun Chandhok's drive for Hispania Racing for the 2010 Formula 1 season, India motorsport's importance in the international arena was cemented. This was confirmed further, with Chandhok's drive for Lotus in the next year's F1 season, followed by his most impressive debut at the 24 Hours of Le Mans, behind the wheel of an HPD ARX-03, becoming the first Indian to race at the legendary French race. Sharing the drive with seasoned veterans David Brabham and Peter Dumbreck, Chandhok and his team finished a very creditable sixth overall.

During the years 2013, 2014 and 2015, Chandhok raced the Nissan-engine French Orecas, which gave him a best overall fifth for the last year. Chandhok is now seen as a Le Mans regular, and he clearly loves racing there.

'When you're in the car at 2 a.m. . . . . you're just floating,' explains Chandhok. 'It's a surreal experience where you're behind the wheel, you're driving along. It feels like a video game sometimes. You've slept for a couple of hours, you're a bit tired and you're trying to drag the lap time out of it in the dark—it's hard. But, it's so rewarding to do good lap times in the night. I remember the stint in 2013 particularly as it was probably my best stint ever in a race car. It started to rain, it was wet at one part of the track. We put intermediate tyres on and I made a full lap back on the leaders. I was ten seconds a lap faster than them. It was so rewarding to drive a stint like that. And I think that's what makes Le Mans special.'

Chandhok's passion for racing reflects the Indian passion for motorsport. Not only are Indians crazy about motorsport, Indian television spectators contribute massively to the all-important viewership figures. Yet, India's own tryst with Formula 1 remained a short-lived tale. India's only purpose-built Formula 1 track hosted the Indian round of the Formula 1 world championship for just three short years: 2011, 2012 and 2013. And, none since 2013. What went wrong?

'The Buddh International Circuit was a very good track,' believes Karun Chandhok. 'The drivers all enjoyed it and the racing was good because the track layout promoted good wheel-to-wheel action. We had a good crowd in year one of 1,05,000 and then after that it settled at around 65,000.'

When asked by the author why that had happened, he continued, 'I guess in the first year there were a lot of people who wanted the novelty of being seen at an F1 event and once they had ticked that box, they weren't keen any more,' explains Chandhok. 'Even so, 65,000 is what they get at most cricket matches around the country and more than a lot of other races on the F1 calendar, so it was still a very decent number. The problem was that the government never got behind the race and therefore it was unrealistic to expect the Jaypee Group to keep pouring money into the project as they had already invested around $500 million over five years into it.'

The fact of the matter is that Formula 1 circuits are not sustainable without government backing, as the requirements for hosting the race have become prohibitively expensive, since Bernie Ecclestone ran the circus. Even after he has gone, it remains very expensive. The then Prime Minister Dr Manmohan Singh's justification that his ministry did not see Formula 1 as a sport which needed government largesse, is, arguably, very valid. At the same time, the argument that a Formula 1 circuit may have been more sustainable in a city which has a longer and greater culture of motorsport may be very valid too. A relevant automotive culture can go a long way in sustaining an important movement, whether it be preserving our automobiles, or our motor racing history.

6

Sports Cars and Convertibles

Henry Ford said, 'Auto racing began five minutes after the second car was built.' As we have already discussed, it did not take very long for racing to catch on, as the very early races in France announced the debut of the automobile as a device for sports. Neither did it take too long to develop cars which were sports cars, as compared to specific-purpose racing machines designed to compete. These sports cars were developed to serve the niche for automobiles, which enthusiasts mainly drove for pleasure, and less for practicality.

During the early years of the automobile, sports cars were essentially toned-down racing machines, cars which could be used for the daily commute during the week, yet raced during the weekend. That, perhaps, is the reason why they were very expensive, with prices close to the exorbitant racers themselves. Yet marques like Bugatti, Bentley, Ballot and Alfa Romeo built up their reputation—and good business cases in most instances—making exclusive, sporty and very attractive and desirable automobiles—cars, which caught the imagination of all automotive enthusiasts.

One such enthusiast was a young Indian studying in Paris, J.R.D. Tata, who needed a car to tootle around town, and what better than a lightweight and quick Bugatti Type 35A? Initially refused by his father, the scion of the Tata family, Ratanji Dadabhoy Tata, but surreptitiously encouraged by his French mother, Suzanne 'Sooni' née

Brière, J.R.D. did manage to get his dream car, the Bugatti, which he brought back to Bombay. He used it regularly, and raced occasionally, with considerable success.

Several other rich, and mostly young, Indian enthusiasts imported high-performance European sports cars too—Alfa Romeos, Bentleys, Lancias, even a Vauxhall Hurlingham, which was imported by Raja Prafulla Nath Tagore. They remained very rare though, as most of the wealthier Indians preferred big and luxurious limousines and tourers, with capacities to move many, including the mandatory attendants on the footboards.

By the late 1920s, early 1930s, though, a whole host of accessible sports cars, derived mostly from inexpensive popular cars, became very fashionable. The most famous of these was MG. Founded by William Morris in 1912 and headquartered in Oxford, WRM Motors Limited launched itself by making the 'Bull-Nose' Oxford model in 1913, followed by the formation of Morris Garages in 1913. After the end of the First World War, Morris turned to the British subsidiary of the French carmaker Hotchkiss & Cie for engines and gearboxes, and by 1925, Morris Motors Limited (what came of the liquidation of WRM Motors in 1919) had become England's number-one carmaker. By then, the offshoot of Morris, Morris Garages (in short MG), had started making and selling modified, sportier roadster versions of the Morris saloons, designed by Cecil Kimber, who had joined the company as the sales manager in 1921, rapidly graduating to the post of general manager, by March 1922.

By the late 1920s, Cecil Kimber's MG had become quite a success story, with over 400 of the Super Sports 14/28 roadsters finding buyers. The launch of the MG M Midget at the Olympia Motor Show of October 1928 cemented the reputation of MG as makers of affordable sports cars, as these 30bhp 847cc sportsters set the sales charts afire, with as many as 3235 of them sold over a three-year period. Several of them found their way to India.

Rarer were the even more exciting French Amilcars. Staying within the limit of a cyclecar, with a maximum dry weight of 350 kilograms and maximum engine size of 1100cc, to take advantage of lower annual car tax, the Amilcars were lightweight sportsters, which were quick and handled brilliantly. Fewer Amilcars came into India, but one of the more famous ones was the Amilcar raced regularly by J. Mehta in Bombay during the late 1920s.

The real surge for sports cars though was after the Second World War, when the very pretty and accessible MGs became quite popular, and dozens of the TCs, the TFs and the TDs were imported into India. Yet the idea of making a sports car did not quite catch on. Of course, there was the issue of needing a licence to manufacture a car, and the licences for making cars had been limited to the Small Three of the Indian automobile industry. None of these three though had the initiative, nor the desire, to develop one. With supply chasing demand, they did not need to think of developing any derivatives—whatever was made was sold, as there was a waiting list for these cars.

With the racing scene in Calcutta getting very competitive, the relatively more expensive imported sportsters, the MGs, the Rileys and the Singers, from the erstwhile colonial country, the United Kingdom, all sported pretty, but not particularly aerodynamic bodies from the pre-War era. Continental Europe, as well as the United Kingdom, had been developing and exhibiting very attractive and aerodynamic coach-built specials on plebeian Fiats, Simcas and Volkswagens. Inspired by these trends, several enthusiasts in India began looking at rebodying and reworking mundane saloons into pretty, little sportsters.

And then came the dreamers

Since the early 1950s, India has had several of these dreamers amongst the enthusiasts, who set about making their own little sports car. Ramachandra Arni, better known as Chandru Arni, was one of the first to make his own sportster. Having seen the very early races at the Alipore Mint airstrip in Calcutta, started by the Calcutta Motor Sports Club, Arni wanted to have his own car, one with which he could go fender-bashing with the regulars.

Arni came from a family of *jagirdars* (like zamindars, wealthy landed gentry), and apparently his father 'owned as many as 182 cars

over the years. I used to watch the motor races at the Alipore airstrip,'
explained Arni to this author on 14 March 2018, 'which was held by
the CMSC on weekends during the winters. I would go there in my
Morris Minor. I was so taken up by one Geoff Budd in a green 1950
Morgan Plus 4, that I wanted to make a special to race with him in that
class, which was the class for cars above 2000cc.'

The first step was to acquire a car, at the lowest possible price.
Chandru Arni approached his father's friend E.K. Srinivasan, who was
the managing director of Hercules Insurance. 'To my immense luck, the
deal went through on 6 June 1953. I got a "completely smashed" 1952
Vanguard for Rs 2500.'

Rs 2500 was not that small a sum of money, when a brand new Fiat
500C Topolino could be bought for Rs 5400. Next, he needed to find
the people to build the car. Through frequent inquiries at the race meets,
Arni came across marshal and track equipment officer of the CMSC,
Nick Carapiet, who advised him that his boss, an Englishman working
for Shalimar Tar, Robin Davies, could help. Arni made an appointment
with Davies at his factory. 'He came out of the factory wearing soiled
clothes in overalls,' remembers Arni, 'He appeared to be quite friendly
with the Indian technicians in the factory, which was a great sign.'

Robin Davies readily agreed to take up the task at Arni's cost, with
minimum labour overheads, which was to be provided by his garage.
As all the cars owned by the shipping company Turner Morrison
used to be serviced there, Arni felt confident that Davies was seriously
interested and that the labour costs would be correct. Arni also paid for
the material.

Davies was keen that his friend, Frenchman Henry Ribordy, assist
him in developing the car. Thus, with the association of Davies and
Ribordy, the car was eventually badged the ARD Special, after the
three names of Arni, Davies and Ribordy. 'Many of the foreigners
were under contract not to take part in risky sports and hence, as they
couldn't race themselves, they had a deep interest to see me do what
they had visualized for themselves,' explained Arni.

With the help of a specialist panel-beater, Arni designed the
shape, which, in all likelihood, may have been inspired by some of the

lightweight sportsters in Europe, showcased at motor shows in Turin and Paris. With a super smooth flowing all-enveloping body, tapered at the rear, the ARD Special looked a lot like the Fiat 1100C Spider, which had been constructed by Italian designer Pietro Frua, in 1946, to catch the attention of potential customers. The car had received very positive coverage in several Italian magazines,[1] during 1947. It was innovative enough to influence many of the little sportsters constructed in the Italian and French coachbuilding industry of the late 1940s, early 1950s.

Unlike Frua's Fiat one-off, the ARD had no doors and no glass— apparently for safety. The chassis was shortened, cross-braced for strength, and the steering column lowered. As the Vanguard's rear axle was carried over, the rearward weight bias remained, and Arni explained that this did affect the driving, especially while coming out of the chicane, with a tendency to swing the rear out into a pronounced oversteer. Arni, though, learnt to control that. There were also round hollow openings in the front. These were positioned so that, when racing, they acted as ducts to cool the brakes. When not racing, sealed headlamps were put in, so that Arni could enjoy his evening jaunts and partake in Calcutta's famous nightlife then, at Firpo's, Princess, Golden Slipper and the 300 Club. Incidentally, the total cost of making the ARD special came up to Rs 6500, which was a significant sum then.

Around the same time that the ARD was getting ready, several other racing specials were also under construction in Calcutta. Unlike the ARD, these were purpose-built single-seaters, all fascinating 'home-grown' specials with a surprisingly quick turn of speed, developed specifically for the track.

One such special was the Ixion, an interesting-looking single-seater racer powered by a much-modified Ford V8 with Mercury crankshaft, Edelbrock high-compression aluminium heads and Allard racing camshafts, with the engine fed by two big Stromberg carburettors. All these goodies made the Ixion a quick beast, which went on to win at least a dozen-odd times at the Alipore track.

Another special was the Rustam, inspired, no doubt, by the mid-engine Coopers and Lotus of that period. Designed by B.P. Ferozeshah (and named after his son), the first Rustam used the power train from the Fiat 1100, but the gearbox broke soon enough. The Rustam II followed the Rustam, which featured a Vincent 998cc motorcycle engine and sequential gearbox (not from a Black Shadow, but in all likelihood, from a Black Knight). This tiny single-seater was a real giant-killer.

The Delilah was a special, which was, in all likelihood, inspired by the Maserati 250F. Unfortunately, it housed a more modest 1.5-litre Riley four-cylinder engine, which was fed by as many as four carburettors (one for each cylinder!), as well as featured a cross-flow high-compression cylinder head with hemispherical combustion chambers.

Cars that could be used on the street, and raced as well, were rarer. A few years after Arni's ARD Special, another Calcuttan, Dickie Richards, constructed a two-seater sportster, the Bijou. No relation to the model Bijou, made by Citroën in its UK factory from 1959 to 1964, Richards' Bijou (French for jewel) was a pretty little spider, with rounded profiles.

An even more convincing design though was the Cheetah, designed and made by ICI boss, Mike Satow. Looking a lot like some of the Ferraris made in the late 1950s, or the early 1960s, the Cheetah built up a reputation for being an excellent handler, and thus saw considerable success on the tracks. Advertised as a sports car available on sale, it seems that the Cheetah was under consideration for series production. Whether any homologation or certification procedures were ever executed, or whether Richards had ever applied for a licence to manufacture the Cheetah, is not known.

The most famous of the Calcutta one-offs though was the Q'marri. Moreover, the Q'marri had many lives. Born as the Tiger, an open-wheeled wasp-like racer with a receding rear, and built by Englishman Alan Morley, another of Calcutta's inveterate racers, the car was sold to Suresh Kumar (the brother of tennis star Naresh Kumar), when the former quit the city. Suresh and his sons Ravi and Rishi Kumar then decided to transform the Tiger into a much prettier, Mercedes-like sportster, renaming the car Q'marri (a stylized take on the family name Kumar, and Kumari).

Next, the Q'marri needed an exceptional driver. That was Kinny Lall, who debuted the Q'marri at the Alipore Mint airstrip in 1968, and who raced the car until the 1970 season. It was in 1971 that the Q'marri made its debut at Sholavaram, with Kinny Lall behind the wheel. Competing against the Amby-engine sportster was Cesare Rossi in his Ferrari 275 GTB/C, Ghanu in his Jaguar-based single-seater (the Godfather), and several other specials from across the country. The Q'marri led the supercars until the car's brakes failed.

The car, though, lived to fight again, when it was back the next year in the Formula India, created for 'home-grown' specials with Indian mechanicals. The regulations for the Formula Indian were changed, and so the Ambassador's engine was replaced by a Fiat's, but bored out to 1198cc. Fully ported, with double sprung valves, and an F3Y cam ground by Piper in England, the engine was mated to a Fiat gearbox. The Weber carburettors were swapped for Solexes. This year it was the turn of Niaz Ali to race with the Q'marri. They were one of the fastest of the weekend, finishing the Grand Prix race at third overall, beating Porsches and Triumphs in the process.

Through the 1970s and the early 1980s, the Q'marri continued to be raced at Alipore and then Barrackpore, driven mostly by the brothers Ravi or Rishi Kumar. The shape evolved over the years, and in its third iteration took on a Corvette-like nose. In its fourth evolution, it received a wrap-around windscreen, and by the fifth, the Q'marri had arrived at a more definitive profile.

Calcutta was not the only city trying its hand at designing sportsters. Chennai had several specials too, most of them developed to meet the Formula India norms. These were once again racing cars, with two seats, but were not 'equipped' to be driven on the streets, as lamps, windscreens and other conveniences were missing. Noteworthy was the Standard Herald-engine, Formula India developed by Chennai-based Vicky Chandhok in 1975, from a chassis designed by Mumbai's Adi Malgham, which was conceptualized to be a two-seater, one that could be roadworthy. Of an interesting wedge-like design, with decent ground clearance, Chandhok's 948cc Formula India, the Carex Special, could be fitted with lamps for street use.

The first of one-off two-seaters

Attempts at developing a practical and usable sports car though happened far away from the racing tracks. In 1959, two Pune-based enthusiasts, Cyrus Poonawalla of the Serum Institute of India, and garage-owner Don Patrick, decided to make their own sports car. They came up with the idea of modifying a Fiat 1100-103 (the one that is referred to as the 'dukkar' Fiat today), into the car of their dreams. Patrick designed a tubular space-frame chassis, within which the engine and the gearbox of the Fiat were shoehorned into, at the front, keeping the drive to the rear. A stylish convertible body was shaped out in aluminium, with a form inspired by the Jaguar D-Type, the car that had won the 24 Hours of Le Mans race in 1955, '56 and '57. In a two-tone red-and-silver, the Cydon (from Cyrus and Don) as it was called, was pretty, practical and most enjoyable to use, so much so that the car remains in the ownership of Poonawala even at the time of writing.

Sadly, the Cydon remained a one-off, as did the other pretty-looking one-off from Bangalore, the Jayaram GT. A. D. Jayaram was a motorsport enthusiast with a passion for engineering. In the late 1960s, he decided to design his own sports car. He toiled over it for some five years, in his garage, and by 1973, the Jayaram GT was ready to hit the road.

Though many have speculated that the purple two-door coupé looked like a Jaguar, one would hazard to say that the real source of inspiration for the design of the body was the Bizzarrini 5300 GT Strada, launched in 1965. The Jayaram GT had a very similar deep curved glass fastback rear, Perspex fairings over headlamps at the front, a flowing wedge-like snout, though the opening at the front was a Jaguar/English sports car oval.

The Jayaram GT was developed from the Jayaram Special, a Lotus Seven-like racing special. The Special used the engine from a Standard Herald, but highly modified, and had a claimed top speed of 145mph (or 233 kmph) in 'normal' tune, though this figure may be more plausible with the version which had the engine supercharged with a Rootes supercharger. It was very quick, no doubt, and it did beat the Jaguar E-Type of the Maharajkumar of Wadhwan, Chaitanyadev Sinhji.

The Herald engine from the Special was later used to power the Jayaram GT. The engine was bored out to 1060cc, and then later to 1360cc, and featured a racing cam, fully ported head, as well as Weber carburettors. The engine was mated to a four-speed gearbox with overdrive in each ratio, making it like a close-ratio gearbox, and a limited slip differential transmitted the power to the rear wheels. Though the car did get on to the road by 1973, A.D. Jayaram was never fully satisfied with it, thus he kept tinkering with it and developing it mechanically.

Underpinning the Jayaram GT was the shortened chassis of a Standard Herald, with the power train also taken from a Herald, even if modified extensively. Suspension was independent for both the front and the rear. The Herald's windscreen was retained, as was the basic structure of the doors, which was reskinned with an outer skin, which went with the 'surface language' of the rest of the body's design. Rear lamps were specifically made for the car. With its rolling sculpted look, the two-door coupé remains a very pretty design, even if it looks a bit disproportionate in its 'truncated' Bizzarrini look. The wheelbase of the Jayaram GT's 2.11 metres is as much as 34 cm shorter than the Bizzarrini's 2.45, and that reflects in a slightly distorted profile. With overall dimensions of a tad over 4 metres in length, a width of 1.6 metres and a height of just 1.15 metres, there is no denying the car's curvaceous sleekness.

As the chassis and the power train of the Standard Herald was utilized (even if shortened markedly) the legitimacy of registering the car for street legal use was retained, as per the rules followed in India those days. As long as the chassis and the engine were the same as the 'original' car's, the Jayaram GT, for the Indian authorities, was just another rebodied Standard Herald. This means that the Jayaram GT could have seen limited-series production. That, unfortunately, did not happen.

What did happen though was a series of Heralds, which received a coupé body style, branded as the Cobra. Gave Cursetjee, a fibreglass specialist from Bangalore, developed a design in which fibreglass panels replaced several of the body sections of the Standard Herald. The Herald, designed by Italian design legend Giovanni Michelotti, was like a jigsaw puzzle, with entire sections which could come off.

Interestingly enough, Madras-based Standard Motors advertised and offered a convertible version of the Standard Herald. Whether any were 'made' by the factory is not known, as all the convertible Heralds extant in India are either English-built ones, or ones, which have been converted from the Indian-assembled hardtop version to the convertible—by the relatively easy task of removing the top.

For his next ones, Cursetjee removed the front end, as well as the greenhouse of the car, the roof with the side and rear windows, and the boot. Taking these sections off, he replaced them with fastback coupé-style sections in fibreglass. Voila! The run-of-the-mill Herald metamorphosed into an attractive, sporty-looking, exotic coupé, with a front end looking a lot like one of the 'characters' from the cartoon movie *Cars,* albeit with a slightly shark-like snout.

Cursetjee made several of these coupé as turnkey projects. The client needed to take a Standard Herald to Cursetjee, and the latter transformed it into a sporty-looking coupé. He also supplied the kits, from which his distributors in other cities remade a few Heralds. Famous collector (the late) Ramesh Thakker, from Pune, re-bodied as many as five Heralds. As many as thirty-six of these Herald-based Cobra coupé were fabricated by Cursetjee and his distributors during the 1970s. The Cobra, at the end of the day, was essentially a kit car custom job, a bespoke modification made to a regular-series production car, with each piece personalized to address the requirements and specifications of the client.

Cursetjee carried over the refabricating of car bodies to the Premier Padmini/Fiat 1100, too, reworking the front ends as well as the rear roofline with flying buttresses, all in fibreglass. Replacing the metal boot, grille, headlamps, tail lamps and bumpers with new fibreglass panels, the looks of the Padminis/Fiat 1100s were updated to a more modern 1970s style. Some ten of these were made by Cursetjee.

The advent of the Maruti range of cars, most specifically the little 800 and the Gypsy, signalled a new era in automotive enthusiasm, specifically that of customizing cars to distinctive personal tastes. A journalist colleague of this author, Bob Rupani, was one of the earliest to transform one of the earliest Maruti Gypsys, into a colourful and extrovert expression of 'automotive art'.

Rupani soon had competition in Dilip Chhabria, a recent graduate of the Art Center College of Design, from Pasadena, California, who executed several cosmetic modifications to Maruti 800s and Gypsys. These though were all one-off custom jobs. In fact, the execution of customizing monocoque cars, whereby the body-as-chassis itself was being changed, was legally not sound (let alone structurally), and was against the rules and regulations of the CMVR (Central Motor Vehicles Rules). Though Chhabria rapidly built up an excellent reputation, he was operating in a somewhat 'grey zone' for many of his custom jobs.

Dreamin' sports cars

Around these years, in the later 1980s, Uganda-born enthusiast Jay Mehta started dreaming of making a sports car in India. Mehta had moved to India from Uganda with his family. He had had to leave Uganda when Idi Amin began an 'economic war' against the Asians and Europeans, who had been living in Uganda for generations.

Rallying and a passion for exciting automobiles brought Mehta and the author together, whereby the latter expressed his desire to build a sports car based on the chassis-mechanicals of the Sipani Dolphin, the fibreglass-bodied two-door, four-seater car, which was then being manufactured in Bangalore. Mehta confided to this author his strong desire, as well as plans, to make a replica of the Lancia Stratos HF in India.

Unveiled at the 1971 edition of the Turin auto show, the Lancia Stratos HF was a purpose-designed sports car, specially conceptualized to compete in the world rally championship. Designed by one of the greatest designers of all time, Marcello Gandini, the Stratos HF was startlingly beautiful. Stubby, short, muscular, yet chunky, the lower part of the body was a heavy-set wedge. All purposeful and aggressive, with a lighter turret-top greenhouse sitting on it, marked out by a striking glass section made up of the deep windscreen, which wrapped around to upswept side windows, creating a helmet-visor-like profile for the rally driver-gladiator, the Stratos looked all set to attack the competition. It did this so successfully—following the Lancia's first victory at the Firestone rally, in Spain, in April 1973, there was no looking back. On 15 May the same year, a Stratos finished second at the Targa Florio, and on 23 September, a Stratos won the Tour de France Auto, its first major victory. The Stratos took on fifteen events in 1974 and the year ended with two thirds, two seconds and ten victories!

From 1974 onwards the Lancia Stratos dominated the world of rallying and road racing, winning the World Rally Championship that year, and then again in '75 and in '76, and would have, in all likelihood, kept winning, if it wasn't 'forcibly retired' to make way for the other group company product (and another Gandini-designed car), the Fiat Abarth 131 Rally. Despite more powerful and much modern competition, the Stratos remained a force to be reckoned with until 1981, when it won the world championship Tour de Corse rally (in Corsica) for the last time.

Built by the coachbuilding arm of Stile Bertone, Carrozzeria Bertone, between 457 and 492 Stratos may have been produced (to meet homologation requirements), according to various sources, all in left-hand-drive form. Production stopped in April 1976, and cars remained unsold for years. Yet, with the resounding success of the Stratos in rallying, combined with its amazing design, the car became much sought after, into the later 1980s. So much so that several tiny garage operations began fabricating replicas of the Stratos, mostly in the United Kingdom.

The first time Jay Mehta saw the Lancia Stratos was at the 1977 edition of the East African Safari Rally. Even though he was there to root for his cousin, the legendary Shekhar Mehta (who was driving a Datsun 160J), Jay was completely spellbound, by the dramatically quick and astoundingly stunning Lancia Stratos HFs of Sandro Munari and Simo Lampinen. Since then, he wanted one.

What Jay did was to acquire two kits from the most famous of the British replica makers, Hawk Cars, who had, in a short time, built up a very fine reputation for making perfect replicas of the Stratos, identical not just in the shape, but also in the fabrication of the chassis and suspension components. The choice of power train though was left to the person ordering. Gerry Hawkridge, the owner of Hawks Cars, suggested either a Fiat/Lancia 2-litre engine (similar to what one of the early prototypes sported), or the Alfa Romeo V6 of 3 litres, but Jay chose to go with the 2-litre from General Motors then, a modern four-cylinder unit developing 148bhp, as he believed that availability would be easier. These were the engines powering the Vauxhall Cavalier then.

The two Hawk 'Stratos' kits with Fiat/Lancia engines, as well as two GM power units, were transported to the facilities of Gerry Johnstone, who had prepared Jay's rally cars, and who had an excellent reputation preparing and competing with Vauxhalls. We visited Johnstone's facilities in Shepreth, in the United Kingdom, in October 1990. We also visited the facilities of Gerry Hawkridge's Hawk Cars, at Tunbridge Wells, a tiny three-garage set-up where he assembled customer's cars. The body panels and the chassis parts were all bought-out, and were of very fine quality.

During the same visit, we also had a look at several British sports car manufacturers, such as Caterham, Ginetta, TVR and Westfield. What was most impressive was that all these famous specialists had relatively tiny, almost cottage industry scale of operations, working with a handful of highly skilled technicians in small, innocuous sheds and garages in the English countryside. A real revelation for all of us, we came away confident that small could not only be beautiful, but that a very beautiful sports car could easily be made in India, once its development was completed.

However, the completion of the two 'prototypes' at Gerry Johnstone Motorsport's facilities never happened. Managing the project long distance became difficult, and with Jay's move to Switzerland for a post-graduation programme, as well as the problems of funding during the economic slowdown of the early 1990s, this dream project faded away.

The idea though of developing sports cars from kit cars seemed to have come up elsewhere in India. Coimbatore-based Sundaram Karivardhan, who had designed several racing single-seaters and other sports cars during the 1980s and early 1990s, and who we have written about in the motorsport chapter, also made plans to make sports cars in India. Karivardhan signed up with one of the other British kit carmakers, Dax, who were making a range of replicas based on the Lotus Seven and the AC Cobra, as well as the Ford GT40. He imported one each of these kits and his plans were to make them in India too. Whether they were being planned as street legal, homologated and certified series production cars, or as one-off kits, or for the racing circuits only, is not known, as Karivardhan's plans were cut short when he was killed in an air crash on 24 August 1995.

Milind Thakker, who was running San Engineering & Locomotive Company, a highly respected private locomotive manufacturer in Bangalore, had a somewhat similar idea when he approached this author in 1992. 'What do you think is the potential of making kit cars in India,' he asked. 'The motor vehicle rules applicable do not allow for this, as it is necessary to certify and homologate every series production car which is for regular use on the street, at the Automobile Research Authority of India (ARAI), in Pune,' was the author's explanation to Thakker.

Unlike the United Kingdom, the USA and Europe, India did not have at that point of time the provision to allow for exceptions, which enabled single-vehicle-type approval, or approval for small-volume production runs, as was possible in these countries. The UK's Individual Vehicle Approval, as well as its National Small Series Type Approval (and which is similar to the European Community Small series Type Approval) have both been very important incentives to encourage a burgeoning 'parallel industry' of specialist manufacturers. Disappointingly enough, India has never encouraged this.

There was a possibility though—an opportunity.

Frustrated by the slow progress with Jay Mehta's Hawk 'Stratos' project, the author had gone ahead, on a purely private basis, with an inexpensive little dream project. The author had acquired a second-hand Sipani Dolphin car, in good mechanical nick (after the promise of acquiring Vijay Mallya's McDowell-sponsored rally Dolphin had fallen through), and had begun converting it into a two-seater sports convertible. Going through the proper process of designing the car, a coloured rendering was executed by the author. Following which, a fibreglass scale model, in 1:5 scale, was carved out in soft wet clay by master sculptor, Bhagwan Rampure.

Next, with Rampure's help, the author built a full-size scale model on the chassis and power train of the Dolphin (still using the traditional wet clay process!). The Dolphin featured a square-section perimeter frame chassis, on which sat the power train, which was a 848cc four-cylinder engine located longitudinally, mated to a four-speed gearbox, from which the drive went to a rear rigid axle. The fibreglass body of the car was bolted to the chassis. All that was needed was to unbolt the Dolphin's body, take it off, and plonk on the new two-seater convertible shell of the author's design (which was to be badged the Stenella, a beautiful genus of dolphins).

The process had yet to be completed, when Milind Thakker saw the work in progress. He proposed to acquire the project and commercialize it at his facilities at San Engineering & Locomotive, to which the author agreed. The yet unpainted but almost complete project was sent off to Bangalore for completion and commercialization.

As Thakker's engineers worked on solving several issues such as developing the windscreen and doors and the other many details, San went on to acquire the rights to the Dolphin from Sipani Automobiles' R.K. Sipani, who had stopped making that model and its derivatives (as he was shifting to the assembly of the Rover Montego for the Indian marketplace). San's first activities were to recommence the manufacturing of the power train of the Dolphin, exporting them back to the original manufacturer, Reliant Motor Company, for use in their popular three-wheeler, the Reliant Robin.

It is one thing to ready a prototype; it is another matter altogether to ready a car for series production. As San's engineers struggled with several issues, the age of the Dolphin (née Reliant Kitten from 1975) was also telling on the vehicle dynamics. Thus, by early 1996, Milind Thakker took a sensible decision: to develop a new car.

Going French

The task for this fell upon the Le Mans Design Group (LMDG), based out of the famous town of Le Mans, some 200 kilometres south-west of Paris. Constituted from essentially three separate legal entities, with facilities adjoining each other, LMDG was located at the Antarès-Technoparc technical centre, next to the famous Bugatti Circuit, which was an integral part of the larger circuit for the 24 Hours of Le Mans race.

LMDG was, at that point of time, made up of Automotive, a prototype-building shop owned and managed by long-time artisan Christophe Bihr; Godfroy Design, a design studio owned and run by ace French designer Gérard Godfroy; as well as Meca Systeme, an automotive engineering outfit founded by Philippe Beloou, the engineer who conceived the 1980 24 Hours of Le Mans-winning car, the Rondeau M379B. Beloou's curriculum vitae until then was most impressive, as he was not only a brilliant race engineer, he was also an equally gifted technician who could conceive practical engineering solutions for low-volume niche cars.

Designer Gérard Godfroy was the one who had designed the legendary Peugeot 205, when working at the design studio of the French giant. Later he moved to the French coachbuilding house of Heuliez, before conceiving his own sports car, the Godfroy Ventury, which evolved into the Venturi sports car, the high-quality and very competitive French response to Lotus and Porsche. Bihr had been associated with both Godfroy and Beloou in their many varied projects. Given their fascinating history in developing several low-volume niche products (Venturi, Hobbycar, Chatenet, Ponticelli and so on), LMDG was chosen over the more famous—but decidedly more expensive—Italian design houses.

As the chassis was going to be brand new, the brief for LMDG allowed for a slightly larger car than one based on the Dolphin, which had a rather short wheelbase of 2.15 metres. It was decided that the wheelbase would be increased by 10 centimetres, to 2.25 metres, but to keep overall length under 3.55 metres (as compared to the Dolphin's 3.33 metres), so that the kerb weight would remain within a reasonable figure, as the power train would remain the same as that of the Dolphin.

The engine though was going to be modernized extensively, changed from an overhead valve unit, to overhead camshafts, a sixteen-valve head and electronic fuel injection system. Tim Bishop, from the United Kingdom, who had a fine reputation for tuning and updating engines, promised that he could get maximum power to go up to around 55bhp, from the Dolphin's 38. Unfortunately, it was not possible to get an additional ratio into the compact gearbox, but then keeping the ratios close for better acceleration was considered more important, as top speed in the Indian context was seen as much less relevant those days.

The brief (provided in April 1996) also specified that the design should be so that three different models, serving three different niches, were to be developed from the same platform. A two-seater convertible, a 2+2-seater (two adults, plus two teenagers) hardtop coupé, and a four-seater leisure vehicle, something like the very popular Citroën Mehari, available both as a soft-top, as well as with a removable hardtop, were the three distinctive models envisaged.

The coupé version was chosen as the starting point as it would be the model, which would be 'halfway between' the two-seater and the leisure version. It was also the version which would, in being a two-door hardtop car, be the one with the greatest torsional rigidity amongst the three. Unlike most designers, Gérard Godfroy's design process was to work on a clay scale model directly, with a few rough sketches as reference, kneading the soft material into the shape he had visualized, scraping away the imperfections, chiselling out the window profiles, but giving material into the form of a very pretty automobile. With the overall profile defined—and dictated by the aforementioned packaging constraints—Godfroy came up with two different proposals, with the left half of the clay scale model showing one, the right half showing the other.

Alternating between the clay model and photographs taken of the model, from which lines were sketched and etched upon, refining the details and the overall form, the two definitive proposals—left and right sides—were converted into renderings, a process, which was just the opposite of what is usually followed.

The decision though as to which design to finalize had been left to the author; the two sets of renderings explaining the two different design proposals were shown to Milind Thakker and his father, Shubhash Thakker. The one with the beltline curving upwards to the C-pillar was the one preferred by the Thakkers, as well as the author, over the one with the window line sweeping down in a conventional arc (which was Godfroy's preferred design). This was by the summer of 1996, barely two months after the project had commenced in April 1996.

That was the easy part. Then began the more complicated set of activities. The finalized shape was finished to sheer perfection on the 1:5 scale model, with Gérard Godfroy aided by a master craftsman, one who had had years of clay modelling experience. Though the entire scale clay model had been converted into the definitive shape (the one with the upward-curving beltline), work was mainly on one side (the left side) of the scale model, in refining it over and over again, until a superbly finished side of the model had been arrived upon. This side was used for digitizing, the process by which the surface was scanned in three dimensions (3D).

In time, the mock-up was completed and then painted a glossy black, so that under neon lights it would be possible to see in the reflections of the (highly reflective) black colour coat, any flaws or distortions on the surface of the mock-up. Sure enough, a few minor imperfections did show up, which were sanded and/or filled in. The mock-up was repainted black once again, for another round of final inspections under the blaze of the neon lights, for a final sign-off.

After the final sign-off, the mock-up was repainted in white, with the windows at the side, the front and rear windscreen and the headlamp areas marked out in dark grey.

After the Thakkers had seen the mock-up, once they had given their sign-off for the design, the process of making 'female' moulds from the mock-up commenced. When Godfroy had readied the one-fifth scale model, he had taken moulds off it to test whether there were any 'undercuts,' any parts of the panel that may not come off when the fibreglass had set in, and the mould needed to be released. Thus, when Bihr and his team made the moulds off the mock-up the concerns regarding undercuts had been addressed. The process turned out to be routine and the moulds were ready by early 1997. Following which the first set of body panels were realized off the moulds, which in turn were bonded together to create the very first body shell of the coupé.

At the same time, the process of designing the interior had begun. Godfroy had made some quick renderings of the dashboard and the door trims and the interior layout by March 1997, when work began on the full-size mock-up of the interior. Taking the dimensions of the interior of the body shell, Christophe Bihr was able to define the width of the dashboard. After discussions with Milind Thakker, it was decided that the dashboard, the centre console and the door trim panels would be vacuum formed from either leather-finish-looking ABS or polypropylene.

As the mock-up of the dashboard proceeded, and work on the interior continued, with the seats in place, as well as the steering wheel and column (right-hand-drive, mind you), and other finer details, Philippe Beloou began work on drawing up the design of the chassis and suspension system. At the outset, the decision was taken that the suspension set-up would be state of the art. Beloou's design was for a double wishbone set-up for the front, and a three-link non-independent set-up with a dead axle, transverse rod and anti-roll bar, at the rear. The chassis though, was more of a sophisticated tubular steel, with a platform-plus-space-frame type of design, compensating for the rigidity lost by the absence of a roof for the convertible version. The convertible was to have a roll hoop at the A-pillar. For the coupé (and the leisure vehicle variant), there would be another roll hoop over the B-pillar.

Whilst the design development and engineering work was proceeding at Le Mans for what would be India's first home-made sports coupé and convertible, a race had begun to get other sports convertibles into the Indian marketplace. All of a sudden, there were at least three projects all aiming for the same untapped niche for aspirational sports cars.

Others in the race

The first announced, out-of-the-blue, was the Quantum, by a Chandigarh-based business house called Overseas Concept Auto Limited (OCAL), when they unveiled a 2+2-seater sports convertible at the Delhi International Motor Show in January 1997. OCAL had signed up with little-known British kit car manufacturer, Quantum Sports Cars. Unlike most of the British kit carmakers, who were mostly into making replicas, Quantum had on offer a modern 2+2-seater convertible sports car, using the front-wheel-drive mechanicals of the UK-made Ford Fiesta.

Powered by a 115bhp 1.8-litre Ford Zetec engine, and badged the OCAL Quantum, it was a handsome convertible, with occasional seats for two children aft of the two bucket seats for the driver and passenger. Featuring an unusual fibreglass monocoque, with integral steel sill members, and a steel subframe at the front, to carry the power train, most of the mechanical bits and pieces of the Quantum were Ford-sourced. Thus, it had the Fiesta's MacPherson struts at the front, as well as its solid rear axle with trailing arms. The steering system and the brakes too were from Ford. Dynamically sorted out, with 'handling that was quite good,' remembers automotive journalist Rajiv Mitra, who had tested the prototype car for *Auto India* magazine in the summer of 1997, adding to the author that, 'there was no pitching or rolling, nor any tendency to back-end wagging'.

A third sports-car project was also rapidly gaining traction. It was another one with which this author was associated. At the 1996 edition of the Mondial de l'Automobile, the Paris motor show, in October, one of the stands which really caught this author's fancy was that of specialist French carmaker de la Chapelle. On the stand were two of De La Chapelle's well-known Bugatti replicas, the Atalante and the

Type 55 Roadster. Plus, a brand new modern design, a mid-engine two-seater convertible, the De La Chapelle Roadster.

An all-new design by Lyon-based design studio, Barre Design (with the chassis designed by Jacques Hubert, ex-René Bonnet), the De La Chapelle Roadster was very attractive in a neo-retro way, with voluptuous lines, which curved over the wheels in an undulating slim-hipped form, a design that managed to look both sensuous, yet muscular. With the engine located amidships, aft of the two seats, but ahead of the rear axle line, the layout was very modern, and was very similar to that of the Porsche Boxster's, which went on sale soon after (by late 1996).

With the Roadster, Xavier de la Chapelle, the owner of carmaker DLC, had hopes of vaulting from being a tiny dozen-cars-a-year carmaker (of the Atalante and the Type 55) to the relatively bigger league of small-volume sports carmaker, such as Lotus, with numbers of, perhaps, a hundred cars every month, 1200 cars in the year. If the Peugeot-sourced 167bhp 2-litre engine car's pricing was right, at about 1,20,000 French francs, the volume could be attainable, reasoned de la Chapelle with the author. Just that with French labour costs that seemed very difficult. Would it be possible to get the Roadster made competitively in a low-labour-cost country like India?

A little over a month later, in late November 1996, ace rally tuner/preparer Shrikant Shah, called this author from Mumbai, explaining that he had the funding, and the mandate, for a sports-car project. 'Instead of developing a car from scratch, would you know of a recently developed car, which we could make in India?' Shah asked. The De La Chapelle looked like the best option.

In December 1996, a few days before Christmas, Shrikant Shah and his business partner, Nikesh Thakker (no relation to Milind Thakker, but the son of Mumbai-based property developer Vallabbhai Thakker), arrived in Paris, and we three took the high-speed train, the TGV, to Lyon, where Xavier de la Chapelle was based. Charles Wilhelm, a French lawyer who was an expert on both French and Indian law, joined us at Lyon. Shah and Thakker checked out the prototype Roadster, and had a short ride in it. Then, over the next three days of intense negotiations, a collaboration deal was concluded.

On 4 January 1997, the contract between Xavier de la Chapelle's company, DLC, and DLC-Sagitta, the company founded by Shah and Thakker, was signed and sealed. Plans were made to exhibit the prototype Roadster at the Indian Engineering Trade Fair (IETF) at the Pragati Maidan, in New Delhi, in late February 1997. The car was shipped out, reaching Delhi in time for the expo. De la Chapelle flew in, with a French model Livie Maschio in tow, and the beautiful Roadster went on display at the IETF.

The De La Chapelle Roadster was a sensation at Pragati Maidan. For many of the visitors it was the star of the show. Scores of enthusiasts wanted the car there and then, ready to plonk their money down for the full cost of the car as advance. Though costs and prices had yet to be figured out, people did not seem to balk at a suggested Rs 12 lakh price point, which was considerable then. At the end of the show, given the sheer enthusiasm and excitement caused by the car at a show which was not a true motor show, de la Chapelle, Shah, Thakker and everyone associated with the project was convinced that they had a winner at hand.

With the IETF over, the prototype was shipped back to France, whereas de la Chapelle, Shah and Thakker moved to Mumbai to discuss the finer details of the project, see the site of the factory near Pune, and finalize the next course of action. As the prototype Roadster was in a European-market left-hand-drive layout, it was decided that a second prototype would be made, in right-hand-drive form. It was also decided that the dashboard design, as well as the door trim panels, would be changed to a more modern and luxurious look, the pair of doors made a wee bit longer (as ingress-egress was seen as a bit too tight), and a few of the parts (wipers, door locks, and so on) converted into Indian componentry. Most of the rest of the car, in terms of the exterior design, and the mechanicals, with the entire drivetrain from the Peugeot 307, in its 135bhp 2-litre four-cylinder configuration, would remain the same as the first two prototype cars.

For the redesign of the interiors, the job went to Barré Design, who had designed the car in the first place. For making the second prototype with the changes to the doors and the componentry, as well as developing the right-hand-drive configuration, it was decided that Meca Systeme's Philippe Beloou (the same engineer who was developing the chassis of the San sports cars), would be entrusted with it. Beloou also decided to redesign the chassis from a tubular space frame to a more sophisticated pontoon-cum-space frame, with independent double wishbones at the front and a five-link, with coil-over-shock, at the rear. Working with him would be Christophe Bihr and his team at Automotive—once again, the same team assisting with the prototyping of the San sports cars.

With maximum power at 135bhp, and with the kerb weight at around 800 kg, the De La Chapelle Roadster, topped out at an estimated 210 kmph. With very sharp handling and excellent dynamics, the Roadster was a delight to drive, despite the rather high sound levels of the engine just aft of the driver and passenger's ears. The pontoon-space-frame chassis, though complicated in its engineering, was not too difficult to make, with the aid of jigs and fixtures, which were to be fabricated in France and then shipped across to India. The moulds of the body were to be prepared in France, too, and shipped across as well. Thus, making the Roadster did not look too complicated, as the entire drivetrain from Peugeot, the engine and the six-speed gearbox, as well as the half shafts from the 307 could be bought as a 'single unit' and installed in the chassis of the Roadster, thereby simplifying the assembly process markedly.

At a customer price north of Rs 10 lakh—more than twice the planned pricing of the San sports convertible—there seemed to be enough potential for both the sports cars to address two ends of the market, and coexist comfortably. Fate, though, deemed otherwise.

In May 1997, Nikesh's father Vallabbhai Thakker, died unexpectedly. After the initial sums put into the project, money became a problem, as there was a falling-out between Nikesh and his brothers. Though developmental work on the right-hand-drive prototype of the De La Chapelle Roadster continued and the car for the Indian marketplace was ready by early 1998, the funding for the rest of the project, for the factory, the toolings and the moulds, dried up, and despite many efforts on the part of Shrikant Shah, the project died a natural death.

Long before the end of the De La Chapelle project, the Quantum project quietly disappeared too. Though the factory to make the cars, at Rajpura, near Patiala (in Punjab), was set up, funding issues seem to have put paid to the dreams of the Chaudhary family at launching India's first home-made sports cars. The San project, though, would eventually have that honour.

Yet the steps were not easy. By the summer of 1997, when the De La Chapelle project's problems had begun, Philippe Beloou completed the design and the prototyping of the chassis of the San coupé. After mounting the body on to it, painting it a metallic Bordeaux, then fitting the interiors in a grey fabric and completing the dashboard and the instrumentation in a matt grey, the first running prototype of the San coupé was ready by July 1997.

Milind and Shubhash Thakker came across to have a look at the car, and we all took turns at the wheel. Despite the excitement of a job well done, it became obvious that the Reliant mechanicals—the 848cc engine and the four-speed gearbox—in spite of all the modifications made to it, just did not have enough grunt, nor refinement. The mechanicals seemed out of place in the sophisticated body draping it. There was also the issue of getting the ageing engine certified to meet ever-stringent emission regulations.

Perhaps a more modern power train would make for a better option. The option of finding a small longitudinally located engine seemed non-existent. All the modern power trains then were for front-wheel-drive cars, so the engines were all transverse, with the gearbox located at one end, driving the front wheels. Amongst them, one of the smaller units was the 1149cc four-cylinder unit made by Renault, the D4F, for their bestselling models, the Twingo and the Clio.

As this author knew Jean-Claude Pie, the commercial director of Renault Moteur, the division of Renault selling power trains and suchlike to others, the latter was approached. Within a couple of days,

San and Renault Moteur came to an understanding, and Renault agreed to supply the power train. As well as agreeing to assist in the homologation of the power train, Renault also agreed to support warranty claims, but only if the engine, in its entirety, remained stock, without any modifications.

Two Renault D4F power train units were sent across to LMDG in Le Mans in double quick time, and Beloou and his team went about reworking the chassis of the red coupé prototype, to reinstall the brand new power train. As the engine bay was designed to take on a longitudinal unit, it was a tight fit for the wider D4F engine, but Beloou and co. did manage to shoehorn the transverse power train unit in. However, the need to accommodate the front-wheel driveshafts, forced Beloou to locate the spring above the top wishbone, instead of between the wishbones. With the double wishbone suspension system retained at the front eventually, the San became one of the very few front-wheel-drive cars with such a sophisticated arrangement.

In the meanwhile, Godfroy worked with Christophe Bihr and his team in readying the two-seater convertible derivative, from the coupé. Retaining the front end of the coupé, the convertible shared panels up to the B-pillar, aft of which it was different, though the body language and surface treatment remained the same.

Once the convertible's bodywork was to be completed, it too was going to receive the second D4F unit, supplied by Renault. But with the changes in the chassis and the reworking of the front subframe and mounting points, the process was delayed, and the objective of getting the two cars ready, to be shipped out to Delhi, in time for the 1998 edition of the Auto Expo looked almost impossible.

The teams from Beloou's Meca Systeme and Bihr's Automotive, as well as Gérard Godfroy and his smaller team, all worked day and night, through Christmas 1997, on until 31 December . . . just in time for the two cars, the metallic red coupé and the convertible painted a mellow yellow, to be airlifted to Delhi. The cars arrived the day before the start of the fourth edition of India's premier motor show, the 1998 Auto Expo.

Badged in a hurry, the coupé was called the San Storm (playing on the San without a 'd'), and the convertible was given the moniker San Streak . . . which had many quipping on the car's 'topless, streaking abilities!' Not surprisingly, the branding was changed, to San Storm for the convertible and San Storm Coupé for the coupé.

The San Storms in

At the Auto Expo, the two Sans were a sensation, almost matching the excitement caused by India's first all-Indian car, the Tata Indica, and its two all-new rivals, the Daewoo Matiz and the Hyundai Santro. Thousands thronged to the San stand, admiring the two red and yellow cars, taking photographs and posing next to them, and wanting to order one right away. Amongst the many who came by and appreciated the design and the concept were the likes of Anand Mahindra and Mahindra & Mahindra CEO Alan Durante, as well as Ratan Tata.

San Motors believed that they could have the car ready for series production by late 1999. Yet, it took another two years, into 2001, before the first cars rolled out of the purpose-built factory that San had built in Goa. From working prototype to production was not an easy process.

Moreover, the production engineering of the car—transforming it from a nicely working prototype to an efficient and reliable series production car meeting all standards—was the most difficult.

At the beginning, many of the component makers came forward eagerly wishing to be associated with the project, despite the small volume. Thus, many went out of their way to specifically develop components, or adapt existing components to San's specifications. At the same time, several of the cosmetic details were reworked, for the worse, to ease production of the body. Philippe Beloou and Christophe Bihr travelled to Bangalore to address some of the developmental issues, yet the process took unusually long, and cost San considerable sums of money, as well as goodwill, especially in terms of opportunity lost.

The first three cars were produced by 31 March 2001, more than three years after the car had been unveiled. Fortunately, Milind

Thakker had the sense not to take advance bookings. The three-year delay though did dim enthusiasm for the car, even after several glowing reports in the Indian automobile magazines.

The May 2001 issue of *Autocar India* featured one of the earliest reviews of the San Storm. The report said: 'First comes the admiration, the walk around. "Wow, fantastic, really cute." Then slack-jawed disbelief; another quick look at the car. "Made in India? You can't be serious." That the Storm is a real eyeball magnet, a neck snapper, is indisputable. People—middle-aged accountants, giggling college girls, mamas with kiddies in tow—all seem drawn in by the car's cheeky and cute styling.'[2]

'The quicker you go the more the chassis comes alive,' said the *Autocar India* report. 'The handling is extremely balanced (despite a disproportionate amount of weight over the front wheels) with that killjoy understeer well under control. You soon realize that the limits of adhesion are much further away than you initially imagined as both your confidence and your cornering speeds begin to grow. Even when pushed hard the San manages to retain its composure, cornering flat with minimal body roll, the anti-roll bars at both ends doing their job effectively.'

The magazine, in the same report, also praised the ride quality of the car: 'We were pretty amazed with the ride quality of the San given its short wheelbase and short suspension travel. Despite being stiffly sprung, the ride is surprisingly pliant and you seldom get tossed around or jolted.'

In conclusion, *Autocar India* wrote in its test report: 'Look at the Storm as a sports car and you will be disappointed, maybe even embarrassed as cars like the Alto VX beat it off the line. This car is not about getting from point A to point B in the shortest possible time. Rather, it is a car that offers the unique pleasure of open-top motoring. The tidy handling also makes the Storm fun to drive and owners will enjoy the nimble responses of this roadster. This car is all about image and driving for driving's sake.'[3]

To get that image and driving right, automotive enthusiast and Alfa Romeo collector Behram Ardeshir came on board. Ardeshir and the author had also known each other for over a decade, and had had parallel discussions on a sports-car project with entrepreneur Yogesh Wadhwana. With his exposure to the way European specialist sports carmakers functioned, Ardeshir jumped in to try and sort out operational aspects at San Motors.

San Motors was initially set up as a division of San Engineering, and was eventually spun off, into an independent entity. When the Government of Goa came up with an attractive scheme to woo industries to set up shop in Goa by offering certain tax and other benefits, San Motors decided to set up its assembly operations in Goa. San built an 80,80,000-square-feet factory on a 2-acre plot in Verna, Goa.

Production picked up by 2002, and by 2003, the factory was in full swing. During 2005–07, production was at its peak, with more than 200 cars produced during these years, of which nearly half were exported, to several right-hand-drive markets such as Malta, Cyprus, Nepal, Bermuda, Bahamas and the United Kingdom.

With the changeover to the transverse Renault engine, there was no room left to install a left-hand-drive steering system. Yet the potential for the United Kingdom, with the possibility of low-volume-type approval, called SVA (Single Vehicle Approval), made it easy to certify the San Storms at a nominal cost, as well as GSP (Generalized System of Preferences) certification, which reduced the import duty to just 6.5 per cent.

Importer Anthony Waite, of Dream Machines, at Sussex, was the top dealer for TVR at that point of time, selling an average of 120 cars every year. Dream Machines was also an important dealer for Lotus and Marcos, and 'the San Storm fitted in perfectly well with what we were selling', explained Waite to the author. 'We needed a less expensive soft-top to complement our range of sports cars, and at an ex-showroom price of £5995, it was excellent value for money. The other coupé-cabriolets then were more than two times the price and the Mazda MX-5 was almost four times!'

'Yes there were a few quality niggles, but the car handled extremely well, and was really fun to drive as I covered a completely trouble-free tour of the country of over 20,000 miles,' pointed out Waite. 'We were planning to address the minor quality issues, and there was considerable enthusiasm for the car. We had signed up 32 dealerships across the UK, and even one in Jersey, and had imported the first batch of demonstrators, when the 2008 economic recession hit us.'

Before Dream Machines had been signed on, during autumn 2004, as part of a survey of the UK market, journalist Jon Pressnell was roped in to take Behram Ardeshir around the country, in a San Storm, on a whirlwind three-day trip to meet various dealers to decide upon the viability of entering the UK market.

San Storms also participated in the quarter-mile drag races in Mumbai, during 2004, 2005 and 2006. It was a non-works team, which was based in Bangalore, and which participated in the quarter-mile drag races around the country and won several of them. The cars were supported, from the outside, by San Motors. Some of them were even fitted with NOS (nitrous oxide system). At under 700 kilograms (with some weight shedding done), the power-to-rate ratio was competitively good.

By 2009 though, it was time to take stock. With impending changes in emission standards, and with the decision by Renault to stop making, and thus supplying, the D4F engine with Euro 3 specifications, San needed an altogether new engine to continue. PSA Peugeot Citroën was more than happy to supply their 120bhp 1.6-litre engine. One such power train was shoehorned into a San Storm, which turned out to be blisteringly—and dangerously—quick. It became obvious that it would be necessary to rethink the chassis and brakes, as well as the design of the car. And then re-homologate the entire car all over again. Which would mean an altogether new car, with considerable new investments.

With Shubhash Thakker falling ill, and with the other business complications cropping up, Milind Thakker took the decision to close down the car-making activities of San Motors, and instead concentrate on the highly profitable fibreglass part of the business. The last San Storm rolled out of the factory in December 2010, ending the saga of India's first sports convertible.

Enters the Avanti

It was around the same time too, when the saga of India's first 'supercar' began. Legendary 'customizer', Dilip Chhabria, decided to embark on his long-held dream of designing and making his own sports car, one which would have his name emblazoned on it. Since the 1980s, Dilip Chhabria had progressed to formalize his activities and founded DC Design, a design studio. DC Design's bread, butter and jam had essentially been from preparing luxurious and high-tech vanity vans and travelling caravans for the movie stars, which included the likes of Salman Khan, Amitabh Bachchan, Hrithik Roshan, Sanjay Dutt, Anil Kapoor, Vivek Oberoi, Mahesh Babu and Ram Charan, amongst others.

DC Design specialized in making yacht-style caravans with swaths of high-quality leather, specially imported wood, with massive high-definition television screens. On a relatively 'mass scale' level, DC Design had also been outfitting the interiors of some luxury buses as well as the Toyota Innova minivans. The Innova, badged as a DC Lounge had been in series production, and was on sale through DC Design showrooms across India. What Dilip Chhabria though was rightfully proud of was DC Design's many prototyping projects executed for the likes of automotive majors such as Aston Martin, BMW, Ford, Mahindra, Mercedes-Benz, Mitsubishi, Renault and Tata. Starting with the Aston Martin AMV 8 concept, which was prototyped at DC Design's Andheri facilities in late 2002, Chhabria's more modern Chinchwad (Pune) facilities—which he set up later—had prototyped many concepts and pre-production cars for several international majors.

Given such a background, Chhabria was confident that he could design the ultimate sports car. The starting point of Chhabria's project was the dimensions of Lamborghini's Aventador. As he wanted to design India's answer to Italy's most dramatic supercar, he decided to use the wheelbase and the width of the Aventador as the reference point for his concept: 4.7 metres and 2 metres, respectively. Having fixed the position of the four wheels, Dilip Chhabria drew out a sweeping, yet complicated and astounding shape, with a brutal nose, and a tapering, squashed rear, ending in an inverted, grimacing countenance. Aggressive and awesome at the same time, the DC Avanti (as it was badged), was a sensation at its unveiling at the eleventh edition of the New Delhi Auto Expo, in January 2012, with the launch of the car made even more newsworthy by the presence of Amitabh Bachchan as the chief guest.

Not unlike the story of the San Storm, it took Chhabria longer than he had thought it would to put the Avanti into production. The first street legal roadworthy cars rolled out of DC's Pune factory in the summer of 2015, some forty-odd months after the car had been unveiled. Instead of a 700bhp V12 located amidships (behind the driver and passenger, but ahead of the rear axle line) as in the case of the Rs 5 crore-plus Aventador, the 'Indian Lambo' featured a relatively modest 1998cc four-cylinder engine developing 248bhp, with a top speed restricted to an underwhelming 180 km/h.

A veritable sheep in wolf's clothing, Chhabria seemed to have hit the right spot with the Avanti, as, at its unveiling in Delhi in 2012, potential buyers lined up rapidly, clamouring for a piece of the action. Soon thereafter, DC Design took 500 advance deposits—at Rs 5 lakh each—for a total kitty of Rs 25 crore, for the first year of production, with internal accruals and debt funding the rest of the project cost.

'But the going has not been easy,' revealed Chhabria to the author in March 2015. The prototype featured a Ford engine, acquired through a Ford engine supplier, as Chhabria had been informed that sourcing a power train from the American carmaker's British arm would not be difficult. Ford though was not that forthcoming. Instead, Chhabria had to turn to the French giant Renault (sounds like a San-style déjà vu), with whom he had good relations, as DC Design had developed several Renault prototypes, starting with the Dacia Logan Steppe concept in 2006.

Renault, it seems, was happy to supply the 2.0-litre engine, which used to power the Renaultsport Megane RS, one of the world's fastest mid-sized cars then. Even though DC Design had been involved in the prototyping of top-level concepts and prototypes for many of the international majors, as well as having experience in the customizing of hundreds of cars for the Indian marketplace, developing a car grounds-up for series production was far from being a cakewalk.

Except for the power train from Renault, just about every component for the Avanti was proprietary—developed specifically for the Avanti—with DC Design having to pay for the tooling-up costs to the many vendors, in the process raising the cost of the project significantly.

When production began in 2015, Chhabria's priority was to clear the backlog of the first 500 clients who had been waiting since 2012, by the end of that year. Yet when DC Design went into production mode, the manufacturing of the space-framed, carbon fibre-bodied sports cars took much longer than anticipated, and DC could barely make ten cars every month.

On its launch, the DC Avanti received good press. 'Overall comfort levels are surprisingly good, all things considered,' said *Autocar India*'s Shapur Kotwal, in his road test of the car, adding, 'what I also found quite ample was ground clearance.' Kotwal also went on to say, 'It feels nicely poised around corners and the flat attitude of the chassis goes a long way in allowing the fundamentally strong "physics" of the mid-engine setup to work well.'

Though more than fifty cars had been delivered by 2016, DC stopped delivering for a while, as it became imperative to address the many issues of the highly flawed chassis design. Pune-based motorcycle tuning ace Ashraf Sheikh was called in to solve the issues, but he was not able to. Next, Shrikant Shah (he of the De La Chapelle project fame) was consulted, but he suggested a complete redesign of the chassis.

There was some optimism when BBC's *TopGear* magazine (the British edition) drove and reviewed the Avanti in Pune in February 2018. Writer Jack Rix found the design . . . err . . . interesting, saying that 'the rear looks like it's been parked up against a radiator, and melted, the front end has a fish-like quality and the ride height is more SUV than supercar (all will be explained), but for sheer traffic stopping drama it does the job, and then some'.

Rix also wrote that the 'build quality is seriously flimsy in places', and that 'the seats are covered in plasticky leather with more plasticky coloured stripes stitched on top'. Yet the overall impression was good:

'Honestly, I don't think we would have turned as many heads, or cause the rickshaws to swarm around us in such a crazed manner, if we were in a McLaren 720S. And when onlookers realized the car was one of their own, not some exotic import, smiles turned to cheers.'[4]

Yet, all the cheering may not save the Avanti. As the advance orders disappeared, and money had to be returned, the debts multiplied. In a 9 June 2019 dateline report[5] by Devesh Mishra in the web magazine *CarToq*, it was mentioned that 'a report by *Pune Mirror* says that Pune-based The Cosmos Cooperative Bank will auction the property of car design firm Dilip Chhabria (DC) Design for defaulting on a loan. According to the report, the company had defaults on a loan of Rs 37.20 crore.'

After delivering less than 150 cars by 2019, DC had ceased operations. At the time of writing, in late 2020, Dilip Chhabria was in serious legal problems. DC's problems, as well as those which San Motors faced, are not a reflection of Indians' desire to own a sports car, a desire, which has been evinced time and again, by the demand and popularity of Lamborghinis, Porsches, Ferraris and Maseratis, as well as Audi TTs, Mercedes-Benz SLCs and BMW Z4s.

Indians love sports cars as much as the European, American and Japanese aficionados. It's just that access to affordable ones has never been easy thanks to a homologation requirement, which is expensive and prohibitive for a small-scale manufacturer. Yet it would be important to remember that some of the most famous automotive marques began as cottage industry niche makers, such as Bentley, Bugatti, Ferrari, Jaguar, Lamborghini, Maserati, and several others. If they had to face the Indian certification system, they would never have made it. If the Indian government wishes to encourage innovative new carmakers, a system of small-volume-type approval will need to be available for start-ups.

7

Bikes and *Bikernis*

As we have discussed earlier, there were several attempts to make automobiles in India, and the assembling of cars began by 1928 with Graham-Paige at first, followed by General Motors and Ford. There does not seem to be any evidence of any assembly of two-wheelers, before India's Independence. The space and cost of transporting a motorcycle (most two-wheelers then were motorcycles) in kit form, versus a fully assembled one was similar, so it did not make any sense to assemble two-wheelers in India. What did happen though was that most of the motorcycles imported into India until the start of the Second World War were British. Not surprisingly so, as at that point of time, Great Britain was the greatest manufacturer of powered two-wheelers. (Yet a few American and German marques did make it into India as imports, specifically Harley-Davidson, the other great American brand Indian, and BMW.)

With over eighty different makes of motorcycles manufactured in the United Kingdom—from AJS to Whitwood—and the few non-Brit bikes imported into the country, the motorcycle consumers in India were spoiled for choice, including lightweight runabouts of around 100cc, to superbikes of 500cc and over. Except for a few sporting specials imported for competition, most of the motorcycles were for getting from point A to point B, and were bought mostly by those who could not afford to acquire a car.

Leading up to the Second World War, several of the bigger motorcycles for military use came to India. During the War itself, and soon thereafter, a large number of Harley-Davidsons (as well as a few Indians) were imported for the use of the US Armed Forces, based in India. The forces left, but they also left the motorcycles behind.

With India's Independence, and then the Industries (Development and Regulation) Act of 1951, followed by the increase in import duties from 1954, the mantra of self-sufficiency came into force for the two-wheeler segment of the automobile industry too. The decision by the government was to restrict the manufacturing of two-wheelers to a few too, not unlike what was happening with the carmakers and the manufacturers of commercial vehicles.

The first ones off the line

One of the first off the line was Automobile Products of India (API) Limited, from Bombay, as they had the facilities up and running for the assembly operation of cars from the English Rootes Group: assembling Hillman, Sunbeam, Singer and Humber models. Incorporated in 1949, by the Rootes Group, API's factory was at Bhandup, in Bombay. In 1955, the Rootes Group exited, after import duties shot up, selling API to the M.A. Chidambaram Group, from Madras. The same year, API received the licence to manufacture scooters, when it switched to the manufacturing of Lambretta scooters, in collaboration with Innocenti of Italy.

Known internationally since 1923, the Innocenti group had initially made their money from the scaffolding business, having patented the steel tubes, which, once assembled, made for lightweight, yet strong scaffoldings for the construction of buildings. Soon after the end of the Second World War, Ferdinando Innocenti decided to get into the manufacturing of scooters, as demand for inexpensive transport exploded in post-War Italy.

Not unlike Piaggio and the Vespa, scooter manufacturing would become Innocenti's main activity, with the first in-house designed scooter, the model A, launched in 1947. Made at a factory in Lambrate, near Milan, the place became the inspiration for the brand name of Lambretta. In no time, the Lambretta would become the icon for the Mods fashion movement in the UK of the 1960s.

The Lambretta A was a two-stroke, 123cc, single-cylinder, two-seater scooter, with its engine located amidships (unlike the Vespa's side-mounted engine), which was mated to a foot-operated, three-speed gearbox, with maximum speed at a useful 70 km/h. The tubular frame comprised a central portion with a square section surmounted by round tubes carrying the saddle, tank and 'trunk'. There was no rear suspension.

Following feedback, the model A evolved to the model B by 1948, which had a rear suspension, wider wheels, hand-operated rotating gears and a speedometer. The model C followed in 1950, and the model D by 1951, which was available in 125 and 150cc versions, with the latter capable of a top speed of 80 km/h.

In 1954, Innocenti launched the Lambretta 48, a single-seater, 48cc moped. Featuring a two-speed transmission and rear suspension (which was not so common for a moped those days), the Lambretta 48 was the first product that API began assembling in India from kits supplied by Innocenti. From 1955 to 1960, API was the only Indian company producing mopeds. The Lambretta 48 moped was later branded Laxmi (the Hindu goddess of light, wealth and happiness), and when Innocenti stopped the production of the 48, the licence to build the Laxmi went to Kirloskar Ghatge Patil Auto Ltd (KGP).

Around the same time when the assembly of the Lambretta 48 began, in 1955, API also began assembling the Lambretta D and LD, Li 150 Series I, and later the Series II scooters, in 125cc form. By 1958, the Lambretta LD was replaced by the Lambretta Li 150 Series I, which had a fixed headlight on the horn console and a thick chrome rim to ornament its speedometer, which was located on the handlebar. By 1959, the Series I was replaced by the Li 150 Series II, which had its headlamp, speedometer and a green pilot light on the handlebar. The mechanicals, with the 6.6bhp, 148cc air-cooled engine, mated to a four-speed gearbox, remained the same as its predecessor. This 150

Li Series II model became the mainstay of API's model range in India, with all the scooters sold with the Lambretta branding.

As API was also entering the two-wheeler business in Bombay, a Madras-based enterprise the Royal Cycle Importing Company imported the first set of Royal Enfield 350 Bullet bikes for the Indian defence forces with specifications as desired by the Armed Forces, mainly for use by dispatch riders. Not unlike the situation with most of the other Indian automobile manufacturers, the parts were initially supplied in 'knocked-down' form, to be assembled in India. The model chosen was the Royal Enfield Bullet from 1954, powered by a four-stroke 350cc single-cylinder engine.

The origins of Royal Enfield date back to the mid-nineteenth century, when George Townsend, born in 1815, established the manufacturing of sewing machines, in Hunt End, a hamlet less than 5 kilometres from Redditch, in Worcestershire, United Kingdom. With the death of George Townsend in 1879, his elder son George Jr took over. In November 1891, George Jr sold the company to Robert Walker Smith, a mechanical engineer at Rudge in Coventry, and Albert Eadie, sales manager at Perry & Co. in Birmingham. The new company, the Eadie Manufacturing Company Ltd, ran into financial difficulties, and the situation eased with the signing of a contract with the Royal Small Arms Factory, located in Enfield, a northern suburb of London, which manufactured the Lee-Enfield rifle to supply machined parts. To celebrate this life-saving contract, the new bicycle tyre manufacturer was renamed Enfield, and a company created to market bicycles, the Enfield Manufacturing Company Ltd.

In 1893, Eadie and Smith added Royal in front of Enfield, and the commercial brand of bicycles became Royal Enfield. This was the era when the famous slogan 'Made like a gun' was coined. On 1 July 1896, the board of directors decided to create the New Enfield Cycle Company to consolidate everything related to bicycles, and then, in 1897, it was consolidated to The Enfield Cycle Co Ltd.

In 1899, the Enfield Cycle Co. Ltd embarked on the production of motorized vehicles, making tricycles and quadricycles at first, all powered by French De Dion-Bouton single-cylinder engines. It was in 1901 when the first two-wheeled motorcycle was unveiled, a bicycle equipped with an air-cooled Minerva engine placed in front of the handlebars above the front wheel, though drive was to the rear wheel, using a long belt.

Over the years, the company went through several mutations, and many models of motorcycles were launched, but the most important to us, the Bullet, made its first appearance in 1932, when this moniker was given to three sports models with 248, 346 and 488cc single-cylinder-engine motorcycles. In 1938 an interesting 350 Bullet with all-aluminium engine came out with a new cylinder head with two separate rocker covers. This provision, which foreshadowed the post-War Bullet, allowed for larger valves and better performance.

During the Second World War, Royal Enfield provided motorcycles for military use, with approximately 55,000 units supplied. Amongst them was the very light 125cc two-stroke single-cylinder engine motorcycle, the legendary Flying Flea—these were parachuted into enemy territory, placed in a cradle made of steel tubes. After the Second World War, the mainstay of the brand was the 346cc single-cylinder Bullet G2, launched in 1948. The Bullet G2 went on to win many enduro victories, both for individuals (the Scottish, and the British expert) as well as a team in the ISDT (the international six-day tournament of national teams), with Johnny Brittain as the star rider.

Madras-based K.R. Sundaram's the Royal Cycle Importing Company, established in the 1930s, wase already importing Royal Enfields. 'They were located in Broadway, which was then the commercial hub of Madras,' remembers C.S. Ananth, a veteran automobile enthusiast and senior industry executive, reminiscing to the author. 'Royal Cycles were importing BSA, Royal Enfield, Hercules, Raleigh and Armstrong bicycles. They were also retailing these cycles.'

It was in the 1950s, after Independence, when Sundaram decided to get into manufacturing. With the help of R. Venkatraman, the then minister of industries, Sundaram managed to obtain a licence for manufacturing motorcycles. With the connection that they had importing Royal Enfields, Sundaram signed up with Royal Enfield, setting up a factory at Thiruvottiyur, near Madras. Thus Enfield India Ltd was born.

The robustness, reliability and the ease of maintenance of the Royal Enfield Bullet 350 were the reasons why the model was considered appropriate for the Indian Armed Forces. It also proved to be a product which made the most sense for the relatively difficult conditions in India.

The start though was slow: Enfield India (as the company was named, in India) assembled just 419 motorcycles in 1955. For that matter, API did hardly any better: just 533 two-wheelers (Lambretta 48 mopeds and Lambretta scooters) were assembled that year. The year after, in 1956, Enfield assembled 1022, whereas API managed as many as 4735. Until 1959, Enfield and API were the only two-wheeler assemblers in India, and between them, they managed to sell 7179 mopeds, scooters and motorcycles that year.

A certain 'socialistic' school of thought in the Indian polity then believed that for industrial growth and progress, priority ought to be for the segments of buses, commercial vehicles and two-wheelers rather than cars. The last was seen as a product accessible only to the very rich, senior government officials and corporate executives, whereas it was conjectured that India's emerging middle class would opt for two-wheelers. Yet the sales figures until 1959 did not seem to reflect that perception.

The figure for 1960, though, changed significantly, with as many as 16,878 two-wheelers made and sold, a growth of 135 per cent over one year! The contribution of Enfield India in this growth story was just short of four thousand, at 3998 Bullets sold. API led the surge with as many as 10,345 mopeds and scooters sold. The 2535 came from the new kid on the block: Bajaj Auto Limited. It was just the year earlier, in 1959, when the government of India approved Bajaj Auto's plans for the domestic manufacture of Piaggio's Vespa 150 GS VS 5 (GS for Gran Sport) scooter, and granted permission to produce 6000 units annually.

The wasp buzzes in

Bajaj Auto, the company founded by the highly influential Jamnalal Bajaj family and the Firodias (with whom they had already founded Bajaj Tempo Limited), signed up for a technical collaboration with the Italian industrial group Piaggio. This was because by the end of the the Second World War, it could not manufacture aircraft any more, as this activity was now prohibited to the Italians. Enrico Piaggio, the son of the group's founder, decided to develop a two-wheeler to create a new activity for his factory. The industrialist asked one of his aeronautical engineers to design a modern and economical mode of transport which could be used by men and women, and did not dirty one's clothes (unlike motorcycles). Engineer Corradino D'Ascanio came up with the Piaggio 'Vespa' (wasp in Italian) in 1946, six months after the Japanese Fuji Rabbit, which could be considered the first modern motor scooter.

The Vespa was distinctive in many ways. The wheels were attached laterally (with the suspension arm on one side only), just like aircraft landing gear, a legacy, no doubt, of the 'aeronautical' origin of the Vespa, and the fork was a simple arm, which facilitated easy changing of the tube and tyres. The engine was protected by the central hull and was mounted directly on the rear wheel, which freed a place for the feet at the front, and which in turn was protected by a fairing. The rear wing on the right side could be used as a storage box, or for the installation of a spare wheel.

By the time the Vespa was launched in India, it was already a resounding success in Italy. The initial batches had the option of two-tone shades, made available for about a year. The first year sales, in India, was not unimpressive either, and despite the impressive growth in the two-wheeler sector, the attraction for relatively inexpensive mobility remained far short of the desire to own a four-wheeled vehicle, what with sales of cars, buses and trucks in India topping 51,000 during 1960.

There was a need for the government to create more capacity for the segment to progress. Thus, the government gave two more licences, both for the manufacture of motorcycles, in quick succession: to a Bombay-based company called Ideal Jawa Private Limited, and another one to Escorts Limited, from New Delhi.

With the Czechoslovakian state-owned export house Motokov looking for Indian distribution possibilities of the Czech motorcycle brands CZ and Jawa, they managed to get Bombay-based importers of BMW and Sunbeam motorcycles, Ideal Motors, interested in representing these two brands for western India. Owned by brothers Rustom and Boman Irani (and in time joined by their nephew Farrokh Irani), Ideal Motors was ideally placed to import and sell these reliable and easily maintained two-stroke motorcycles from behind the Iron Curtain. The motorcycles came in semi knocked down form, and Ideal Motors assembled the CZs and the recently launched Jawa Perak for sale in Bombay, Poona and other parts of India.

Jawa becomes the ideal bike

When the government made clear that the import of kits had to come to an end, and that India needed to transit to making its own vehicles, the Iranis applied for a licence to make motorcycles in India. With their successful, ongoing relationship with the Czechs, the Iranis decided that the motorcycle that they would make would be one of the Jawa models.

Jawa was a Czechoslovak brand of motorcycles created in 1929. Its name comes from the merger of the workshop of Janeček (named after its founder, the engineer František Janeček) and the motorcycles made under licence from the German Wanderer. The production during the communist regime merged Jawa with that of the factory of Česká Zbrojovka (CZ) in Strakonice. Jawa was the top of the range, with CZ making the lighter single-cylinder motorcycles, Jawa, the twins.

František Janeček, a brilliant engineer, was running a small armament factory, but with business limitations, he decided to diversify into motorcycle manufacturing. In 1928, he signed up for a licence to make the 500cc Wanderer, of German origin. It was a commercial failure, but the following year, František Janeček created Jawa, a combination of JAneček and WAnderer. In 1932, the factory began making a small motorcycle, powered by a 175cc Villiers of English origin, which was a resounding success. The range then grew from 98cc two-strokes to 350cc four-stroke motorcycles. With Germany invading in 1939, the design development of a 250cc two-stroke was executed in secret. Sadly, Janeček never saw the motorcycle getting into production, as he died in 1941.

In 1948, all Czech industries were nationalized, as a part of the move into communist rule, and the sales networks of CZ and Jawa were merged. It is then that the production of the smaller engines became CZ's responsibility, and the larger 250cc upwards, to Jawa, which went into producing its two-stroke twin exhaust motorcycle, the Perak, and then the Kyvacka, which remained in production for a long time, mostly unchanged.

When it came to the decision regarding which model to focus upon in India, the Iranis zeroed in on the latest iteration of the Jawa 250 Kyvacka, the evolution known as the 353 Type 04, the most modern in the line-up then. With its distinctive rounded form, its simple and reliable two-stroke single-cylinder and two exhausts flowing out in perfect symmetry, the Jawa 250 was a stylish and practical motorcycle, one which slotted in perfectly well, in terms of price and positioning, below the bigger thumper, the Enfield Bullet.

The kick-starter, which was located to the left, doubled up as a gear lever, a unique feature for Indian buyers, who soon fell in love with the brand Jawa. The OE Zikov carburettor was concealed behind a panel. The handlebar was partly hidden too, within the headlamp nacelle. The ignition key was also unconventional and universal for all similar bikes, with no teeth or sutures, but in the form of a lollipop stick with a head and an indentation just above its base. Once inserted, and then turned, it would complete the electrical circuit to the kick-start. Many reportedly used a nail of a similar size to start the Jawa bikes, as a substitute for the original key. The appended accessory, of a handlebar lock, was important, to save the motorcycle from the easy temptations of stealing.

For the assembling of the motorcycles, and then phased manufacturing, the Iranis founded a new legal entity, Ideal Jawa Private Limited. Though the company was incorporated in Bombay, the manufacturing was located in Mysore—because, at that point of time, the government believed in distributing the manufacturing. As Bajaj Auto had been given the licence to make scooters in Poona, for Ideal Jawa it was not possible to make their two-wheeler in the same region.

Farrokh Irani's friendship with the Maharaja of Mysore then, Jayachamarajendra Wodeyar, helped. The latter offered land in Mysore instead. The first set of Indian-assembled Jawas rolled out in 1961, with close to four thousand (3954 to be exact) sold by the end of the year.

The year after, in 1962, was when the first set of thirty-eight motorcycles rolled out of the Escorts' factory, in Faridabad, near Delhi. Branded Rajdoot, the 173cc two-stroke motorcycle was another model sourced from behind the Iron Curtain. The Nanda family-owned Escorts Limited had turned to Polish motorcycle manufacturer KZWM Polmo-SHL, which was, at that point of time manufacturing the model M11.

Launched as recently as 1961, the SHL M11 was the successor to the 150cc M06T, from which it adapted the distinctive Earles fork front suspension—a swing-arm with two telescopic shock absorbers with hydraulic damping. The suspension travel was also increased, and the steering system was equipped with a friction shock absorber, all of which contributed to the excellent ride quality of the Rajdoots—reason enough why rural India, with its terrible road conditions, took to the motorcycle from Escorts.

In successive years, the numbers for the Rajdoots increased exponentially, and by the year 1965, Escorts produced and sold a tad over seven thousand motorcycles that year. Yet they were behind their motorcycle manufacturer rivals, Ideal Jawa and Enfield India. By then though, the situation was changing. It was more a case of 42,181 lucky buyers who found two-wheelers, as demand had started outstripping supply, and one had to book a vehicle well in advance and await delivery, which had started taking months, even years, and in some cases, a decade.

Transferring a new scooter to a second owner's name for the initial two years was illegal, yet this rule did not curb the thriving grey market. The government not only restricted licences to the chosen few, it also stipulated the maximum volume that the manufacturer could make. For instance, Bajaj Auto was licensed to manufacture up to 6000 scooters every year, a figure which they reached by the fourth year of production, in 1963, when they made 6148 units. The government then agreed to increase capacity to 8000 units per year. Bajaj produced 8339 in 1964, and then 8376 the next year.

Adding to the woes were price controls, approved by the government, for each of the vehicles on sale. The price controls remained in force for much more than a decade for each automobile, whereas the taxes, in the form of central excise, state excise and octroi, would keep going up (along with the taxes on alcohol and tobacco). This was necessary though, to keep in check the premium that the manufacturers could have mopped up, if there was no price control.

Rising demand

Seeing the spiralling demand for two-wheelers, the government decided to give three more licences, all for mopeds. One was to Pearl Scooters Limited, who tied up with Yamaha of Japan, launching the Pearl Yamaha moped in 1962, a model that remained in production for a decade. The Pearl Yamaha was fitted with a battery, and thus had a more effective horn (which has always been important in India!), as compared to most other two-wheelers of its time.

One more licence was given to Saund Zweirad Union (India) Private Limited, a Gwalior-based company, which went into the manufacturing of the Vicky moped, with technology licensed from the German Victoria, another cycling-motorcycling veteran constructor, which became a part of Zweirad Union. The Vicky was a stylish 48cc two-stroke machine, which had seen considerable success in Europe. Motorcycling enthusiast Dr Anjan Chatterjee remembers that an owner had once quipped to him, 'If a Vicky moped is fully submerged in water for quite a while and resurrected, it would fire back to life with a single kick-start!' (Saund Zweirad, later, also went on to make the Saund, a derivative of the Victoria/Vicky III, but in the frame and shape of a motorcycle.)

The third licence went to Mopeds India Limited. Incorporated in Coimbatore by K.L. Varadarajan, the manufacturing facilities were set up in Tirupati. For technical know-how, Mopeds India turned to French two-wheeler giant Motobécane. Founded in 1923 by Abel Bardin and Charles Benoît, Motobécane (slang for motorized bicycle in French) began by making light two-stroke motorcycles for several years, before it moved into the realm of heavier machines with the models called Confort, and later, Motoconfort. Soon Motobécane's range comprised 98–344cc two-stroke motorcycles, as well as 346–498cc four-stroke models. The latter featured Blackburne engines, and in the other models, Zürcher engine blocks were used. In the early 1930s, the heavier models of 498cc and 746cc used four-cylinder, four-stroke engines from JAP.

After 1945, in the post-War situation, Motobécane decided to focus on light two-stroke machines, and in 1949 unveiled the legendary Mobylette moped. Mopeds India chose to bring the 50cc Mobylette into India, branded as the Suvega. Launched in 1965, the Suvega had a relatively slow start, as it had to compete with the Vicky moped, the Pearl Yamaha and the Jawa Colt/Jet 50 (based on the Jawa Type 555 Pionyr), made by Ideal Jawa. The other three could comfortably seat two, and featured rear shock absorbers. Buyers had to add a rear seat to the Suvega, atop the rear mudguard, where it had a carrier rack. Later, in the early 1970s, Mopeds India launched a model with rear shock absorbers, as well as a factory-fitted rear seat.

Moreover, mopeds did not seem to find that much favour with the Indian consumer: as the market share of these tiddlers did not even represent 10 per cent of a grand total that had just topped 1 lakh sales (1,05,877 units) for the first time ever, in the year 1970. What most of the Indian two-wheeler consumers seemed to desperately want, though, was scooters, as between Bajaj, with 32,091, and API, with 25,335 units sold (which included some mopeds though), they had cornered more than half the total market. Also, the demand for two-wheelers had begun to outstrip the demand for all four-wheeled vehicles, with total sales in India in 1970 for cars, buses and commercial vehicles adding up to a tad over 76,000.

By the turn of the decade, from the 1960s to the 1970s, the demand for scooters went 'through the roof', as eager consumers booked scooters in anticipation of deliveries years later. This author remembers how his father, a doctor in the Indian Army, had booked and received earlier than usual, a Lambretta scooter through the Army 'canteen quota', upon which, he booked his next one. As soon as the next one arrived, the first scooter was sold at a markedly higher price, with the second one replacing the first at, not only no extra cost, but a noticeable profit . . . an inconceivable state of affairs today.

As the government took, after much deliberation and considerable debate and controversy, the decision to award a fourth licence to the prime minister's son (as well as an inconsequential fifth one to Madan Mohan Rao) for the manufacture of cars, it also took the decision to open the market, or rather, the industrial opportunity for the manufacture of two-wheelers. Not only that, it also decided to jump into the business of making two-wheelers itself!

Thus, in 1972, as the Government of India incorporated Scooters India Limited, it also began looking around for acquiring the licence to manufacture a range of scooters from Europe. Advising the government was M.A. Chidambaram, the owner of API, and a highly influential industrialist then. Chidambaram was aware that his company's erstwhile technical collaborator, Innocenti, was looking to sell the scooter business, which was in rapid decline in Europe then, and refocusing on its car division (as there was a spurt in the demand for small cars in Italy and Europe).

Innocenti, through the 1960s, had had considerable success with its car manufacturing activities, whereas the sales of scooters had plateaued by the mid-1960s, with the beginnings of a decline soon thereafter. Even after Innocenti had replaced the Lambretta Li with the Li Special, and the TV Series III, and then with the handsome SX, sales had slowed down.

It was in 1968 when Innocenti turned to the leading Italian design house then, Carrozzeria Bertone, for a redesign of its big scooter after a very happy and successful design experience with the latter, for Innocenti's 'scooterino' project, the Lambretta Lui scooterette. With the request to update its ageing mainstay, Innocenti specified that the basic design of the strong backbone frame, as well as the mechanical elements, had to remain exactly as they were, but the sheet metal panels at the side, the mudguard at the front and the leg shield of the bestselling scooters needed to be changed. Bertone chief designer, the legendary Marcello Gandini (who had wowed the world with the Lamborghini Miura, Marzal and Espada by then), was tasked with the job. He smoothed out the bodywork, which received subtle surface treatment and cleaner lines. A squared-out headlamp unit was added, the mudguard and the leg shields were redesigned too, and the rear lamp unit modernized.

The facelift was much appreciated—most Lambretta enthusiasts believe that the DL/GP series (as it was badged) are the best-ever Lambrettas. Yet, with the market for two-wheelers in both Italy and Europe on a downward spiral, the production life of Lambretta's last scooter model ended in 1971 (though launched in January 1969) with a little over 46,000 made until then. As Innocenti shifted focus to the development of a new car model (which would be unveiled in 1974 as the Innocenti Mini), the option of selling off its scooter business was very much on. It was around the same time that Scooters India Limited (SIL) came shopping. A deal was concluded, with Innocenti selling the design and tooling of the DL/GP to Scooters India in 1972.

It took three years for Scooters India to shift all the toolings, the dies and equipment of Innocenti's scooter factory at Lambrate, to Scooters India's brand new set-up in Lucknow, and to commence production, with the first scooters from the latter rolling out in 1975. Scooters India's 'made in India' scooter's branding was Vijai Deluxe. This was despite the fact that Scooters India had acquired the legendary Lambretta brand. It was a period of time when the Indian government insisted that all Indian products needed to have an Indian branding—the Fiat 1100 had been renamed the Premier Padmini (after two years of being branded the Premier President), the Vespa 150 a Bajaj Chetak, and Ideal Jawa was calling the Jawa a Yezdi. For exports, though, Scooters India continued with the Lambretta branding.

As Scooters India received a licence to make two-wheelers, a dozen-odd others were also awarded licences by the government. Strangely, the government insisted on maintaining a 'maximum capacity' system for the manufacturers, with the hot-selling Bajaj vehicles pegged at 30,000 per year, despite the endless waiting periods!

The government must have expected to mop up the extra demand with Scooters India, and to bring about a revolution in the manufacture of two-wheelers in India. Five more state government-owned two-wheeler manufacturers came up—Punjab Scooters Limited, Karnataka Scooters Limited, Andhra Pradesh Scooters Limited, Rajasthan Scooters Limited and West Bengal Scooters Limited—all assembling the Vijai Deluxe at their facilities, rebranding them as Vijai Kesri, Vijai Falcon, Allwyn Pushpak, Aravalli and Digvijay, respectively.

The next phase

During the first round of bookings, Scooters India asked for advance payments of Rs 500 from prospective buyers in a post office savings bank account, which was pledged to Hindustan Petroleum Corporation Limited. The bookings opened on 10 March 1974, with the forms needing to have the details of the account. As dealers advertised for the bookings, buyer expectations were so high that punters and potential customers queued up since the previous night at the outlets.

Emulating Scooters India, Bajaj Auto inked deals to supply their scooter models in kits, to be assembled, rebadged and sold as the Priya and the Girnar (later Narmada) by the Maharashtra government-owned Maharashtra Scooters Limited and Gujarat Small Industries Limited (later Gujarat Narmada Auto Limited), respectively.

It was also an opportunity for others to get on to the bandwagon. Pune-based Kinetic Engineering Limited, floated by the Firodia family, who had had a falling-out with the Bajaj family, with whom they had collaborated for the Bajaj Tempo and Bajaj Auto projects, launched an indigenously designed moped, the Kinetic Luna, in 1972. Kirloskar Ghatge Patil Auto Limited, a Kolhapur-based manufacturer of mopeds, bought out the rights to the Lambretta 48 from API, to launch the Laxmi 48, in 1975.

API, after 1978, lost the rights to use the Lambretta badge since Scooters India had acquired it. Thus, API rebadged its scooters MAC 175, the initials of the owner M.A. Chidambaram, in 1978, and then later Lamby 150. It is possible that Scooters India began with the Vijai badging because API still had the rights to use the Lambretta badge until 1978.

Kirloskar Consultants helped develop the short-lived Aravalli scooter for Aravalli Svachalit Vahan Limited, which was launched in 1976. In Jamshedpur, another indigenously developed moped manufacturer, India Automotives Limited, joined the fray with a vehicle branded Hitodi (from Hindustan Tools & Dies). Sonepat-based Atlas Auto Cycles Limited, who were already making cycles, launched the French-licensed Velosolex powered cycle, branded AtlaSolex, with a 49cc engine directly driving the front wheels, in 1975. With cow dung making the front wheels slip, traction became an issue in the Indian context, and the highly popular Velosolex (the AtlaSolex in India) met with a quick, untimely demise in India.

In contrast, the other French-inspired moped, the Hero Majestic, launched by Ludhiana-based Majestic Auto Limited, in 1978 was much more successful. Initially, the Munjal family-owned Majestic Auto had looked at inking a technical collaboration deal with French two-wheeler (and car) veteran Peugeot, but then they changed their mind. Instead, they copied the classic Peugeot 103 moped family, and launched an almost identical product in India.

Thus, by the end of the decade, by 1980, when the latest kid on the block—Sundaram Clayton Limited, established in Hosur, near Bangalore—launched the TVS fifty moped, as many as twenty-odd two-wheeler manufacturers were scrapping for a slice of a 4 lakh-plus market (4,10,457). The Indian market though, was dominated by Bajaj Auto's scooters, with more than a quarter of the total sales accounted for by the Pune-based giant (not counting the 24,390 Priyas and 3417

Girnars made by Maharashtra Scooters and Gujarat Small Industries). In a distant second and third were Escorts and Kinetic Engineering. Contrary to expectations, Scooters India was trailing a poor fourth, having made a tad over 36,000 scooters that year.

With the two dozen-odd two-wheeler manufacturers, the waiting list for most of the two-wheeler models had disappeared by the early 1980s. Waiting lists remained only for the Bajaj 150/Super and the Priya, as well as the Bajaj Chetak, which was available against foreign exchange payments.

Even though industry experts and economists tend to cite the moves by the Narasimha Rao government and the measures introduced by Dr Manmohan Singh in the early 1990s as the moment when India's economy was first liberalized, the earliest moves, in the opinion of this author, were the 'doling out' of licences to the two-wheeler industry in the early 1970s.

During the 1950s, barely three two-wheeler manufacturers received licences. Into the 1960s, another five were able to get licences to make mopeds and motorcycles. It was in the 1970s, when almost two dozen received new licences. It was also the decade when several two-wheeler manufacturers shut shop, as competition weeded out the inefficient and the less competent. Aravalli Svachalit produced their scooters from 1976 to 1979, before calling it a day. Atlas' AltaSolex slipped out of the market by 1978, too, barely three years since they began producing their powered cycles. Pearl Yamaha had given up the ghost by 1972.

Punjab Scooters, who made the Kesri, a licensed Lambretta/Vijai Deluxe, survived barely three years, from 1977 to 1979. The Ramona moped, made by Ramona Engineering, was around from 1976 to 1980. Calcutta-based Sen & Pandit Engineering Products Limited made the Dart moped for a few years starting 1974. Tamilnadu Mopeds Limited's Mayuram was in production for a few years since its launch in 1976. A company from West Bengal launched the Banrex (with Banrex coming from entrepreneur Banerjee), a 50cc moped in the early 1970s priced at around Rs 1600. Pre-production examples were sent to several showrooms, and bookings invited, but barely any Banrex were ever sighted.

In retrospect, the 1970s was the first of the automotive bloodbaths. It was also a strange mix of initiatives, with more than half a dozen government-funded scooter manufacturers set up, several home-grown indigenous developments, and innumerable forays away from core competencies, like when Escorts and Enfield both felt that they could be more successful getting into the scooter business with the awkwardly designed Rajdoot Runabout and the Enfield Fantabulous. Though the Runabout was powered by the same engine as in the Rajdoot motorcycle's (thereby keeping costs under control), and the Fantabulous made do with a 7.5bhp 175cc two-stroke single, sourced from Villiers, both failed to excite the customers.

The same Villiers engine had powered the Royal Enfield Sherpa of the 1960s, whose predecessor was the 125cc, two-stroke Royal Enfield Ensign, launched in the late 1950s. The Sherpa's successor was the Royal Enfield Crusader, launched in 1974, with nearly the same 175cc engine. The Royal Enfield Fantabulous was launched in 1962 (also 175cc, two-stroke, 7.5bhp), and was fitted with a self-starter, operated by a battery. It had foot-operated gears. The self-starter had some issues, and by 1968, the Fantabulous changed over to a kick-starter.

In the meantime, in 1974, Bajaj Auto launched the Chetak, inspired by the Vespa Sprint. Named after the legendary horse of the warrior king, Rana Pratap Singh, the Chetak became the most desirable scooter in India. To the dismay of potential buyers, the Chetak was available against payment in elusive foreign exchange. The waiting list was not so long, and delivery was possible within a month, but was possible for only those who had a 'foreign connection'.

The most exciting news though in in the 1970s was the advertisements put out by Bajaj Auto in the back cover of *Time* magazine. These ads ran from 1977 until 1979. As there was a cap on what could be sold in India, and Bajaj had the capacity to manufacture more, they chose to export the Chetak scooter in the international market. To facilitate that, Bajaj put out a series of advertisements on the back cover of *Time*, which pointed out that the Bajaj Chetak had 'scootered a long way to the international scene. This fuel-saving beauty from India is real sleek, compact and durable.'

Given that Bajaj had never advertised in India (it never needed to do so), and given that no one remembered ever seeing a Bajaj scooter advertisement in India, the back cover of *Time* magazine was not just astounding, but a matter of huge pride. This was at a point of time, 1975, when no engineering product—made in India—was known to have been on sale in the international market.

In another back-cover advertisement on *Time* magazine, from 1978, Bajaj Auto once again mentioned that the 'Bajaj Chetak is made by Bajaj Auto of India. One of the two largest scooter manufacturers of the world.' The other presumably being its erstwhile collaborator Piaggio, with which Bajaj Auto had tangled in Europe, with the former taking the latter to court over design infringements, when Bajaj redesigned the 150 into the sharper-edged Chetak, which seemed to emulate the styling evolution of the traditional Vespa to the Nuova Vespa. Bajaj though had won, and India was prouder. That same advertisement also listed out the countries where Bajaj had successfully licensed out production: Indonesia and Taiwan.

If the scooter was good enough for Indonesia, Taiwan and other parts of the world, it was more than good enough for India. Even if the Vijai Deluxe was dynamically superior, more modern, and was winning at Sholavaram and dominating the scooter class in racing, it could not quite match up to the image of the 'world-class' Bajaj Chetak. The fact that Scooters India was exporting the Vijai as the Lambretta DL and GP 200 in Europe, and that in Spain it was being imported in kit form, and assembled and sold as the Serveta, and then later as the Lambretta, was something that the Indian consumer had no clue about. Somehow, Scooters India made it a point to be so self-effacing in their achievements that they systematically effaced themselves off the market.

It was the Bajaj Chetak, which had become the 'vehicle for the people' of India, the one two-wheeler, which everyone wanted. It was the family vehicle, the one which the man of the house used to get to his workplace, dropping off his child at school, the one which then carried the family in the evening for dinner at the grandparents. It was the all-purpose vehicle, which had the space between the legs for ferrying the gas cylinders, or carting the shopping from the market, or for carrying young Munna, standing between the legs, on the footboard, looking over the handlebar.

If the Bajaj Chetak became the central backbone, the vertebra to the Indian two-wheeler industry, some of the other two-wheeled vehicles took on different roles and images. The moped was the most basic, inexpensive runabout, the one which was convenient for young boys and girls to get to college, to university, as well as the poorest in the villages to get about. The better off in the villages and the countryside would opt for the rustic Rajdoot motorcycles, with its supple suspension system, smoothing out the rough dirt terrain of rural India. The wealthier amongst the 'ruralites' opted for the Enfield Bullet, as it was robust, more imposing, and was strong enough to carry half a dozen heavy milk cans. The army and the police also remained faithful to the classic thumper, the Bullet.

For the trendier lot, the young men about town, the Jawa/Yezdi 250 was the set of wheels to own. Funkier and faster, the Yezdi 250 had already built up a reputation for winning at racing, and was the one for the smart set, the bike to pick up the babes with. The younger men, army officers, and young executives in multinationals, all made a beeline for the Yezdi, never realizing the most exciting of all the two-wheelers in India then was one which was being made in India, yet was not available for sale in the country.

Scooters India was making and exporting the Lambretta GP 200, the 12bhp, 198cc version of the Vijai Deluxe, which had a top speed of over 110 km/h, faster than the Yezdi 250, and the fastest scooter in the world when it came out in 1969. Innocenti had also explored the possibility of a twin-cylinder version of the 200. For styling, Bertone had again been contracted, and Marcello Gandini's take on what a powerful sports scooter could look like was very startling, made all the more distinctive by a pentagonal headlamp casing, a beaky, pointed front mudguard and an inverted wedge side panel. Alas, nothing came of it, except for a mock-up. If the senior executives at Scooters India (and the bureaucrats at the ministry of heavy industry) had any vision whatsoever, this super scooter ought to have been developed for the international market.

Yet no denying that the creation of Scooters India, and the subsequent industrial policy which allowed for the awarding of a dozen-odd licences, not only provided the necessary fillip to get the market to quadruple over a decade, but also acted as an amazing engine of growth for the revitalized two-wheeler industry in India. Into the 1980s, it was time for the next lot of reforms.

Going international

In all likelihood, the death of Sanjay Gandhi and then Indira Gandhi's desire to revive the 'people's car' concept with the Maruti project, which needed a joint venture with an international carmaker, may have acted as the trigger for the next phase of policy changes with regard to the two-wheeler industry. If the newly 'reconstituted' Maruti Udyog needed a new licence, as well as a technical collaboration and some investment commitment from an international carmaker, then similar facilities needed to be afforded to other sectors of the industry.

Maruti Udyog contributed to the Indian automobile scene in many ways. It was because of Maruti Udyog that Bangalore-based R.K. Siplani was awarded a licence to manufacture cars, with technical collaboration with English specialist carmaker Reliant Motors. Maruti also enabled Honda, Kawasaki, Mazda, Mitsubishi, Nissan, Suzuki, Toyota and Yamaha, as well as Piaggio and Ford to sign collaborations with several Indian vehicle manufacturers.

The first of these Japanese technology transfers was one of the most exciting of all the two-wheelers launched in India until the 1980s. In 1983, Escorts rolled out the Rajdoot RD350, which was the legendary twin-cylinder Yamaha RD350, in markedly detuned form. Launched in 1973, the Yamaha RD350 was a model derived from racing, with RD standing for 'race derived', and was one of the quicker motorcycles on sale in the international market. With 39bhp from the 347cc air-cooled two-stroke twin-cylinder engine, the motorcycle was capable of a top speed close to 170 kmph. When Escorts took the licence to make the 350B version in India, it detuned the engine—for the sake of improved fuel efficiency—to 30.5bhp for the 'high-torque' version and to 27bhp for the 'low-torque' version. Though performance was noticeably blunted, the RD350 was easily the fastest motorcycle available in India during the 1980s.

With the RD350, Escorts was hoping to take on the Enfield Bullet, but the police and the army hesitated to take to a motorcycle, which they could barely handle. (With the exception of the Calcutta Police, which acquired a fleet of very smart-looking red Rajdoot RD350s with big polycarbonate visors, a siren and panniers.) Consequently, sales of the RD350 remained rather confidential.

Escorts' joint venture with Yamaha for the motorcycle model, the Yamaha RX100, launched in 1986, was much more successful, aided no doubt, with a series of smart advertisements: 'You have seen the crowd, here comes the leader', followed by 'Born to lead', 'Ride the international favourite' and 'Ahead of the 100s'.

Similarly, all the other joint-venture products: the Kinetic Honda scooter between Kinetic and Honda, the Ind-Suzuki AX100 motorcycle launched by TVS and Suzuki, the Kawasaki KB100 motorcycle launched by Bajaj Auto, were very successful. The greatest success though was the Hero Honda CD100, launched by the joint venture between Hero and Honda, and its brilliant advertisement: 'Fill it. Shut it. Forget it.' The company also claimed an astounding 80 kilometres per litre, as compared to the rivals' 40-55 kilometres to the litre.

Grabbing the headlines

What really grabbed headlines in the early 1980s, and with that the imagination of all punters, was the technical collaboration between LML (Lohia Machines Limited), a Kanpur-based company, and Piaggio of Italy, to make the latest Vespa models. The grandson of the mother of the Bajaj Chetak was coming to India, and everyone thought that the new LML Vespa XE was going to be the next big thing. With close to 22 lakhs punters putting down money as advance bookings, LML collected Rs 110 crores, which was a lot of money then, more than the entire project cost.

Piaggio's other technical collaboration was with Andhra Pradesh Scooters Limited, and the latter switched from making the Vijai-licensed Allwyn Pushpak to the 96cc Vespa PL170. Another prominent Italian two-wheeler manufacturer Benelli agreed to provide technical know-how to a Calcutta-based company, Arvind Benelli Limited, for the manufacture of a modern automatic scooter, the Benelli S125. The fourth Italian technical tie-up was between refrigerator manufacturer, Kelvinator India Limited and Agrati-Garelli, for a range of scooters and mopeds branded Avanti.

Peugeot, which had had some issues with Majestic Auto, agreed to provide technical know-how to Bangalore-based Shree Chamundi Mopeds Limited, for the latter to make Peugeot's most modern moped, the 105D, badged the Sportif for the Indian market. Austrian automotive conglomerate Puch sold the designs of a high-quality step-through two-wheeler with a 65cc two-stroke engine to Hero Motors (a part of the Hero Group), with the latter launching the Hero Puch range. (The range, later, included a model called the Hero Puch Shakti, which was designed by this author. The author also designed a full-fairing sports motorcycle version too, but that never went into production.)

The most unusual of all the technical tie-ups was the one between the legendary British brand, BSA, which under new ownership was making 50cc tiddlers, and Brooke Bond, the tea company! The one-time rival of BSA, Royal Enfield's India-connected survivor, Enfield India, took a different route. They decided to buy out some of the models from the product line-up of Zundapp, a German motorcycling veteran which was closing shop (eventually selling the factory lock, stock and barrel to the Chinese). Enfield bought the rights and the toolings for two 50cc models (launched as the Silver Plus step-through, and the Explorer motorcycle), and a more powerful 175cc, sold as the Enfield Fury 175DX.

Thus, through the 1980s, the Indian consumer had an amazingly wide range of two-wheelers to choose from: a 22cc spindly thingummy called the Mofa (and made by Enfield India) to the dangerously quick Rajdoot/Yamaha RD350. In between, there was the very pretty and beautifully finished moped, the Peugeot Sportif, with distinctive alloy-style pressed steel wheels (Honda Comstar-style rims) and electric start—both were firsts for a moped. The Hero Puch was another alloy-wheeled wonder, with quality details.

Then there were those motorcycles from BSA, the Bond, the Mascot and the Falcon, all 50cc tiddlers, which handled beautifully, rode excellently well, as they featured monoshocks at the rear (a first for India), and had a good turn of speed. Enfield's Silver Plus, Explorer and Fury featured alloy wheels for the first time in India, and the latter had the distinction of Brembo disc brakes at the front, as well as Paoili shocks for the front fork. Yet, most of these were short-lived and sold in rather dismal numbers.

However, some of the others just sank without a trace. Though Benelli had sold the toolings of the Benelli S125 to Arvind Benelli (when erstwhile owner Alejandro De Tomaso sold Benelli in 1986 to industrialist Giancarlo Selci, who preferred to concentrate on only the 50cc models), except for an initial batch of scooters for dealerships, none of the scooters made it to customers. This was so despite a unique transmission system, which was a four-speeder, with hand control, allowing one to start from standstill at any gear, as well as the possibility to change gear, even without engaging the clutch lever.

Meanwhile, the Indo-Japanese two-wheeler brigade did much better than their commercial vehicle counterparts, so much so that the Hero Honda CD100 dethroned the Bajaj Chetak as India's bestselling vehicle ever. The others fared well too, even if they were not quite in the same league as the redoubtable CD100, with the AX100, the KB100 and the Kinetic Honda, all selling in lakhs. Over the years as models changed, or replaced, many were scrapped or reduced to rust heaps. The best survivors though have been the Yamaha RX100, as this one model took on cult status.

Despite the popularity, none of the joint ventures survived. Eventually, Kinetic and Honda went their respective ways, as did Hero and Honda, as well as TVS and Suzuki. Escorts sold out to Yamaha, and exited the two-wheeler sphere altogether. Suzuki and Honda restarted from scratch in India.

No matter the fate of individual companies, the market though grew in leaps and bounds: by 1985, two-wheeler sales crossed a million that year (to 1.13 million). By 1990, sales had topped 1.88 million. By 2000, the end of the last century, more than 4 million mopeds, scooters, motorcycles and three-wheelers had sold in India that year. Yet, during these two decades, the composition of the Indian market changed drastically. For the year 2000, motorcycles accounted for more than half the market, scooters were now a distant second, and mopeds had shrunk considerably in importance. Despite the introduction of a modern and fuel-efficient four-stroke engine for the Bajaj Chetak, by 2006, the vehicle, which had been the preferred set of wheels for three generations of Indians, was dead.

During that period, Ideal Jawa died, as did Andhra Pradesh Scooters, API, Chamundi Mopeds, Gujarat Narmada, India Automotives, Karnataka Scooters, Karnawati Auto, Kelvinator India, Kirloskar Ghatge Patil, Mopeds India, Saund Zweirad Union, Sen & Pandit and Tamilnadu Mopeds. Scooters India, the one that may have been the cause célèbre for the industry to change so much, stopped making scooters altogether (by 1997), though three-wheeler production continued.

By 2006, the Indian two-wheeler industry doubled once again, producing over 8 million vehicles (8.4 million) that year. It took another seven years to double that: with over 16 million (16.4 million) two-wheelers sold during 2013. In 2017, when India made 21.8 million two-wheelers, it became the world's largest producer of fossil-fuelled two-wheelers, overtaking China, which has been in a decline. During 2018, more than 25 million two-wheelers rolled out of factories in India.

Since 2017, the gap between China and India has been widening—whether that is a matter of pride is debatable. The reason why China's numbers have come down is for the single reason that they have been discouraging the use of fossil-fuelled motorized two-wheelers, whereas encouraging the use of electric ones, which, for the sake of counting, are seen as 'bicycles'.

The future is not ours to see

As the Doris Day song goes, 'que será, será, whatever will be, will be, the future's not ours to see'. Instead, we can discuss the immediate past and bemoan the passing of Kinetic Engineering and Kinetic Motor, both swallowed by Mahindra & Mahindra. After an initial burst of sales, Mahindra Two Wheelers has seen its sales curve diving down.

By 2018, India's two-wheeler industry had narrowed down to squaring out between the Indians and the Japanese. The three Japanese giants, Honda, Yamaha and Suzuki, between them had almost one-third of the manufacturing pie, with the remaining two-thirds mainly Indian (not counting the irrelevant numbers by Harley-Davidson and Triumph, as well as the joint venture between TVS and BMW). With a tad over 8 million two-wheelers produced in 2018, Hero MotoCorp remains India's biggest manufacturer. With almost 6.4 million (64 lakh) scooters and motorcycles made in 2018, Honda remains a close number two. Bajaj, at a tad over 4 million, is a distant number three, and TVS remains at fourth place with 3.77 million produced. Yamaha made a little over a million, and Royal Enfield sold 8,73,567 motorcycles in 2018.

Ten years ago, in 2008, Royal Enfield had sold 42,626 motorcycles, its best year ever since its inception as Enfield India in 1955. From 2008 to 2018, in a decade, Royal Enfield grew twenty times!

By 2018, Royal Enfield was claiming to be the world's biggest manufacturer in the mid-sized motorcycle segment. By comparison, Harley-Davidson sold 2,28,000, BMW 1,65,000, Triumph 64,000, and Ducati 53,000. Europe's biggest motorcycle manufacturer, KTM, shifted 2,61,500 in 2018 (with more than a little help from their friend, and 49 per cent owner, Bajaj Auto). Royal Enfield, interestingly, outsold the combined sales of these five. All thanks to the one driver, which has been the Indian market made up of a set of highly enthusiastic motorcycle riders.

It was in this last decade, or at the most two, that the Indian two-wheeler landscape changed completely. Even as stability came in, in terms of makes and manufacturers, and consistency in volumes and growths, the market matured rapidly into one where fewer vehicles are being perceived as mere transport. Of course, the market for mopeds and scooters, which is a third of sales, remains mainly one for moving people from point A to B, but a significant percentage of the motorcycle buyers are buying one for pleasure and leisure, and less so as a commodity.

This phenomenon is reflected in the revival of the Jawa brand, as of 2018. When Ideal Jawa ceased operations in the mid-1990s, one would never have imagined that the marques Jawa and Yezdi would resurface one day, with designs, which harked back to the halcyon days of yore. In fact, at that point of time it was the outdated design which seemed to work against the Yezdi's market success.

This author designed a sportier version of the Yezdi 250 Roadking, which had the moniker Super Sprint. It was a fully faired version, more modern to look at than anything else available then in the country. The mechanicals though remained the same as that of the Roadking's, except for expansion chambers for the exhausts. Other changes included 18-inch alloy wheels. Though enthusiasts believed that the Yezdi Super Sprint's 'striking graphics and attractive design gave it a very special appearance and that it could have been a winner amongst superbikes', it was too late for a manufacturer, which was bleeding profusely.

With the advent of a newer breed of serious enthusiasts who appreciate and understand the history of a brand and what it stood for, marques such as Jawa, Yezdi, BSA and others are in the process of being revived. Aiding this are a handful of enthusiasts of historic vehicles, who have saved the older motorcycles and two-wheelers from disappearing, by acquiring vintage and classic two-wheelers, preserving them, and as well as restoring them back to their old glory.

Just like the movement for historic vehicles in the car segment, several collectors in India have built up very impressive collection of historic two-wheelers. Car collectors such as Harit Trivedi, Dr Ravi Prakash, Diljeet Titus, M.S. Guhan and Pestonjee Bhujwalla have sizeable collections of two-wheelers too, but there are several other Indian collectors, who specialize mainly in collections of motorcycles, scooters, even mopeds. The most prominent of them being Rakesh Jain, Norton Singh (yes, named after the motorcycle brand), Sandeep Kapoor, Raju Sharma, Gurmukh Singh and Desh Deepak Singh, all from Delhi, as well as Reuben Solomon, Jazil Mehta, Shiraz Ginwalla, Guru Prasad, Lokesk T.L. Dnyanesh Sawant, Dr Anjan Chatterjee and several others, from other parts of India. Mention must be made of the many lesser-known collectors of two-wheelers who have managed to save some of the most magnificent machines, as well as the most innocuous of tiddlers India has known.

Rebels with a cause

The fact that motorcycles are being acquired increasingly for pleasure rather than for convenience became obvious with India's first Bike Week, organized in Goa, during 2–3 February 2013, when several thousands of motorcycling enthusiasts from different corners of India rode to Goa for two days of riding, sharing and partaking the joys of wind-in-the-face motoring. Patterned along the lines of the famous Sturgis Motorcycle Rally, in the United States, Indian Bike week promised much for all the motorcycling aficionadas.

Even if Sturgis managed more than 7,00,000 bikers that same year, and Goa less than 7000, it was a good start. The main attraction though was the promised ride of a Harley-Davidson, by the Indian HOG (Harley Owners Club), which did not come through, even though Harley had the most important presence, with Royal Enfield presence a distant second. Over the years though, the Royal Enfield clubs have gone on to dominate the scene amongst the 100-plus clubs that assemble in Goa every year since.

Important events at the India Bike week are the dirt race, the flea market, live bands, custom parade and the display of historic motorcycles.

Since 2013, India Bike week has grown to a meet, which claims to be Asia's largest motorcycling festival, though numbers remain at a modest 'less than 20,000'. With over 200 motorcycling clubs attending, India Bike week is a heady mix of adventure, motorcycle culture, music and biking 'brotherhood'—as well as sisterhood, as it has also given space and recognition to another recent phenomenon, the *bikernis*, a group of women who are as passionate about motorcycling as the men.

When the monopoly ended

For most of India's two-wheeler history, motorcycling has been mainly a monopoly of the men. Women rode mopeds most of the time, to get to school, university and to work. Some graduated to using scooters, specifically the Kinetic Honda in the 1980s, as it had the convenience of an automatic. In fact, the popularity of the Kinetic Honda with women eventually damaged the image of the scooter, reducing it to an also-ran, a vehicle for the ladies, despite the scooter winning several rallies and races. Some of the braver women rode a geared scooter. One or two 'crazy Parsees' would turn up at the occasional historic vehicle event, astride the odd BSA.

Thus, it was a most pleasant surprise when this author came across a pretty, young eighteen-year-old in 1986, on a Rajdoot 175, in the streets of Bombay. Natasha Alpaiwalla had just turned eighteen, and had just bought herself a ten-year-old Rajdoot, with money earned baking and selling cake, as her parents were not going to buy her a 'dangerous two-wheeler'.

For Natasha, motorcycles have stood for, 'freedom, independence and the pleasure of speed and mobility. I did not want a motorcycle because it looked cool, but because it stood for so much more, because there was so much pleasure to be had, with the wind in your face. Not your hair, mind you, as I have always used a helmet when riding,' points out Natasha, adding, 'my parents bought me the first helmet. Once they reluctantly agreed to my use of a motorcycle, and not a car to move around in, they were insistent that I use a helmet, which I have always happily done.'

In the meantime, a Bajaj Avenger replaced the Rajdoot. After being away from India for a few years, Natasha has been back in Mumbai since 2001, where she runs her very successful confectionary business. A Kawasaki 700 LTD joined the fleet subsequently, on which she went for several long cross-country rides to the south of India, Bangalore, Pondicherry and then back to Mumbai via Goa. Amongst her motorcycle-touring holidays, the one she enjoyed the most was one on a dirt bike in Cambodia.

For Natasha, looking good on a motorcycle was the last thing on her mind—the sheer pleasure of what motorcycling offers has been the overriding factor. Thus, she has stayed away from the new phenomena of the Bikerni, a pan-India association of female motorcycle riders. 'I had been invited for a couple of their meets, but I prefer riding alone or with a couple of close friends, whether female or male,' explains Natasha.

The *bikernis* mark an interesting trend. Capturing it is an article from the blog *Moterrific*, titled: 'Don't date a girl who rides a motorcycle.' It goes on to say, 'If you are able to read past the title, you will appreciate the sarcasm.'[1]

Written by Cristi Farrell, the article lists out several reasons why someone must not date a girl whose 'idea of having a good time is to pack the bare essentials in her tank bag, gas up, and just go riding—no destination in particular, just an emphasis on the in-between.' As well as one 'who has no qualms about running out of gas in the middle of nowhere or improvising near a cactus when restrooms are scarce'.

Amongst the most telling reasons is the one on how she would be the one who 'is often independent and capable, not playing part to the ploy of batting her eyelashes in hopes of your swift rescue'. Farrell sums it up by saying, 'Don't date a girl who rides a motorcycle because perfection won't be tantamount. The simplest journey and the most mundane tasks will become the greatest adventure and your life will never be the same. Don't date a girl who rides a motorcycle. Marry her.'

Women riding motorcycles in North America or Europe is not that unusual—more than a third of the riders of Harley-Davidsons in Paris are women, for instance. In the Indian context though it has become a very powerful statement, a symbol of a new-found freedom, a form of assertion, and an instrument of liberation and women's rights.

One of the most prominent of these newly assertive young ladies, is Sonia Jain, who has made riding a motorcycle her vocation. It all started when Jain was at her job and she received 'a random text to audition for India bike rally, for twenty-one days, thirty-odd cities, 2500 km. Generally, I ignore spam but it had the word bike in it and the prize was a new Yamaha. All I knew was that this was my chance to get a bike. I did not have to ask anybody or save up for years. I just have to win it. I auditioned and made it to the rally'.

Which she won, after a slow start, as she was not yet an expert rider. 'I had achieved a dream I had dreamt of since when I was sixteen,' remembers Jain. 'As I could not get off from work for twenty-one days, I was unemployed when I came back home, but I had made my dad proud.'

'In 2010, Yamaha asked me to participate in another rally, only this time it was for thirty-three days, over 4500 km and solo riding, nobody to correct my mistakes,' recounts Jain. 'But as it hadn't stopped me earlier, it didn't this time either. I came back home with another bike.' Since then there has been no looking back as Jain has made a profession of riding motorcycles for launches of new models, of being a professional 'influencer'.

Sonia Jain has been an influencer in more ways than just promoting products and brands such as Yamaha. She has been quite an influence on a whole generation of young women, all with a passion for motorcycling, riding, adventure tourism and using the motorcycle to assert themselves against the various societal pressures and issues.

Ridhi Nahata is one such rebel with a cause, one of Sonia Jain's many fans. 'I was ten years old when I saw a woman riding a Bajaj Chetak scooter, and asked my father whether I could ride one, one day,' recounts Nahata. "Of course, just be healthy to balance your vehicle ", said my father. This simple answer ignited in me a fire for independence, freedom, speed and a decision, which I will always be proud of. I was raised in a middle-class Marwari family, and was lucky to have open-minded parents, but they were also balancing social norms, which is to limit a girl and the first answer for her is always a no!'

'I learnt to be opportunistic, and each time I got a chance to ride a two-wheeler I would grab it,' remembers Nahata. 'The rebel was with a cause, to be the change that I want to see in society, to accept that a female could drive a light or a heavy motor vehicle. I started reading about females who were working as auto-rickshaw drivers. I researched more and realized that I was normal. Vehicles are man-made machines, and the only criteria to drive or ride them is to be an expert rider, as machines don't differentiate between a male rider and a female rider.'

Ridhi Nahata, Sonia Jain and Natasha Alpaiwalla are just a few of the many young Indian women who are using the motorcycle to carve out a place for themselves in a new India, which is more open, broad-minded and emancipated. The motorcycle has become a symbol of the India of the future, a vehicle which provides liberty, mobility, independence and equality to a large swathe of the populace, as well as weaving a new social fabric, technologically and culturally. In the inescapable transition from fossil-fuelled versions to electric and lesser-polluting variants, the motorcycle will, hopefully, be at the vanguard of a cleaner, sustainable future for mobility, liberty and freedom, as well as a form of emancipation and gender equality.

8

The Art of the Automobile

Even though it is known that the very first automobile was invented by a Frenchman, Nicolas-Joseph Cugnot, in the year 1770, it would not be amiss to also point out that the idea of an automobile, a self-propelled vehicle, was under consideration for centuries before that. Many may have dreamt of such a device, a vehicle, but it needed a Leonardo da Vinci (1452–1519) to conceptualize one. Around 1478, the redoubtable genius gave expression to that dream in the form of a series of rough sketches in his *Codex Atlanticus*.

It is believed that Leonardo da Vinci may have sketched this as an idea (though the sketches are uncommented and thus presumed incomplete) for one of his many wealthy patrons who regularly employed him to create complex showpieces. It is possible that one of his patrons had commissioned this 'concept' for the famous artist from Anchiano, Italy, to execute, as a way for them to show their wealth to their guests. The device may not be considered a car, though, as it had no provision for seats, but it could be steered and, in theory, was able to move on its own power for up to 40 metres, or so.

Da Vinci's three-wheeler was spring-driven so it had to be wound up before it could move. Inspired by the first clocks and the study of perpetual motion, he conceptualized a vehicle, driven by two independent wheels, with a rudimentary differential, and a mechanical gear assembly, rack, gear wheel, and pinion. A complex clockwork and escapement system—

inspired by watchmaking—based on two symmetrical leaf springs, 'powered' the vehicle, and regulated the speed. A third tricycle wheel at the rear provided for steering, acting as a 'rudder'.

A machine with perpetual motion would, in theory, self-power energy from nothing, or very little, but da Vinci eventually concluded from his experiments, the dynamic impossibility of this principle. This was around 1490.

In 2004, a team of scientists from the Museo Galileo in Florence produced a model of this incomplete vehicle concept. The prototype works, thanks to the addition (which was not in the original diagram) of a double motor spring (invented around the same period, the beginning of the fifteenth century, with the first spring-actuated clocks) based on two spiral springs, placed under the two large gears, capable of driving the wheels independently.

Thus, it was an artist who dreamt and conceived the very first automobile. Yet, the very first automobiles actually made were the work of engineers such as Nicolas-Joseph Cugnot, and later the Franco-Swiss François Isaac de Rivaz and a Belgian, Jean-Joseph Etienne Lenoir, as well as the Germans, Karl Benz and Gottlieb Daimler. The vehicles produced by these engineers were far from pretty, and aesthetic considerations were the last thing on their mind, as they tried to get their fledgling invention working properly.

The aesthetic aspect, specifically the design of the body and the construction of the interior, gained importance during the 1920s and later, with the coachbuilders bringing their art into the shaping and the colouring of the exterior and the interior. By the end of the nineteenth century, though, the automobile itself had the beginnings of an impact on the world of art, sculpture and culture.

One of the first amongst the renowned artists to incorporate the automobile was Frenchman Henri de Toulouse-Lautrec. His lithograph *The Automobilist*, from 1896, was perhaps the earliest example of the image of the automobile in the work of a major artist. 'Fascinated by the kinetics and rhythms of modern life, particularly that of dance halls and cafes, Lautrec expressed the tempo of modernity in a portrayal of his cousin as a supercharged extension of a fuming vehicle,' is how the book *Automobile and Culture*[1] explained Toulouse-Lautrec's diagonally divided composition. The book, published on the occasion of the museum's hosting of a special exhibition on automobile and art in 1984, in Los Angeles, went on to describe how the 'vibrantly delineated, forward-surging explosive form of the car and its possessed driver are contrasted with the somewhat sketchy background figures of a promenader and her dog. The centuries confront one another: the tranquil nineteenth-century world of Impressionist imagery is pitted against the tumultuous vision of twentieth-century technological invention.'

If art had already acknowledged the automobile, could sculpture be far behind?

It was again the French who took the lead, when they erected the Monument to Emile Levassor, at the Porte Maillot in Paris, in 1907. The monumental sculpture was a tribute to racing hero and inveterate 'automobilist', Émile Levassor, a pioneering car inventor, racer, and winner of the legendary Paris-Bordeaux-Paris race in 1895. What was normally accorded only to war heroes and political leaders, in the liberal atmosphere of late-nineteenth-century France, it was the turn of heroes of a different kind, the gladiator who had covered 1178 km, averaging close to 25 kmph, enduring nearly forty-eight hours of virtually non-stop driving! A feat that is yet to be bettered in the annals of motoring.

Winning with an automobile powered by an internal combustion engine, Levassor embarked on manufacturing with René Panhard the Panhard et Levassor cars, which helped propel France into a prominent position in early automotive history. It was a year after Levassor's death in 1897, when the recently founded Automobile Club de France (ACF) commissioned the monument, selecting sculptor Aimée-Jules Dalou to execute it. Working from photographs, Dalou made two bronze models.

After Dalou's death in 1902, his pupil Camille Lefèbvre took over the project, completing a Greco-Roman style triumphal arch (in 1907), within which the car of Levassor bursts forth, with Emile Levassor leaning forward, egging on his victorious machine, amidst the cheers of the spectators surrounding the car.

Yet, it would be some more years before the world of art and sculpture would look at the automobile as a subject once again. Instead, it would be the art of the poster, which would become the perfect canvas to illustrate and promote these new-fangled machines, and their successes at winning races, with the advertising poster of French carmaker Richard-Brasier winning the Gordon Bennett race of 1904, as one of the early examples of this new art form.

Illustrated by H. Belléry Desfontaines, the poster is dominated by an image of a windswept mythological figure preceding the speeding Richard-Brasier bolide. As the book *Automobile and Culture* explains, the illustration 'makes an allusion to Aurora, the classical harbinger of the dawn, here leading the way for an internal combustion version of Apollo's sun-chariot. Fuelled by contemporary millennial sentiments, the car became the symbol of the dawning of a new age, the incarnation of a technological energy akin to the power of the sun.'[2]

Belléry Desfontaines was one of several artists and illustrators who became known for their Art Nouveau-meets-La Belle Epoque style of celebrating the automobile and the vibrant aspects of modern life, including racing, beautiful women and technology. Georges Gaudy, E. Montaut, Gamy, Henry Meunier, André Névil and Umberto Boccioni were some of the many others who painted and drew illustrations which tackled the subject of showcasing speed, motion and excitement, with renderings which illustrated dust-shrouded cars lurching forward, madly spinning wheels, careening wildly, coaxed and cajoled by determined, forward-crouched brave men, battling machine and the elements. (Always men driving and the women draping the automobile—a rather sexist attitude which prevailed for decades, unfortunately.)

The advent of photography

It was, of course, the most recent of technologies which captured the excitement of the automobile best: the new art of photography. Amongst the ones who were the early champions of this new art and its use to capture movement, speed and thrills, was the young genius,

Jacques-Henri Lartigue. Another Frenchman, or rather, boy, seven-year-old Lartigue was completely enamoured of the automobile. Born into a creative, stylish and bourgeois family, in 1894, Jacques-Henri was surrounded by family members (his grandfather, brother) who tinkered with automobiles, monorails and airplanes. Photographing cars on Parisian streets, as well as family outings in automobiles, and documenting many important racing events in the early part of the twentieth century, Lartigue captured some of the most important moments during the 1905 Gordon Bennett Cup race, as well as the 1912 Grand Prix of the Automobile Club de France.

'Breaking with photographic convention, he often produced intentionally blurred and cropped shots, using the edge cutting off the image to capture the spirit of flux characteristic of the modern world,' explains *Automobile and Culture*. 'For example, one of a series of photographs taken of the Grand Prix of the Automobile Club of France in 1912 emphasizes speed and motion by slicing the image of the race car and counterposing it and its blurred wheels with the strange leftward tilt of spectators and poles. In its contrast between speeding car in the foreground and pedestrians in the background, *Grand Prix* compositionally recalls Toulouse-Lautrec's *The Automobilist*.'[3]

Lartigue went on to influence an entire generation of photographers, many of whom went on to use his style of snapshot aesthetic, which was the instantaneous recording of actual events, for automobile magazines. Many of these magazines—mostly specifically the English ones, such as *The Autocar* and *The Car*—found their way to India, bringing with them the art of photography and illustrations as used for product advertising within the pages. The Indian princes and the wealthier educated class of Indians, as well as the resident British, acquired the magazines, the posters, as well as some of the early prints and automotive postcards.

Local enterprise though seems to have been limited. Amongst the paintings in the havelis of Shekhawati, most of which have been executed during the early twentieth century, there are a few of automobiles, amongst several of elephants with howdahs, horse carriages, bullock carts, even an occasional train, and a very early airplane. The automobiles seem to be mostly veterans, from the pre-First World War era, though some may very well be from the 1920s, executed in a 'two-dimensional' Indian miniature style, which make it difficult to identify them, but they seem to be mostly of tourers, with either the princely types sitting in them, or Europeans, with bowler hats and parasols.

There are a few which are illustrations of Radha and Krishna driven by Gopika, or Arjun driving Krishna and Rukmini, as well as other deities, in elegant, long tourers. One of the paintings seems to be that of an elongated, chariot-like vehicle, with an elaborate umbrella-like cowl for a covering, and with a steering wheel. There is another one, which is a decent replication of a landaulet-style body, which could very well be that of a Napier or a Rolls-Royce from around 1910 or earlier. Whether the painters had actually seen these vehicles and then painted them, or whether they were 'copied' from photographs and illustrations is not clear, though it could very well be a case of the latter.

It is interesting to see them juxtaposed in the Indian context, with mythology playing a role in their symbolism as 'chariots of the gods', as well as the importance of the colonial masters and how the automobile, which was their invention, took on the role of technological importance, glamour and superiority.

Even if the leading artists of the twentieth century did not go back to the automobile as a subject—or as a canvas—until much later, it did give rise to a lesser-acknowledged group of automotive artists, such as Géo Ham. Born in 1900, Georges Hamel, who worked under the pseudonym of Géo Ham, rapidly established a reputation as one of the finest painters of automobiles and airplanes, for which he was recognized as the official painter for French aviation, in 1931.

Beginning with the very prestigious magazine *Omnia* as an illustrator for them, he was later illustrating the cover of *L'Illustration* magazine from 1927. Soon leading carmakers such as Amilcar, Rolls-Royce, Talbot, Delahaye, Chenard et Walker benefited from his talent, as he made posters and advertisements for them. Controversially, his illustrations may have also influenced the designs of certain coachbuilders—one of the finest-looking automobiles of the pre-War era, the Figoni et Falaschi coach-built Delahaye 135 (one of which survives in Jodhpur), may have been inspired by one of his illustrations, though this hypothesis has been challenged by the Figoni family.

Even though Géo Ham went on to influence an entire generation—as well as subsequent generations—of artists, painters and sculptors who specialized in the automobile as a subject, his influence did not quite reach India. Except for a set of a dozen-odd watercolours of cars from the palace of Bhavnagar, probably executed in the early 1930s, not many such automotive paintings seem to be extant in India. These Bhavnagar paintings are all unsigned, and may have been directly 'copied' from photos and postcards, as they look like cut-outs, without any shadow under the cars, as if floating in the air.

The art of the word

It would be decades before automotive art would finally catch on in India. The same lacunae would be in the realm of literature. Even as Europeans and Americans wrote and pontificated on the effects of the automobile on modern society, Indians rarely touched on the subject. In the West, motoring was 'seen as providing pleasures and thrills comparable to that of horseback riding'.[4] In the book *The Complete Motorist*, written by British author A.B. Filson Young in 1904 (and re-published by Palala Press in 2016), he requested the likes of Rudyard Kipling and John St Loe Strachey to contribute their feelings about the car. One respondent, Lady Mary Jeune (the Baroness of St Helier), wrote in *The Complete Motorist*:

> 'There is a monster in the stable who has to be exercised, and from time to time you hear his brothers hooting to him as they rush past along the road. . . . There is no sensation so enjoyable—except that of riding a good horse in a fast run—as driving in a fast motor. The endless variety of scenery: the keen whistle of the wind in one's face; the perpetual changing sunshine and shadow, create an indescribable feeling of exhilaration and excitement; while the almost human consciousness of the machine; the patient, ready response which it makes to any call on its powers; the snort with which it breasts

the hill, and the soft sob which dies away when it has reached the summit, make it as companionable as any living being.'[5]

By giving the automobile human and animal traits, Lady Jeune was establishing a communion of an erotic nature, an intimacy between man and machine, which has since been a part of the history of automotive iconography. One of the early connections (more in the nature of man-machine than erotic) in Indian literature is in the works of Bengali author Subodh Ghosh (1909–80). In his short story *Ajantrik*, Ghosh captures the tragicomic relationship that a taxi driver in a small provincial town in Bengal has with his taxi (named *Jagaddal*).

In Ghosh's short story, the automobile reflects a human's physical regularity. Like a tired labourer, the writer narrates the story: 'Kantikumar starts his day at 9 am in Hazarimoll Automobile and gets free by 6pm sharp, when the gnawed pistons are getting dizzy in the head, and the nervous system crumples when the sparks shock, and the breath runs out when the fan belt tears in the chest.'[6]

In Ghosh's story, Bimal's acute affection for *Jagaddal* expresses itself when his counterpart Piyara Singh, or the mechanic Gobinda, or any passers-by make fun of his car. Most people, though, tend to avoid Bimal due to his irritable temper, and his intolerance for jokes about *Jagaddal*. When Piyara Singh suggests that Bimal should get a new car like his, Bimal compares the new car to a whore. *Jagaddal* is described as one with a torn hood, a broken windshield, dented bonnet, the tyres retreaded, dirty seats, loose doors, useless headlamps and a dying engine. The adjectives to describe the car are aged horse, lame duck, blind cat, and so on. To Bimal, though, the car is more than a car, it is *Jagaddal*, his closest friend, a god-gifted company, a dependable wish for more than fifteen years. Bimal talks to *Jagaddal*, shares his emotions, and asks if he is thirsty or feels regret for his inability to get him repaired.

The automobile in cinema

Converted into a movie by legendary Bengali film-maker Ritwik Ghatak (1925–76), *Ajantrik* (known internationally as *The Unmechanical*, meaning a machine which is not like a machine), was considered for special entry into the Venice Film Festival of 1959. Described by the renowned French film critic, Georges Sadoul, as 'What does "*Ajantrik*" mean? I don't know and I believe no one in Venice Film Festival knew . . . I can't tell the whole story of the film . . . there was no subtitle for the film. But I saw the film spellbound till the very end.'[7]

According to Bengali poet Alokranjan Dasgupta, *Ajantrik* was a, 'merciless conflict of ethereal nature and mechanized civilization, through the love of taxi driver Bimal and his pathetic vehicle *Jagaddal* seems to be a unique gift of . . . modernism'.[8]

The storyline of the film is simple: Bimal (played by Kali Banerjee), an irascible and eccentric taxi driver, is 'emotionally entangled' with his old dilapidated car, a 1920 Chevrolet, which he calls *Jagaddal*, and which could be translated from Bengali as 'a stone which doesn't budge'. This car is not similar to others; it can be jealous, especially when its driver wants to help a young woman.

In Ritwik Ghatak's book *Cinema And I*,[9] one of the first movies he writes about is *Ajantrik* (which was the second movie the film-maker had made but the first to be released in the cinemas):

'For twelve long years, I had thought about this story before I made it into a film. When it first came my way, accidentally, I was a greenhorn, newly arrived at Calcutta and fresh from the university. *Ajantrik*, caught my imagination and held it for days at a stretch—for more reason than the alliteration with my name. I thought about it for a long time in a vague and general sort of way. Never concretely. What struck me most was its philosophical implication. Here was a story, which sought to establish a new relationship in our literature—the very significant and inevitable relationship between man and machine.'

'Our literature, in fact our culture itself (i.e. the culture of middle-class city-dwellers) has never cared very much for the machine age,' wrote Ghatak. 'The idea of the machine has always had an association of monstrosity for us. It devours all that is good, all that is contemplative and spiritual. It is something that is alien to the spirit of our culture—the spirit of ancient, venerable India. It stands for clash and clangour, for swift, destructive change, for fermenting discontent.'[10]

It also may not be that presumptuous to assume that the character of Bimal in *Ajantrik* may have influenced fellow Bengali cinema giant, Satyajit Ray's 1962 masterpiece, *Abhijan*, and its cynical taxi driver Narasingh (played by the redoubtable Soumitra Chatterjee), which, in turn, went on to influence Martin Scorsese's epochal *Taxi Driver* and the character of Travis Bickle (played by Robert De Niro), from 1976, as admitted by the American film-maker.

In Satyajit Ray's *Abhijan*, the movie is more about Narasingh, the taxi driver, and his complex relationship with people, good and evil, and his trials and tribulations at the edge of society. The car takes a back seat (pun intended) to all the issues that the protagonist tackles, not unlike Martin Scorsese's *Taxi Driver*. Thus, *Abhijan* and *Taxi Driver* were less 'car flicks', unlike *The Italian Job*, *Grand Prix*, *Bullitt*, *The French Connection*, *Le Mans* and *Vanishing Point*.

Bollywood discovers the automobile

A delightful comedy, with mix-ups and confusion, a car, a Ford Model A, from around the late 1920s or early 1930s, had as much a role to play in the movie *Chalti Ka Naam Gadi*, as lead actors Ashok Kumar, his brothers Kishore and Anoop Kumar, and Madhubala. Directed by Satyen Bose, *Chalti Ka Naam Gadi* was about brothers Brijmohan (Ashok Kumar), Manmohan (Kishore Kumar) and Jagmohan Sharma (Anoop Kumar), who run an auto repair shop.

One day, the beautiful Renu (Madhubala) comes to the workshop because her car—an Austin Somerset—has problems. After Manmohan repairs her car, Renu leaves the workshop with her Austin, without paying for the repairs. Manmohan discovers her purse in the workshop and finds in it a ticket for a concert. Manmohan decides to go to the concert to get his money—however, as the invitation card is for Renu only, he is not allowed in. So, he decides to wait in Renu's car and falls asleep. As Renu gets into the car, she does not notice him, and drives her car back home and into the garage. When Manmohan wakes up he is surprised by a servant, but he runs away. Meanwhile, Renu's father is busy with Raja Hardayal Singh, who wants to marry off his younger brother to Renu. Renu's father does not suspect that Raja is a criminal who is after his money. Manmohan takes Renu with him to protect her from Raja. However, they are prevented from escaping by Raja's younger brother, and are taken captive.

Of course, in good Bollywood fashion, all's well that ends well, after much song, dance, action and running around trees and driving around roundabouts. There are several endearing scenes with the Ford (which was named Champion in the film), including one where the car keeps going around in circles under its own power (realism be damned), but the car was central to the romance and intrigue. The most exciting though is the race, which is two-thirds of the way through, at one hour and fifty minutes, when Champion proves that she is indeed a champion, beating several other cars in the tenth annual car race.

Filmed, in all likelihood at the Juhu airstrip, in Bombay, Champion lines up at the start of the race alongside a '55 Buick Roadmaster convertible, an MG TC (maybe two), as well as a '54 Plymouth and a '54 Dodge convertible, and a very rare '52 Hudson convertible. A Riley may be the ninth car. When the flag goes down at the start of the race, all the others take off, except Champion, which refuses to start. Much kicking later, Champion takes off, and then rapidly begins drawing in the rest, overtaking one at a time, by means which are, not necessarily, the fairest. At a point in the race, two other cars (which had not taken the start) show up—another rarity, an Austin A90 Atlantic, as well as the car, which is arguably the most precious in India, the Jodhpur Delahaye 135!

Not surprisingly, Champion wins. Perhaps the only time in the history of the automobile when a Ford Model A beat MG TCs, a Buick Roadmaster, a Hudson, even a Delahaye—even if the latter appeared out of thin air!

Five years later, in 1963, another Bollywood thriller, *Bachpan*, was released. Directed by Nazar, the lead roles played were by Salim Khan and Menka Irani. The poster of the movie featured a striking image of cars racing, obviously taken from an event in Europe, in all likelihood a Formula 1 grand prix race, with single-seaters speeding in formation. From the cars that one can see in the poster—BRM, Cooper, Lotus, Porsche and Maserati—indicates that the photo would be from one of the races during the 1962 season.

Sadly, there is no footage of a Formula 1 race; instead, we have the hero Salim Khan shown as someone passionate about his car, a Frazer-Nash BMW 328, from the late 1930s, with which he goes racing. 'The storyline was very thin, about a person who loved his car and liked racing and then meeting the heroine,' remembers Salim Khan, when relating the story to the author. 'I drove the BMW in the race and for all the action. I loved driving, and I owned a Jaguar 1 ½ Litre then, from 1948, as well as a Triumph Tiger T100, from 1956. The movie was about racing, and most of the racing scenes were filmed on the Bombay-Poona highway then, which had sections which were under construction, so was empty. As well as the BMW, there was a Jaguar XK120 and an MG, even a Bentley, which was ex-Holkar, if I remember right.'

Interestingly enough, the Frazer-Nash BMW has survived (and is owned by T.R. Raghunandan, in Bangalore) and is awaiting restoration at the time of writing this book.

Less than ten years after the film *Bachpan* sank without a trace (it was released only in a few halls, remembers Salim Khan), another film with racing on the poster, and within the plot, made the headlines in India. Larger-than-life hero, Feroz Khan starred in a movie, which he had produced and directed himself, and where Khan went racing. The movie *Apradh*, from 1978, once again, had single-seater Formula 1 cars on the poster, and once again from around 1962 or so, despite the fact that the movie was coming out a decade later. The cars, in action, on the poster, were juxtaposed between the two superstars then, Mumtaz and Feroz Khan.

In the movie, though, it was a different set of cars. Instead of Formula 1 bolides from the early 1960s, what one gets to see, immediately after the mandatory black-and-white Censor Board certification, are a bunch of Formula 2 single-seaters from the 1971 season, lined up at the start of a race, at the legendary Nürburgring, in Germany. The scene opens with the cars all set to race, lined up by rows in a proper grid, and the viewer can see that the grid is impressively numerous, with dozens of racing machines, all set to be flagged off. The stands are full of people, and with the mounting tension of a flag-off, a deep voice announces, 'Speed lovers, we welcome you to the Nürburgring, the world's most unpredictable auto racetrack. The event, a 100-km, five laps race for Super V Formula 4 cars, with India's Ram Khanna racing in the blue Volkswagen car number 7, which is his lucky number.'

The camera then pans close to a head in a red helmet, with just a pair of narrow eyes visible through the visor, full of concentration. The camera then zooms out, and we see the driver, sitting deep in a blue car, with the number 7 emblazoned on the side. With the camera zooming away in a wide angle, we see dozens of racers roaring off the start line, jockeying for position, finding gaps as they charge to the first left-hander at the end of the straight. The camera at the corner then takes over, as the action moves on to the other parts of the 22-km circuit of the Nordschleife, at Nürburgring. Of course, after five minutes of very exciting, spellbinding racing action, amplified by the sound and size of a big screen in the cinema halls of yore, car number 7, that of Ram Khanna (Feroz Khan), sure enough wins the race.

Even if the large font used for credits may have irritated the moviegoer, the action glimpsed through the letters, and some behind it, was good enough for any automotive enthusiast in India then. As the race gets over, the scene moves to the streets of a city in Germany, where a red Alfa Romeo Spider draws to a street's kerbside, and a pretty, young Mumtaz steps out of that startlingly beautiful car.

It's only around the twenty-seventh minute of the film that the next racing car appears, and . . . it's a bright-red Ferrari. A gorgeously curvaceous 512M prototype racer, from 1971, one of twenty-five made during 1970 for the International Championship of Makes, we see it storming around the Nordschleife, before the car comes into the pits. When the car stops, the gull-wing door opens upwards, with an eager mechanic helping lift the door, and we see Feroz Khan stepping out of the car, dressed in casuals . . . except that he is wearing a red helmet, which he takes off, and then peels off the protective balaclava from his face.

The enthusiasts watching the movie needed to wait for another twenty minutes before racing action returns on the screen. Even though Feroz Khan and Mumtaz are on the run, chased by the goons, and their lives are in danger, one last race needs to be raced before Ram Khanna can flee back to India with Mumtaz. Mumtaz worries for Feroz's life, but the fearless racer must do or die.

Shortly after the fiftieth minute, we are back at the Nürburgring once again. The same Southern European voice is back commentating: 'Ladies and gentlemen, we welcome you once again, to the Nürburgring Grand Prix, a thrilling forty-five laps of hair-raising excitement, with the greatest sports event of the year, for 5-litre Prototype Formula 1 cars. As per tradition, the cars are being led around for a warm-up lap by a Mercedes. Driving number 60 in a Ferrari is India's Ram Khanna. Driving number 1, a Porsche, is Arno Shear, the favourite to win today. Driving number 15, also a Ferrari, Salvatore Moroni, an Argentinian, who is the South American champion.'

Warm-up lap over, the race begins and then for the next six minutes the moviegoer is treated to some of the finest footage of real racing action. There are long shots, as well as close-ups and in-car camera shots as cars overtake and trail other racers, and then there is magnificent footage taken from the air and other high vantage points. The racing is real, the action is more than real and the excitement is palpable and pulsating, as some of the fastest cars in the world tear around one of the greatest racing circuits ever.

By the fifty-seventh minute, the action is over, as Ram Khanna (but of course) wins the 'grand prix', with the chequered flag waved at a blurry red car. It is time to go home, to leave the theatre, as that was that—the remaining seventy-odd minutes is more of the typical Hindi film action, with Khan and Mumtaz back in India, embroiled in fisticuffs, fights, romance, song, dance and the usual Bollywood razzmatazz. (This author saw the movie several times as a teenager, but chose to leave the hall after the fifty-seventh minute, almost every time.)

Even if the racing action was limited to barely twelve to thirteen minutes, it was the first time that the majority of Indians had been able to see real motor racing on the screen. Films such as *Grand Prix* and *Le Mans* may have been viewed by the privileged few in the bigger cities of India, limited by the language, English. *Apradh* was in Hindi, and both Feroz Khan and Mumtaz were major box office stars, drawing in millions to the movie halls across the country. *Apradh* was indeed a major success.

For the racing action, Feroz Khan seems to have acquired footage from the television channel covering two of the races at Nürburgring during 1971. Even though not many who were involved in the making of *Apradh* are alive at the time of writing (2020) this book, this author believes that the two races from which footage was used, may be the ADAC Eifelrennen Formula 2 race and the Nürburgring 1000 Kilometres race, both from 1971. The opening five minutes of racing may have been from the Formula 2 race of 2 May 1971, and the session when Feroz Khan is 'racing' the Ferrari 512M, is surely from the Nürburgring 1000 Kilometres, from 30 May 1971.

Inspired, no doubt, by *Grand Prix*, the landmark film by John Frankenheimer, from 1966, Feroz Khan managed to make a film with genuine racing footage with a significantly limited budget, using at most two cars for purpose-footage for a few of the passing shots and for a few in-car camera pans.

For the 2 May 1971 Formula 2 race, it is possible that Khan used the car of Vittorio Brambilla, a Brabham BT30, for the 'non-racing' shots. Nicknamed the Monza Gorilla, Brambilla was from Lesmo, Italy—he eventually went on to race in Formula 1, with limited success, winning just one F1 race out of seventy-four starts. During 1971, he was still in the process of climbing his way up the racing ladder, campaigning in the Formula 2 championship in a Brabham BT30 (powered by a 1.6-litre Cosworth FVA engine), and the money earned lending his car for the grid shots, the close-ups and for the fake racing footage must have helped the upcoming racer.

For racing enthusiasts, it may be worth noting that in the short five minutes of footage, the viewers may have had glimpses of several racing legends in action. The race was won by the brilliant French racing ace, François Cevert, who would die two years later, in a dramatic accident at Watkins Glen, in the United States. Runner-up was future world champion Emerson Fittipaldi. Former F1 world champion Graham Hill was also in the race, as was future F1 world champion Niki Lauda and future multiple winner of the 24 Hours of Le Mans, Henri Pescarolo. Several other prominent racing stars competing that day included Carlos Reutemann, Wilson Fittipaldi, Jo Siffert, Patrick Depailler, Derek Bell and Hans-Joachim Stuck.

Incidentally, Brambilla did not get to finish the race, as an accident in the fourth lap (out of ten) ended his run. It looks like it was a similar case of a DNF (did not finish) for the red Ferrari 512M 'raced by Ram Khanna' at the 1971 Nürburgring 1000 Kilometres, with the car meeting with an accident. Feroz Khan 'used' the car entered by Herbert Müller Racing, which sported the number 60. In fact, Herbert Müller Racing entered two cars, one a Ferrari 512M (number 60), and the other a Ferrari 512S (number 61). Swiss racer Herbert Müller raced number 60, with René Herzog as co-driver, whereas number 61 was raced by Austrian Heinrich Wiesendanger and Swiss, Cox Kocher.

The few seconds of footage of Feroz Khan with car number 60 must have been before the race, as the accident in the race disfigured the car, which is why the red bolide, which flashes past at the chequered flag, is deliberately unrecognizable, as it must have been some other car. The 'use' of Herbert Müller's car must have come at a considerable price, as Müller was a much-respected racer, having won the legendary Targa Florio in a Porsche in 1966. Barely two weeks later, Müller would enter the record books as the runner-up in the 1971 edition of the 24 Hours of Le Mans, co-driving with Richard Attwood, in a Porsche 917K.

For the record, viewers would have seen the likes of several racing legends from the era: Pedro Rodriguez, Jo Siffert, Derek Bell and Gijs van Lennep, all in Porsche 908/03s. Then there were Rolf Stommelen, Nanni Galli, Nino Vaccarella, Carlo Facetti, Andrea de Adamich and Henri Pescarolo in Alfa Romeo T33/3s, and the likes of Jacky Ickx and Clay Regazzoni in a Ferrari 312 PB. Winners Vic Elford and

Gérard Larrousse were in a Porsche 908/03, in car number 3, though the favourites—as per the heavily accented commentator—were number 1 (which ended the runner-up), the Porsche of Rodriguez and Siffert, and the Ferrari, number 15, of Ickx and Regazzoni (which did not finish).

The commentator also mentions that the race was for 5-litre Formula 1 cars. The Ferraris featured a 5-litre V12, but the cars were sports prototypes, not F1 bolides—a silly mistake indeed. When the commentator mentioned that the race was for forty-five laps, he was correct, though, as forty-five laps of the 22-km-long roller-coaster circuit adds up to the 1000 km of the Nürburgring 1000 Kilometres, one of the most important endurance races of the era, arguably second only to the 24 Hours of Le Mans, in Europe then. Described by an English journalist 'as if a reeling, drunken giant had been sent out to determine the route', the great Jackie Stewart gave the circuit the name, which it will probably never lose: Green Hell (Grüne Hölle). Yet, Nürburgring was, and remains, one of the greatest racing circuits ever.

Ironically, Herbert Müller, who had lent his car to Feroz Khan for the movie, met a fiery end at Grüne Hölle, when his Porsche 908 Turbo collided with an earth bank, and hit the stalled car of Bobby Rahal, whilst avoiding a car which had spun just ahead of him, during the 1981 edition of the Nürburgring 1000 Kilometres. Müller was planning to retire from motorsport after the end of that race. Müller was Nürburgring's fifty-third victim, amongst drivers.

Müller's co-driver that day, René Herzog, has survived many years of racing at the top level, competing alongside Müller, as well as with the likes of Hurley Haywood, Hans-Joachim Stuck and the legendary Niki Lauda, sharing cars such as BMWs, Porsches, Fords, Nissans, Chevrolets, and the occasional Ferrari.

At seventy-three years of age (as of 2019), Herzog still has very clear remembrances of the Indian film crew shooting at the race in 1971, when relating the race and the filming to the author: 'I met the film team after the race and I can vividly remember a woman who was a fortune teller. But, she couldn't have been very good as she read my hand and told me that I will be very rich one day. I am still waiting for that day.'

'It is correct that the Ferrari 512M was leased to make the necessary footage at the Nürburgring 1000km race,' points out Herzog. 'The lease was only for stationary pictures including the stars. I don't have any other recollection of the movie team.'

About the actual race itself, Herzog said, 'In the second lap we had a small accident hitting the rail. I was able to get to the pit stop, and have the damage fixed. Unfortunately, the temporary repair didn't last so we had to retire the car even though the damage was minor.'

John Frankenheimer's *Grand Prix* was shot at Monaco, and the racing tracks of Clermont-Ferrand (France), Spa-Francorchamps (Belgium), Zandvoort (Holland), Brands Hatch (UK) and Monza (Italy). Nürburgring was mentioned, but no footage was ever shown in the film. Steve McQueen's *Le Mans* was filmed mainly at the circuit of Le Mans. In all likelihood, Feroz Khan must have seen both. Did he choose to shoot at Nürburgring, to distinguish it from the others, as well as pay tribute to one of the greatest and most dangerous of all the racing circuits?

Promoting a product

Even though interesting and exciting automobiles always figured in many of the Bollywood films, the automobile did not play an important enough role until the blockbuster *Bobby* arrived in 1973. Produced and directed by Raj Kapoor, the storyline of *Bobby* was hardly any different from that of scores of other Indian popular movies, which had preceded it. Once again a love story between a boy, Raj, the son of a rich man, and Bobby, a young girl from a poor family, with the two fighting against all odds to make their love possible, despite the social differences. What made the movie special was the way the story was treated, the freshness of the two protagonists, and the amusing little motorcycle that Raj used, the yet-to-be-launched Rajdoot GTS 175.

Moviegoers in India took to the refreshing charm and demeanour of the baby-faced Rishi Kapoor and sheer gorgeousness of Dimple Kapadia, as well as the symbolism of the cute and accessible motorcycle, which transported the two to their trysts for all the song-and-dance sequences. Reflecting an optimistic, young teenage sense of romance and adventure, the Rajdoot GTS 175 became synonymous with the movie, and has since been referred to as the 'Bobby bike', a moniker which stuck, even if that was not the official one.

As explained by motorcycling enthusiast Sonia Jain to the author, the 'GTS 175 was more popularly known as Bobby, a name much more familiar amongst everyone who has heard of this motorcycle. The reason why it was named so, was because it was featured in the hit Hindi movie, *Bobby*. The young and dynamic Rishi Kapoor rode it with the equally stunning Dimple Kapadia as pillion, and they both changed the fortune of this particular Rajdoot forever.'

The success of the Rajdoot 'Bobby' GTS 175 though, was short-lived, unlike the movie, which was rated by *Indiatimes Movies* in the 'Top 25 Must See Bollywood Films'.[11] Not only was *Bobby* one of the top twenty grossers in the realm of Bollywood, it was an astounding success in the Soviet Union, where more than 62 million saw the film.

The use of the film *Bobby* to promote Rajdoot's new motorcycle, the GTS 175, was not coincidental. The moviemaker Raj Kapoor's elder daughter Ritu Kapoor was married to Rajan Nanda, the son of the founder of Escorts Limited, H.P. Nanda. The Rajdoot GTS 175 was an Escorts product. In fact, this was perhaps one of the first cases of a product placement in an Indian movie.

Inspired by the success, no doubt, of using a Bollywood film to launch a product, another motorcycle from Escorts Limited followed a somewhat similar formula. 'The Rajdoot Yamaha RD350 was launched through another Bollywood blockbuster, *Hero*, by Subhash Ghai, with Jackie Shroff and Meenakshi Seshadri,' remembers automotive enthusiast Dr Anjan Chatterjee. 'The film showed the Escorts factory and a race too, where the Rajdoot RD350 walked away with all the accolades, of course.'

The automobile has always been an integral part of Indian cinema, most specifically for the song-and-dance sequence, as much as to provide glamour and make the stars look good. 'It is so much easier to show off a star from all angles in a convertible as the camera can pan in from any angle,' explains Gul Panag (a prominent film star and activist, as well as former Miss India) to the author. This explains why it has been common practice for Bollywood and other language cinema to use convertibles of all kinds in Indian films.

Some of the most memorable uses of a convertible involve the red Corvette of Mehmood in the 1976 film, *Ginny Aur Johnny*. Two years later, in the film *Trishul*, spectators were regaled, not just by the rising stars Amitabh Bachchan and Shashi Kapoor, but also by an Alfa Romeo, a Jaguar E-Type and a 1960 Chevrolet Impala convertible.

Stars and cars: a love story

There was a close association between several of Bollywood's stars and specific models of vehicles. As much as the association between the red Corvette and Mehmood has become the folklore of Bollywood, there are innumerable stories and associations between K.L. Saigal and his inseparable Buick, or Suraiya's Buick Super Eight and Lincoln Continental. 'These two cars would be parked at her Marine Drive residence and would go for all her shoots, with her retinue, which included her grandmother, who smoked a cigarette held between her third and little finger, as well as the uncle, and the make-up man,' related Dr Anjan Chatterjee to the author.

Chatterjee also remembers, 'Raj Kapoor bought an Oldsmobile 98 Convertible, around 1948, after the success of his film *Aag*, his first venture as director. The Oldsmobile was extensively featured in the film *Barsaat* (from 1949), which was another RK blockbuster, starring Raj Kapoor, Nimmi and Premnath. Raj Kapoor had sentimental attachment to the Oldsmobile, and it was parked at RK Studios for decades, before being moved to his Loni Farms, near Pune.'

'As one who owns an MG TC and is a bit of a movie buff, one always keeps an eye out for these stylish cars in movies,' points out Bangalore-based collector and auto enthusiast T.R. Raghunandan (to the author), who also owns the *Bachpan* Frazer-Nash BMW. 'Of course, it is disconcerting for others who are deeply absorbed in the plot, when I leap up and yell "TC!", whenever I see those rakish lines flit by on the screen.' Raghunandan further explains:

TCs were popular with movie stars in India. Mehmood owned one, and it is said that Raj Kapoor gifted Nargis another. That car apparently makes a cameo appearance in all their movies together it is said. It is a story that I have not followed up, though I do remember a TC parked on a side street in the movie *Aan*. Since the TCs are such romantic cars, it is but natural that they should feature in Bollywood movies and in particular, song sequences. One of the most famous scenes is the one featuring Dev Anand and Nalini Jayawant, in the 1955 movie *Munimji*. The song, *Jeevan ke Safar mein Raahi*, sung in a breezy happy version by Kishore Kumar, and in a soulful and sad rendering by Lata Mangeshkar, both feature a TC.

Dev Anand started out with a Hillman Minx and graduated to an olive green Triumph 1800 Roadster. As Dev Anand mentions in his autobiography *Romancing With Life*[12] 'I had become a little richer and could afford to sit in a more noticeable open car, so that I could wave my kisses to the growing number of admiring fans as I swished past them.' He called his Triumph, his Princess. It was fitted with a lover's horn, he said. Dev Anand changed cars regularly, and his 1950s Chevrolet Belair convertible was featured in *Prem Pujari* (1970). Into the 1980s, he preferred his Premier Padminis, when lesser stars were flaunting their imported cars. As Chatterjee explains, 'His logic was that he could evade identification at traffic junctions, where he was often mobbed in imported cars, which were few and far between during those years'.

Lyricist, poet and singer Anand Bakshi acquired a used 1964 Fiat Super Select, in the late 1960s, and he went on to pen a poem on his Fiat! Next, he was gifted a Chevrolet Belair by film-maker Shakti Samanta in 1970, after the success of the film *Aradhana*. Raj Kumar also owned a pillar-less two-tone Chevrolet Belair from the 1950s, which he treasured.

Kishore Kumar kept his Ford Model A, the car from *Chalti Ka Naam Gaadi*, forever parked at his Gauri Kunj residence in Juhu, Mumbai. Kishore Kumar also owned a Chevrolet Nova. Lata Mangeshkar had a Hillman Minx in the early years, and then went on to buy a Chevrolet

Styleline Deluxe. She even had a Fiat 1100D, which was later bought by the then struggling music director Bappi Lahiri, who kept it for a long time due to sentimental reasons. Rahul Dev Burman's first car was a Fiat 1100 Elegant, which he kept until his last breath. It is still garaged and under the care of singer Asha Bhonsle. Chatterjee also remembers that, 'In the early 1970s, after tasting success after success, R.D. Burman bought a mid-1960s Triumph Spitfire.'

As Satyajit Ray's award-winning films were mostly made on shoestring budgets, the best that the Oscar winner could manage was an Ambassador, of which he had a succession of models. 'When shooting for his films, he would be comfortable in the luggage boot of an Ambassador, with its boot lid detached, which would provide for enough space for the six-footer,' pointed out Chatterjee to the author. 'Most of his films featured at least one Ambassador, sometimes many.'

The other famous Ambassador enthusiast was cartoonist R.K. Laxman, who bought a succession of black Ambassadors. When legendary painter M.F. Hussain acquired an off-white Premier 118NE, he must have found the colour a tad dull, as he decided to get the car painted . . . by himself. The result was the most colourful—and perhaps the most valuable—118NE ever. A multiplicity of galloping horses painted in the typical M.F. Hussain style, with broad sweeping brushstrokes converted the 118NE into one of the most attractive artworks on Indian wheels.

In all likelihood, Hussain's inspiration was the famous art cars of BMW. When French racer and auctioneer Hervé Poulain commissioned his artist friend Alexander Calder to paint a BMW 3.0 CSL, which he was campaigning in the 1975 edition of the 24 Hours of Le Mans, he started an extraordinary history in the realm of art, culture and automobile. Since then, nineteen 'art car' BMWs have been executed (until 2017) by the likes of Roy Lichtenstein, Andy Warhol and Jeff Koons, as well as Japanese Nihonga painter Matazo Kayama and South African Esther Mahlangu, from the Ndebele nation, bringing a very varied perspective to the concept of turning automobiles into canvases.

Sadly, M.F. Hussain's 118NE was ignored, not just by BMW, but also by the Indian art establishment, and the car seems to have disappeared, probably destroyed, or just RIP, rusted into pieces. It took the best part of almost three decades before cars became canvases again, when the brilliant initiative by Jaipur-based automobile enthusiast Himanshu Jangid in 2015 had several young artists painting Tata Nanos and other Indian automobiles. Jangid's initiative has burgeoned into a movement, which has had these beautifully painted cars as well as automotive art and sculpture traversing the country with a series of roadshows.

Yet, we must remember that in this subcontinent of ours, thousands of trucks and auto-rickshaws with vibrant, gaily painted folk art have been on the road for decades now. The ultimate roadshow of folk and pop culture criss-crossing the nation, expressing the joy and the aesthetics of a simplistic set of people, providing a cultural fabric, which has been continuously knitting the varied sensibilities of a highly diversified nation—a nation which has loved the automobile for more than a century, one that still loves the automobile in its many-splendoured forms and colours.

Acknowledgements

The author is indebted to the following list of people who helped out immensely with this book; out of convenience they are listed out alphabetically, and not in any order of importance:

Richard Adatto, Gunjan Ahlawat, Allan Almeida, Natasha Alpaiwalla, C.S. Ananth, Behram Ardeshir, Prabal Banerjee, Makarand Baokar, Jaikumar Bhoopal, Karl Bhote, André Blaize, Billy Bose, Partha Sadan Bose, Daniel Cabart, Karun Chandhok, Indu Chandhok, Vicky Chandhok, Avik Chattopadhyay, Anne Castagnos-Sen, Dr Anjan Chatterjee, Grzegorz Chmielewski, Chris Clark, Patrick Delage, Xavier de la Chapelle, Christian Descombes, Cyrus Dhabar, John Fasal, Claude Figoni, Raphael Galdos del Carpio, Cyrus Gandhi, Rajiv Ghosh, Sanjoy Ghosh, Viveck Goenka, Shreya Goswami, Abhay Gupta, Kanishka Gupta, Harikesh Ananthamurthy, René Herzog, Iris Hummel, Himanshusinh Jadeja, Pratap Jayaram, Salim Khan, Sonia Jain, Abbas Jasdanwalla, Shrivardhan Kanoria, Aleksandra Kasztelewicz, Darab Khan, Aparna Kumar, Rishad Kundanmal, Rajesh Malhotra, Harshit Merchant, Jay Mehta, Rajiv Mitra, Ridhi Nahata, Dr Pal Negyesi, Ashok Palyad, Kamlesh Patel, T.R. Raghunandan, Bhisham Rai, Pallab Roy, Bob Rupani, Navaz Sandhu, Shomenath Roy Chowdhury, Shrikant Shah, Jackie Shroff, Amit Sen, Karandip Singh, Hormazd Sorabjee, Sugato Sen, Nandini Sengupta, K.P.

Subbaiah, Chaitanyadevsinhji Surendrasinhji, Prithvi Nath Tagore, Milind Thakker, Tarun Thakral, Harit Trivedi, Jean-Paul Tissot, Diljeet Titus, Hans Veenenbos, Julian Williamson, Sobiesław Zasada.

Notes

Preface

1. Jack Kerouac, *On the Road,* Viking Press, 1957.
2. John Steinbeck, *Travels with Charley: In Search of America,* Viking, 1962.
3. Tom Wolfe, *The Electric Kool-Aid Acid Test,* Farrar Straus Giroux, 1968.
4. Robert Pirsig, *Zen and the Art of Motorcycle Maintenance: An Inquiry into Values,* William Morrow and Company, 1974.

Chapter 1: A Love Affair Begins

1. James J. Flink: *America Adopts the Automobile.* Cambridge: The MIT Press, 1971.
2. *Times of India,* 22 June, 2016, 'The Myth of India's Population Explosion'.
3. *La Pratique Automobile,* May 1908.
4. Ibid.
5. Elizabeth Blackstock, 'The 1910 Brooke Swan Car Is the Most Absurd Thing I've Ever Needed to Drive', Jalopnik.com, 17 November 2018.
6. *The Bengalee,* 25 April 1910.
7. *American Commerce Reports,* Volume II, Issue 80, 1915.

8. Alexandra Henton, *The 1911 Delhi Durbar: A Remarkable Spectacle,* The Field, https://www.thefield.co.uk/features/the-1911-delhi-durbar-a-remarkable-spectacle-21754
9. Ravi Chaturvedi, *Legendary Indian Cricketers,* Ocean Books, 2009.
10. Sharada Dwivedi and Manvendra Singh Barwani, *The Automobiles of the Maharajas,* Eminence Designs, 2003.
11. Interview by email, 24 November 2018.
12. *Time* magazine, 22 February 1937.
13. *American Commerce Reports,* Volume II, Issue 80, 1915.
14. On 28 October 2018 in Hyderabad.
15. Robert Cumberford and Michel Zumbrunn, *Auto Legends: Classics of Style & Design,* Chartwell.
16. Javier Moro, *Passion India: The Story of the Spanish Princess of Kapurthala,* Full Circle Publishing Ltd., 2007.
17. Coralie Younger, *Wicked Women of the Raj,* SOS Free Stock, May 2005.

Chapter 2: The Love Affair Continues

1. Ali Rajabally, 'Vintage Cars: The Parsee Connection', *Parsiana,* August 1984.
2. Ibid.
3. According to a survey done by the FBVHC in 2020: The 2020 National Historic Vehicle Survey, Structural report, by the FBVHC, https://fbhvc.co.uk/storage/downloads/page/11/0310%20FBHVC%20Report%20TEXT%20V0_7W.pdf

Chapter 3: Make in India

1. The National Archives in College Park, Maryland, has archived the publications of the U. S. Department of Commerce. Until the Second World War, the Department of Commerce asked consulates and embassies to gather industrial statistics, which they cumulated and published in order to help American companies understand local market conditions.
2. Gyan Prakash, *Emergency Chronicles: Indira Gandhi and Democracy's Turning Point,* Princeton University Press, 2019.

3. Ibid.

4. L.K. Jha and others, *Report of the Author Committee on Automobile Industry*, Ministry of Commerce and Industry, Government of India, 1960 (http://cslrepository.nvli.in//handle/123456789/2468)

5. Rajinder Puri, *India: The Wasted Years, 1969–1975*, Chetana Publications, 1975.

6. Gyan Prakash, *Emergency Chronicles: Indira Gandhi and Democracy's Turning Point*, Princeton University Press, 2019.

7. Vinod Mehta, *The Sanjay Story*, HarperCollins Publishers India, republished in 2012.

8. Gyan Prakash, *Emergency Chronicles: Indira Gandhi and Democracy's Turning Point*, Princeton University Press, 2019.

9. Ibid.

10. 'Maruti: Gone with the Wind', *India Today*, 30 April 1977.

11. Vinod Mehta, *The Sanjay Story*, republished in 2012 by HarperCollins Publishers India.

12. Khushwant Singh, 'Sanjay Gandhi's Maruti', *Illustrated Weekly of India*, 1975.

13. Case Law Citation: (1978)1CompLJ331(P & H) and Case Law Citation: MANU/PH/0132/1978

14. T.A. Pai, 'T.A. Pai Sheds New Light on Sanjay's Maruti', *Illustrated Weekly of India*, 1979.

15. Ibid.

16. Id.

Chapter 4: A Car For the People

1. Dilip Cherian and Mohan Ram, 'The Maruti Sweepstakes', *Business India*, 12–25 April 1982.

2. Figures from the *Organisation Internationale des Constructeurs d'Automobiles*, http://www.oica.net/production-statistics/

3. Ibid.

4. Internal documents from the Maruti archive.

5. 'Maruti: Salvaging a Wreck', *India Today*, 1–15 November, 1980.

6. '1998 Hyundai Santro Launch in India TVC 4 (Shahrukh Khan & Kim)', YouTube video.

7. https://www.youtube.com/watch?v=HDhVqhlzCN0
8. Tata Motors Press Release, 10 January 2008.
9. Peter Foster and Pallavi Malhotra, 'Protests over "World's Cheapest Car" by Tata', *Daily Telegraph*, 10 January 2008.
10. 'List of countries by vehicles per capita', Wikipedia, https://en.wikipedia.org/wiki/List_of_countries_by_vehicles_per_capita.

Chapter 5: A Love for Speed

1. Pierre Giffard, 'Le concours de Petit Journal', *Le Petit Journal.*
2. *Autocar,* 14 March 1908.
3. *Statesman,* 12 October 1949.
4. 'From Clapham to Calcutta', *Classic & Sports Car,* February 2014.
5. 'First National Speed Record', *Automobile Magazine*, April 1953.
6. Sobiesław Zasada, *Szybkosc bezpieczna Rajdy swiata,* Motopress, 2006.
7. Shreekant Khandekar and Dilip Bobb's 'Himalayan Rally Sputters to a Dismal End as Anti-rally Demonstrations Get Violent', *India Today,* 15 November 1980.
8. Ibid.
9. Id.

Chapter 6: Sports Cars & Convertibles

1. *Quattroroute,* October 1947, and *Auto Italiana,* January 1948.
2. 'San Storm', *Autocar India*, May 2001.
3. Ibid.
4. https://www.topgear.com/car-reviews/avanti/first-drive
5. Devesh Mishra, 'Dilip Chhabria's DC Design's Property to be Auctioned', Cartoq.com, 9 June 2019.

Chapter 7: Bikes and *Bikerni*s

1. Cristi Farrell, 'Don't Date a Girl Who Rides Motorcycles . . .', *Moterrific* (podcast), 15 December 2013, http://www.moterrific.com/blog/2013/12/15/dont-date-a-girl-who-rides-motorcycles.

Chapter 8: The Art of the Automobile

1. Gerald Silk, The Museum of Contemporary Art, 1984, Los Angeles.
2. Ibid.
3. Gerald Silk, The Museum of Contemporary Art, 1984, Los Angeles.
4. Ibid.
5. A.B. Filson Young, *The Complete Motorist*, Library of Congress, 1904, republished by Andesite Press, 2015.
6. Hafiz-Al-Asad, 'Term Paper on the film adaptation Ajantrik by Ritwik Ghatak from the short story "Ajantrik" by Subodh Ghosh', Jahangirnagar University, Savar, Dhaka, 2010.
7. Manoj Srivastava, *Wide Angle: History of Indian Cinema* (published by Notion Press, 2016).
8. *The Shadow of a Kite and Other Essays* (Friends Publishing, 2004).
9. Published by Dhyanbindu & RMT, 2018.
10. Ritwik Ghatak, *Cinema and I*, Dhyanbindu & RMT, 2018.
11. 'Top 25 Must-See Bollywood Films', *India Time*, icheckmovies.com
12. Published by Penguin Global in 2007.

Bibliography

Fast Forward: The Cars of the Future, The Future of Cars (Gestalten, 2017)

Adler, Dennis. *Mercedes-Benz* (Motorbooks, MBI Publishing Company, 2008)

Anand, Dev. *Romancing With Life* (Penguin Global, 2007)

Bhargava, R.C. & Seetha. *The Maruti Story: How a Public Sector Company Put India on Wheels* (Collins Business, 2010)

Brown, Roland. *Fast bikes* (Parragon, 2002)

Buckley, Martin. *The Car: A Book of Classic Motors* (Southwater, 1997)

Chacko, Philip; Noronha, Christabelle; Agrawal, Sujata. *Small Wonder: The Making of the Nano* (Westland Ltd, 2010)

Cheetham, Craig. *Classic Cars: Legendary Automobiles Design and Development* (Metro Books, 2008)

Cheetham, Craig, General Editor. *American Cars: The Automobiles that Made America* (Amber Books, 2004)

De La Rive Box, Rob. *The Complete Encyclopaedia of Saloon Cars 1945–1975* (Rebo Publishers, 1999)

Design Museum. *Fifty Cars that Changed the World* (Conran Octopus, 2010)

Ford, Henry & Crowther, Samuel. *My Life and Work.* (Doubleday, Page & Co., 1922)

Freiberg, Kevin and Jackie. *Nanovation: How a Little Car Can Teach the World to Think Big* (Portfolio, Penguin Group, 2010)

Gay, Jean-Marc & Semonsut, Alexandre. *La Peugeot 205 de mon père* (E.T.A.I. Editions, 2013)

Ingrassia, Paul. *Engines of Change: A History of the American Dream in Fifteen Cars* (Simon & Schuster, 2012)

Mehta, Vinod. *The Sanjay Story* (HarperCollins Publishers India, 1979 & 2012)

Meurie, Benoit. *La Dyane de mon père* (E.T.A.I. Editions, 2011)

Pignacca, Brizio. *Fiat 1100* (Giorgio Nada Editore, 1992)

Pressnell, Jon. *Mini: The Definitive History* (Haynes Publishing, 2009)

Pressnell, Jon. *Morris: The Cars and the Company* (Haynes Publishing, 2013)

Reynolds, John. *André Citroen: The Man and the Motor Cars* (Sutton Publishing, 1996)

Robson, Graham. *The Cars of BMC* (Motor Racing Publications Ltd, 1987)

Robson, Graham. *The Book of the Standard Motor Company* (Veloce Publishing Ltd, 2011)

Sara, Bernard. *2CV l'auto aux mille visages* (E.T.A.I. Editions, 2012)

Sparrow, Andrea & David. *Fiat & Abarth 500 & 600: Colour Family Album* (Veloce Publishing Plc, 1998)